THE MARKSMANSHIP PRIMER

The Experts' Guide to Shooting Handguns and Rifles

THE MARKSMANSHIP PRIMER

The Experts' Guide to Shooting Handguns and Rifles

JIM CASADA

Skyhorse Publishing

Skyhorse Publishing books may be purchased in bulk at special discounts for
sales promotion, corporate gifts, fund-raising, or educational purposes. Special
editions can also be created to specifications. For details, contact the Special Sales
Department, Skyhorse Publishing, 307 West 36th Street, 11th Floor, New York,
NY 10018 or info@skyhorsepublishing.com.

Skyhorse® and Skyhorse Publishing® are registered trademarks of Skyhorse
Publishing, Inc.®, a Delaware corporation.

Visit our website at www.skyhorsepublishing.com.

10 9 8 7 6 5 4 3 2 1

Library of Congress Cataloging-in-Publication Data

Casada, Jim.
 The marksmanship primer : the experts' guide to shooting handguns and rifles /
Jim Casada.
   p. cm.
 Includes bibliographical references and index.
 Summary: "Presents selections from America's gun writers of past and present,
aimed at marksmen of all levels of experience, that give advice on topics such as
sighting, accuracy, and hunting"--Provided by publisher.
 ISBN 978-1-62087-367-0 (pbk. : alk. paper)
 1. Shooting. 2. Firearms. I. Title.
 GV1153.C27 2012
 799.2'13--dc23
                                2012033183

Printed in the United States of America

CONTENTS

ACKNOWLEDGMENTS

As is invariably the case when one writes or compiles a book, others make contributions richly deserving of thanks. Les Adams conceived this project, and his effort along somewhat parallel lines, *The Second Amendment Primer,* provided a model starting point. Amanda Adams has been intimately involved in the undertaking at every step along the way, gently prodding me when needed (which was often), encouraging my efforts, and facilitating everything from links to contributors to dealings with the textual editor. That individual was Katharine Wiencke, who knows little about marksmanship but who is always on the mark when it comes to issues of clarity, consistency, and proper usage.

Two contemporaries in the world of writing on guns and hunting, Bryce Towsley and Wayne Van Zwoll, figure significantly in this book, and in addition to being an admirer of their professionalism, I am proud to claim them as friends. The same holds true, albeit vicariously, for those great gun writers from earlier generations whose collective wisdom forms the heart of this compilation. I have read their words as a boy and a man, and the enduring verities found there tell, in eloquent fashion, of the prominent place marksmanship has always had in the American way of life. They were straight shooters, in person and in print, and theirs is an example well worth emulating.

Finally, as always, I am indebted to my family. My wife, Ann, tolerates the vicissitudes of the writing life; gives me a sense of safe harbor when the dark, gathering clouds of deadlines move uncomfortably close; turns the fruits of my personal marksmanship in the hunting field into delicious meals; and does her part in seeing that all my efforts as a writer reach fruition. Our daughter and son-in-law, Natasha and Eric Getway, ask the right questions about works in progress, and I look eagerly forward to the day when their daughter, Ashlyn, becomes my partner in the field, giving me a welcome opportunity to pass the shooting tradition on to another generation.

A NOTE ON SELECTION

Over the years, an incredible amount of material on rifle and pistol marksmanship has appeared in print. Many of the basic principles of accurate shooting remain constant; others have changed, thanks to study, experimentation, and technological advances. This primer combines the finest advice from old masters and modern writers. Selecting the "best" information on marksmanship is a difficult and ultimately subjective task. However, certain parameters guided me in the selection process. Primarily, I sought material that was readable and writers who were authoritative. In many cases, anecdotal or dated information was edited out of the material presented, my underlying idea being provision of sound, sensible, and easily followed advice.

I have given the origin of all the selections, most of which come from books. The bibliography offers some further guidance on the sources consulted during the process of compiling the book. A goodly number of these works are now out of print. Biographical profiles of the contributors are presented at the end of the book, before the bibliography.

A NATION OF STRAIGHT SHOOTERS: THE EVOLUTION OF AMERICAN MARKSMANSHIP

Marksmanship has played an integral and important role in American history. So much is this the case that we regularly use the phrase "straight shooter" to describe an honest, reliable individual who speaks his mind. Although it could be argued that straight shooters are a vanishing breed in the world of politics, one of our greatest leaders was a staunch advocate of the shooting life and the sport that forms one of its most enjoyable manifestations. Theodore Roosevelt wrote, in his timeless book, *The Wilderness Hunter* (1893):

> The free, self-reliant, adventurous life, with its rugged and stalwart democracy; the wild surroundings, the grand beauty of the scenery, the chance to study the ways and habits of the woodland creatures — all these unite to give to the career of the wilderness hunter its peculiar charm. . . . The wilderness hunter must not only show skill in the use of the rifle and success in finding and approaching game, but he must also show the qualities of hardihood, self-reliance, and resolution needed for effectively grappling with his wild surroundings.

One of our greatest leaders was an advocate of the shooting life

To a considerable degree, it was the wild surroundings of which Roosevelt wrote that gave rise
to the great American tradition of superb marksmanship. Hardy frontiersmen depended on their
wits, woodsmanship, and ability with the long rifle
for survival. The gun became almost an extension
of the body for these men, and they relied on it for
both sustenance and safety.

The use of firearms looms large in our past

Anyone who delves into American history soon
comes to realize just how large the competent use
of firearms looms in our past. In the American
Revolution, a key turning point came in the battles of Cowpens and Kings Mountain. In the latter
engagement particularly, the redcoats (British reg-
ulars and Hessian mercenaries) proved no match
for the Overmountain Boys. These hardy frontiersmen from the area that would eventually become the states of Tennessee and Kentucky had
several things going for them that more than made
up for the superior organization and military experience of their foes.

First and foremost, they had accurate rifles and
understood their performance capabilities completely, whereas the British troops had relatively
ineffective smoothbores. Any frontiersman worth
his salt could "bark" a squirrel (shoot a bullet into
the tree or limb beneath the animal in such a precise fashion that the bushytail was killed, the meat
was undamaged, and the lead could be retrieved
for remolding) at a considerable distance. Add
deadly marksmanship, superior skills as woods-
men, and an intimate knowledge of the lay of the

land, and the Overmountain Boys became formidable adversaries.

The experiences of the Revolution established what in time became a pattern. Highly skilled marksmen have figured prominently in all of America's wars. Take, for example, two of the best known of our country's civilian soldiers. In World War I, Tennessee's Alvin York, a reclusive country boy forced by the press of circumstances to use skills he had learned hunting for the family table in the killing ground known as the Western Front, accomplished feats that almost defy belief. Single-handedly, he captured scores of Germans after they had seen deadly examples of his sharpshooting. Two generations later, Carlos Hathcock, a simple son of the Arkansas soil who was caught up in the maelstrom that was Vietnam, became a legendary marksman. Like York, he acquired his skill through what in essence was subsistence hunting.

Highly skilled marksmen have figured prominently in all our wars

On a more personal level, the finest deer hunter it has ever been my privilege to know, Joe Scarborough, is a native of the North Carolina high country with a quite similar background. He served three tours of duty in Vietnam as a sniper, and so finely honed were his combined skills in shooting and stealth that he instructed other snipers. He could move through the woods like a wraith, took virtually all his deer while they were bedded down, and invariably killed them cleanly with a single shot through the eye.

Skill with rifles and pistols played an important role in what Theodore Roosevelt called, in a book of that title, *The Winning of the West*. To be sure, in everything from classic movies to third-rate westerns, Hollywood has romanticized and mis-represented gun fighting and the use of guns in America's march to achieve its manifest destiny. Indeed, anyone who has ever visited the site of the shootout at the OK Corral in Tombstone, Arizona, has to wonder how there were any survivors. There may have been some notable and notorious gunslingers present, but sharpshooters they clearly were not.

The ways that firearms really figured promi-nently in our country's inexorable expansion west-ward were simpler and far less sensational. Sure, there were skirmishes with "redskins" and shootouts with outlaws, but marksmanship took on its real meaning when it came to putting food on the table, shooting bison for their hides, or mar-ket gunning for deer meat and hides. A man with a bunch of mouths to feed and with the wolf of starvation never far from the door needed skill to survive. Likewise, a skilled buffalo hunter could sometimes take as many as two dozen of the mammoth beasts at a single "stand," dropping each of them in its tracks with a well-placed shot from atop his shooting sticks.

Even later, well into the twentieth century, skill with a rifle remained a given for boys growing up in a rural setting — and for a good deal of the last century, much of the American population still had real connections with the land. Hunting for sport and for the table was as great a part of rural

Hunting for sport or the table was a great part of rural boyhood

boyhood as playing baseball in the summertime, feeding livestock, or picking blackberries for cobblers. Untold millions of youngsters (I was among them) learned to shoot with a .22, although some hand-eye coordination using a slingshot may have preceded these first footsteps in firearms use. In time, we graduated to center-fire rifles, but plinking at cans, hunting squirrels in the fall and rabbits in the winter, or maybe just doing some target shooting with a little .22 with open sights was part and parcel of growing up.

During the mean lean years of the Depression, the meat portion of many families' diets came almost exclusively from hunting, and perhaps a bit of trapping with rabbit gums or snares. Shells cost "cash money" (a phrase in common use at the time because hard currency was so scarce as to deserve the redundancy) and were not to be wasted with careless or ill-advised shots.

Even a generation later, when I was a boy, the common way to buy ammunition was not by the box but by the shell. Shorts for .22 rifles sold for the princely sum of a penny apiece, whereas long rifle cartridges were more expensive, at a penny and a half each. Center-fire shells cost as much as a dime apiece, and no one shot more of them than was required to get a gun properly sighted. Sometimes accuracy meant the difference between a hearty meal and gnawing hunger, and that pressure, combined with a need to account for every shell used, proved a powerful incentive for hitting one's target. Today when a youngster returns from a hunting trip, the first thing he is likely to be asked is "Did you have any luck?" Back then, the first two inquiries directed toward young hunters were invariably "What did you kill?" and "How many shots did you take?" Cost consciousness and simple need placed a premium on marksmanship, and this fact explains that uniquely American phrase "bringing home the bacon."

Similar emphasis on marksmanship unquestionably runs as a shining thread through the fabric of American history. The same holds true of gun making. The making of fine rifles — and, to a lesser degree, pistols — became an honorable, important craft early in our nation's history. These firearms, capable of outstanding performance when placed in skilled hands, have always been recognized as treasures. The production of accurate guns — from the beautiful muzzleloaders such as the famed Kentucky and Plains rifles, fashioned by individuals, to the mass-produced guns of makers such as the Remington Arms Company — has been acknowledged as an area of craftsmanship in which Americans have always excelled.

Americans have always excelled in gun craftsmanship

Good guns lend themselves to good shooting, or, as Townsend Whelen once put it, "only accurate rifles are interesting." As individuals and as a nation, we have always taken pride in marksmanship, and it is by no means a stretch to suggest that marksmanship is one of the building blocks on which this nation was founded. Those who question or challenge the Second Amendment might be well advised to delve a bit deeper into the past. If they do so, they will be constantly reminded of the role firearms and proficient shooters have played throughout our development as a country.

Or, to use a favorite phrase of historians, "you can't know where you're going if you don't know where you've been." We have always been a nation of shooters, and the simple fact that an ordinary man can own a gun and use it for hunting or target shooting sets us apart from the rest of the world. America was founded by hunters and marksmen, nurtured by the food that accurate shooting provided, and sustained in one war after another by farm boys turned sharpshooters. In a real sense our country is distinctive thanks to the role of firearms in our past.

One of America's great sporting scribes who loved his country to the core, Archibald Rutledge, put it wonderfully well. He exposed his three sons to shooting and hunting at a young age, and "Old Flintlock," as he was fondly known, firmly believed he could offer them no finer legacy. "There is something inherently manly and home-bred and truly American in that expression, 'shooting straight,'" he wrote. "If the sentimentalist were right," he continued, "hunting would develop in men a cruelty of character. But I have found that it inculcates patience, demands discipline and iron nerve, and develops a serenity of spirit that makes for long life and long love of life." Rutledge's conclusion was a simple one: "The privilege of hunting is about as fine a heritage as we have." Had he

The privilege of hunting is about as fine a heritage as we have rephrased that to read "hunting and shooting," he would have been squarely on target.

Certainly hunting and the other shooting sports are part of the fabric of American life, and in many senses this book celebrates that fact. This volume serves as a road map to greater shooting proficiency and, in turn, greater enjoyment of shooting. The book's first two sections focus in detail on the various aspects of first-rate performance with a rifle or handgun. A third section is devoted to general aspects of shooting and completes the primer.

This volume serves as a road map to great shooting proficiency

Carefully chosen selections from some of America's great gun writers, of yesteryear and today, touch on the many and varied considerations that enter into the complicated makeup of an accomplished marksman. For the most part, mention of specific guns, brands of ammunition, and accessories has been edited out, because these are matters that change with the advance of technology. The basics of marksmanship, on the other hand, remain the same. That is the essence of this book, the goal of which is to present the fundamentals of marksmanship.

Expensive guns and the finest of accessories undeniably can make a difference in shooting performance, but it is comforting to know that many well-made, reasonably priced firearms offer the potential to fire excellent groups. Any law-abiding American can own a firearm, and that means sound marksmanship lies within reach of all of us. Achieving accuracy and a high degree of competence is an immediate joy; refining it through regular trips to the range or the field can provide a lifetime of pleasure. The pages that follow open the doors to such pleasure, with guidance from a bevy of first-rate writers, teachers, and shooters.

Part I

THE RIFLE

The next six chapters cover all aspects of rifle marksmanship. I begin with an overview of the basics and then turn to the various positions that the rifleman can assume to improve his accuracy. The components of sighting in a rifle are discussed in the subsequent chapter. The vital, frequently misunderstood or underappreciated matter of ballistics receives careful attention, as do long-range accuracy and the hunter as a marksman.

You will discover that many elements enter into marksmanship with long guns, and some of the greatest names in hunting and gun writing share their thoughts on these elements. Occasionally, the selections touch on the same or closely related subjects, and when they do, keep in mind that it is always useful to have different perspectives. In the final analysis, you have to study the thoughts of the experts, apply them in the field or at the range, and reach your own conclusions about what works best for you. Yet it is comforting to have guidance from real shooting gurus, and that is what you get in the chapters that follow.

I
RIFLE
SHOOTING BASICS

Many folks who have handled long guns for years suddenly discover, when in the presence of a master or an experienced teacher, that they have all sorts of bad habits. These may be deeply ingrained and difficult to overcome, which is why, in some senses, a relative newcomer to shooting who gets proper exposure to the basics at the outset actually has an advantage.

Here we have insight from two of the greatest names in the history of writing on rifles: Jack O'Connor and Townsend Whelen. Both bring a research analyst's mind-set to their work, and anything they say about marksmanship merits careful attention. O'Connor touches on "the elements," whereas Whelen describes these aspects as "the essentials." Some of what they say may seem slightly repetitive, but getting things right from the start looms so large in proficient marksmanship that any redundancy is well worthwhile.

●

This selection comes from what many consider Jack O'Connor's greatest work, The Rifle Book *(1964; second edition). For those interested*

*in pursuing O'Connor's thoughts on the matter
even further, related (and sometimes quite similar) information appears in* Complete Book of
Shooting *(1965) and in two booklets:* Rifle and
Shotgun Shooting Basics *(1986) and* 7-Lesson
Rifle Shooting Course *(1981). The former booklet
comes directly from* Complete Book of Shooting.

**Jack
O'Connor
on rifle
shooting**

THE ELEMENTS OF
RIFLE SHOOTING

The average man who has learned to shoot a rifle
has almost always begun his practice in exactly
the wrong way. He has started off without any
supervision whatsoever, and as a usual thing he
has acquired bad habits. He has done his first
shooting from the offhand position, the most difficult of all positions from which to shoot a rifle.
He has never learned to call his shots. He jerks
the trigger and flinches.

The United States is not exactly full of good
rifleshots, and the average man who hunts deer
once a year and who occasionally shoots at a
tin can is really a pretty poor shot. I once
helped three deer hunters who had just purchased
new Model 94 Winchester rifles in .32 Special
to sight their rifles in. From a sitting position
two of these hunters could just about keep their
shots in a 2 ½-foot circle at 100 yards. That is
pretty poor shooting, but even shooting as bad
as that will get deer. The third hunter could not
even begin to keep his shots in a 10-foot circle at

100 yards. He must have been closing his eyes and jerking the trigger. I have seen hunters miss standing deer at 50 and 100 yards, and once I saw five hunters fire twenty-five shots at a running buck that got up within 10 yards of the closest hunter and ran 150 yards up an open hillside and over a crest. One would think that the law of averages would get that buck, but he got over the ridge and out of sight without even having a hair ruffled.

Learning to shoot a rifle is not difficult. I believe that learning to shoot a rifle well enough to kill deer consistently is really exceedingly easy if one goes about it right. Shooting a rifle at a stationary mark is actually one of the easiest of all sports. It is far easier to learn, for example, than good shotgun handling.

All that is necessary to hit a mark with a rifle (assuming that the rifle is correctly sighted in) is to get the sights lined up on the mark and then to let the trigger off without disturbing the aim. This, in theory at least, is utterly simple. If a rifle could be held absolutely steady and the trigger squeezed off each shot, the bullets would land in a very small group on the mark.

All good rifle shooting is based on the rifleman's assuming as steady a position as is possible under the circumstances and then letting off the trigger at exactly the right time. One soon finds out, however, that except from a bench rest it is impossible to hold a rifle even approximately steady, and even with most bench rests a rifle can-

Shooting a rifle at a stationary mark is one of the easiest of all sports

not be held *absolutely* steady. When using iron [open] sights from a bench rest it is possible for a man to believe that he is holding steady, but let us put an eight-power scope, say, on the rifle, and we discover that even when we are sitting at a bench rest with the rifle resting across a sandbag, there still is wobble and tremor to the piece. Whatever the position, then, we learn that we have to complete the trigger squeeze at exactly the right time, when the sights are properly aligned.

Most men begin shooting from the offhand position

Most men begin shooting from the offhand position. The rifle wobbles, and in an attempt to get the shot off when the sights are aligned, the beginner yanks the trigger. He does not learn to call his shots or to have a mental picture in his mind of exactly how the sights looked when he felt the recoil. The yank he gives the trigger throws the rifle off. Anticipation of the recoil and muzzle blast makes him flinch and it adds this flinch to the jerk of the trigger. Many people will fool around with offhand shooting for years and get no better.

If it were possible, it would be best to begin every shooter from the prone position with a sandbag rest, or from a bench rest. Then the problem of keeping the rifle steady does not amount to much. The shooter can concentrate on squeezing the trigger and learn to let off his shot without disturbing the aim. He will gain confidence in his rifle and in himself. He will learn that when the sights are correctly aligned, the bullet strikes within the bull's-eye as he has intended. After a week of rest shooting and concentration on squeezing the trigger and avoiding the flinch, the beginner should be able to shoot a relatively small group at 100 or 200 yards.

The next step should be shooting from the prone position, which is the steadiest of all positions. When the prone position is assumed, the shooter lies with his legs outspread and his body at about a forty-five degree angle to the left of the line toward the target. The left elbow should be directly under the rifle, and the rifle itself should rest on the heel of the palm. In that position there is much less tendency for the rifle to shake and wobble because it is supported by the bones of the forearm, acting as a pillar in direct contact between the rifle and the ground. In this position the rifle is relatively but not absolutely steady even with the help of a sling.

Shooting from the prone position

The ability to squeeze the trigger and to call the shot will increase in usefulness here. For many years the army has taught that the rifleman should not know when his rifle is going to go off. The theory is that when the rifleman gets his sights lined up approximately he should take up the preliminary pull of the double military pull*.

Then when his sights are on the bull correctly,

*This refers to what was, at the time this piece was written, the standard instructional technique that taught military rifle users to tighten the trigger finger, usually to a pound or pressure or so, when he made the initial line-up with this sights. The subsequent sequence leading to the shot was as O'Connor explains it.

he should increase the squeeze by a few ounces. When the sights wobble off he should stop. As the rifle comes back again on the target, he should increase the pull once more. Finally, theoretically at least, the rifle will go off unexpectedly, and because he is not expecting the recoil, he will not flinch. Since he has increased the pressure on the trigger only when the sights are correctly aligned, every shot should land within the bull's-eye. For whatever reason, this theory never worked with me. I have always known when the gun was going off. As soon as I learn the trigger pull I press the trigger until all except the last two or three ounces of pull are taken up. Then when my sights swing onto the target in correct alignment, I squeeze the shot off. Our beginning rifleman, then, should practice from no other position but prone for some time. He should keep shooting until the majority of his shots land within the bull. Not until this essential prone position has been mastered should he move on to a more difficult one.

Under most hunting conditions, the prone position has little value

Under most hunting conditions the prone position has little value. In other words, there is practically no chance that a man can shoot at a white-tail deer or any other forest animal from a prone position. In the Southwest with its rocks and cactus the position can seldom be assumed and it cannot be used in canyon country because to lie down the rifleman needs relatively level ground. For plains shooting at antelope the prone position is very handy. It can also be widely used above timber line in the Rocky Mountains, where a typical shot will be from a smooth, round ridge down into a basin below. The most useful of all hunting positions under any other conditions except the jump shooting of forest game is the standard sitting position, which is almost as steady as prone. The sitting position puts the rifle much higher than the prone position and it can be used in fairly tall grass or small bushes. It can be assumed on a hillside. For my part, I have probably killed seventy-five per cent of the game I have shot from the sitting position. In the canyon country of the West, even when a buck jumps up and goes off at a hard run, I drop to the sitting position and I have trained myself to get the sights on almost the instant I touch the ground.

Shooting from the sitting position

To assume the sitting position, the hunter should face away from the target at an angle of about 45 degrees. Then he should lean over so that the flat part of his upper arm above the elbow comes in contact with the inside of the knees. As in the prone position, the left elbow should be as nearly under the rifle as possible so that the bone of the forearm acts as a pillar to support it. In the standard sitting position the heels are hard against the ground, and if the shooter has the time he should make little holes in the soil so that his heels will not slip. A good variation of the sitting position is the same as the one just described except that the shooter sits cross-legged. Many prefer this cross-legged position on level ground; of course, it

cannot be used from a steep hillside. From a good
steady position it is not too difficult for a good shot
who can squeeze them off and call them to stay in
a ten-inch circle at three hundred yards and to
drive the bullets well within the lung area of an
animal the size of a mule deer or sheep at the
same distance. At four hundred yards, however,
the prone position should be used whenever possible; usually an animal that far away is not
greatly frightened and the rifleman will have a
chance to assume the steadier position.

In the sitting position the most fatal mistake
that can be made is to put the elbows on top of the
knees. When this happens the loose cartilage of
the elbows and the kneecaps causes the rifle to
wobble. It is actually no better than shooting offhand — if, indeed, it is as good.

The sitting position is made much steadier by
the proper use of a good tight sling. If a hunter has
time to get his left arm through the loop of the
sling and tighten up all along the line, he can do
the best work from the sitting position. One of the
smallest groups I ever shot from the sitting position under any circumstances was at a big mountain sheep. He was on a hillside about two hundred yards away. I had been watching him with
glasses to decide whether I wanted his big head or
not. When I decided I did, I laid my binoculars
down, slipped my arm through the loop, drew the
keepers up tight, and then put the cross-hairs right
behind a foreleg. That rifle seemed as steady as

from a bench rest. Because that ram was on a steep slope, his off side was higher than the near side. The bullets I was using did not open up much. The shots went through the body and almost tore the left leg off where it joined the body on the off side. I believe a silver dollar would have covered my three shots.

The kneeling position is much less steady than sitting. In fact, it is not greatly superior in that respect to shooting offhand. There are times, however, when it is useful. It can be assumed slightly quicker than a sitting position and it holds a rifle a little higher. Where there are tail grass and small bushes it is often impossible to sit and yet one can kneel and get the rifle over the obstructions. As I write this, the last deer I shot was from the kneeling position. I was down in the Mexican state of Sonora. I could see two deer across a wide arroyo. They were partially concealed by brush and I was standing in high grass and bushes. I watched those deer for a moment; then I could see that one of them was a big buck. I dropped to a kneeling position and as the rifle steadied I squeezed off the shot with the cross-hairs resting right on the chest of the big buck as he faced me. I heard the bullet plop into him and saw him go off on a mad dash. I crossed the arroyo, picked up his track, and found him dead about seventy-five yards from where he had been hit. The bullet hole was almost exactly in the spot for which I had aimed.

To assume the kneeling position, one should

Shooting from the kneeling position

face away from the target at an angle of about 45 degrees, squat firmly on the right heel, and hook the left arm well over the left knee. The tension of the back muscles causes the upper arm to pull against the knee and establish a relatively steady state of equilibrium. Above all, the shooter should avoid having his elbow right on top of the wobbly kneecap.

The offhand position is the most widely used, one of the most useful, and also the least steady of all positions. It is a position that must be learned, however, and no one who cannot shoot well from it can be called a good all-around shot. Almost all game in wooded areas is killed from the offhand position.

A good shot from the sitting position at 200 yards can keep most of his shots in the 8-inch bull*, but the good offhand shot is one who can keep *all* his shots in the 30-inch 4-ring, picking up an occasional bull as he goes along. If he can average a score of 43 out of 50 he is a good offhand shot. If he can place *half* his shots in the bull with the rest in the 4-ring he is very good indeed. It is seldom, however, that a skillful shot will take a pop at a big-game animal offhand at 200 yards. If

---

* O'Connor refers to bull's-eyes in a fashion that may be confusing to modern shooters. That is because the configuration of bull's-eyes, including the width of the rings and the number or rings present, can vary. The key thing to keep in mind, and this is what O'Connor always stressed, is accuracy sufficient to kill the game animal being hunted in a clean, quick and ethical fashion.

the game is that far away, he'll usually have time to sit or kneel.

For cool, deliberate offhand shooting, the right elbow should be held horizontal, almost exactly level with the shoulder, and the butt should rest on the big pad of muscles thus formed at the conjunction of the shoulder and the upper arm. The work of holding the butt firm against the shoulder should be done with the last four fingers of the right hand and with the thumb *around* the small of the stock. The left hand should be rather far back, just about on the floor plate of the rifle, and the weight of the rifle should rest on the heel of the palm. The elbow should be directly below the rifle itself, as if it is to the side it causes sway and trembling. The shooter should stand so that a line drawn between his toes points almost directly at the target. In other words, he should stand so that if he is shooting east he is just about facing south.

The proper hand, elbow, arm, and shoulder positions for offhand shooting

This is the offhand target position and one which will occasionally be used for a fairly long shot on game if the cover is such that one cannot kneel or sit. The last moose I shot was from the offhand position. I was standing in arctic willows almost waist-high and the bull was about two hundred yards away. My three shots could have just about been covered by a twenty-four-inch circle, which isn't too good, yet not too bad either.

The best offhand shot I ever made — one of those a man will always remember — was down in Sonora many years ago. I was standing on a point in waist-high chaparral when I saw a big buck standing under a tree about 300 yards away across the canyon on the next point. It seemed as if it took me a couple of minutes to get the shot off, but when I did the buck fell on his nose. In that case my single shot for record was a pin-wheel "5" [five-inch target].

For woods shooting at running game, the left hand is much farther forward to control the swing of the rifle and the shooter does not face away from the target so much. In woods hunting the accent is on speed, rather than accuracy, since the target is large, usually not far away, and very often moving.

TRIGGER CONTROL

When good positions are learned and become natural, the next step is to control the trigger and call the shot. No man ever learns to become a good rifleshot unless he develops his coordination to the point where he can let his shot off at the exact instant he wishes. This is as true of shooting running game as it is on the target range. The best trigger is one with a light, crisp pull. It can be a double-stage military pull or a single-stage sporting pull, *but it must be crisp.* If the last stage is draggy, rough, and creepy, no one can use it. A heavy crisp pull is far superior to a light creepy pull.

When a good shot learns his pull, he takes up

The best trigger is one with a light, crisp pull

by his sensitive sense of touch all but a couple of ounces of the pull; then when his sights are correctly aligned, he squeezes off those last few ounces. The final stage of the pull should always be thought of as the most gentle of squeezes, even though the squeeze is a rapid one at a charging grizzly. If the motion that lets the trigger off is anything but a gentle squeeze, it will disturb the aim and the shot will not go where it is supposed to.

The difference between the good shot and the fair shot is that the good shot gets his bullet on the way when he wants it to go, and the fair shot gets his off *about* when he wants it. This getting the shot off at the precise instant takes a lot of practice and the good shot who isn't shooting up to par has let his co-ordination fall down. This is why offhand shooting is such fine practice. You either have to control that trigger — or else!

No one can ever be a good shot unless he can *call his shot*. He should be able to say where his sights are aligned when the rifle goes off. Particularly in the offhand position it is impossible to get the shots off exactly at the right instant every time. In the interval between the time the brain says to let off and when the laggard muscles actually do so, the rifle has moved a bit, from a pinwheel "5" to a "4" at two o'clock let us say. But the shooter should know it. If he calls a "5" and gets the "4" he is getting nowhere.

Shots on game should be called just as carefully. The first moose I ever shot was in very

Calling the
shot

heavy timber along the bank of a little creek up in the Alberta Rockies. I was still hunting and was within thirty-five yards of the moose when it got up. It ran quartering away, and when the rifle went off, the cross-hairs in the scope were against the curve of the abdomen, so that the bullet should have driven up into the lungs.

But away went the moose, giving absolutely no sign of being hit. I thought it over. I just couldn't see how I could have missed the bull. I took up his track. He had gone down in a patch of willow not more than fifty yards from where he had been struck by the bullet. My shot was right where I had called it — which wasn't much of a feat at that, since a moose is a very large target. Many times the fact that I always call shots has paid off in big-game hunting.

Always know how the sights are aligned when the rifle goes off, and you are on your way to becoming a good shot!

Getting enough practice with the rifle isn't easy for the average city dweller. If possible he should belong to a rifle club so he can have range facilities at his disposal and be able to shoot for a half-day every week or two. If he cannot get anything better, an indoor range for three-positional .22 shooting helps enormously. He should not confine himself to the prone position alone, as so many small-bore enthusiasts do, but should shoot offhand and sitting as much as possible.

Handgun shooting is beautifully adapted to training for rifle shooting as the very smoothest trigger pull is even more vital with the handgun than with the rifle. To some extent training acquired at skeet and trap shooting is also transferable. Those games teach one to swing and to shoot fast, both skills applicable to running game.

If nothing better is available, "dry shooting" at miniature targets or silhouettes of game in one's own living-room is helpful and far better than nothing. The man who religiously squeezes off and calls ten shots a day with an empty rifle is going to be surprisingly good if he can also have a little practice with live ammunition between times.

"Dry shooting" is helpful

From the patio of my home I can see a chimney with a dark brick. Every day I take a rifle out and get off ten dry shots from the sitting position at this brick and as many offhand. The neighbors think I'm slightly nuts, but it keeps the trigger finger limbered up!

As Townsend Whelen once suggested, "only accurate rifles are interesting" (a quote often wrongly attributed to Warren Page), and here he offers his thoughts on what is essential for getting the ultimate accuracy out of a rifle. His thoughts and recommendations on trigger squeeze are of particular interest. The material comes from The Hunting Rifle *(1940).*

Townsend Whelen's recommendations for good shooting

THE ESSENTIALS

The primary essentials for good shooting with the rifle are skill in *Holding, Aiming* and *Trigger Squeeze.* The most important of these is *Trigger Squeeze,* although the beginner, at the start, seemingly has more trouble with *Holding.* If the rifle be held steadily and aimed accurately at the bull's-eye, then if the trigger be squeezed off without disturbing this hold and aim, the bull's-eye will be surely struck by the bullet.

The first stumbling block that the beginner encounters is holding the rifle steady or "still." If your instruction is not on proper lines you seldom get over this seemingly difficult job. You make almost no progress in your attempts to hold the rifle steady and you finally give up in disgust.

Also, if you cannot hold the rifle steady, you likewise cannot see the sights correctly ali[g]ned on the mark for more than the briefest moment, and consequently you learn nothing about accurate aim.

Finally, if you cannot hold steady, and see your sights accurately and steadily ali[g]ned on the mark, you cannot learn to coordinate your trigger squeeze so that the rifle will be discharged without any disturbance of hold and aim. Moreover, you cannot continually practice the correct trigger squeeze until its proper performance becomes a fixed habit.

The good shot is the man to whom correct trigger squeeze has become a fixed habit. Everything else in the realm of rifle shooting is comparatively easy and simple compared with the trigger squeeze, but it is difficult to make the beginner see it at first. The first, and seemingly the greatest trouble he will encounter is holding. Therefore at the start it all sums up to teaching you to hold the rifle steadily.

Trigger squeeze is a fixed habit of the good shot

Fortunately a method has been found by means of which we can teach any beginner to hold the rifle practically absolutely steady after only about five periods of daily practice of about 15 minutes each. It merely consists of teaching you to assume the prone position with the gunsling in the precise and standard method by which it is assumed by all experienced and successful riflemen. The place to learn this prone position is in your bedroom or on your lawn. Like any unusual position or exercise, it is extremely uncomfortable at first, and it may make you stiff. As soon as you have become accustomed to the position, and have gotten over your stiffness — about the fifth day — ability comes to hold the rifle so steadily that you cannot see the sights move on the target. Therefore the first step is to learn this prone position with the gunsling.

When you have thus learned to hold steadily,

the next step is to learn to aim accurately. This is comparatively easy, and will be fully explained to you in the chapter devoted to it. Remember that it must be made an accurate operation, more like threading a very fine needle than corking a bottle.

Practicing the trigger squeeze

The third step consists of learning the trigger squeeze and coordinating it with your holding and aiming. This you learn by practicing the trigger squeeze exercise while holding the rifle in the prone position with gunsling, and while aiming at a small target tacked on the wall of your bedroom or set up somewhere on your lawn. The trigger squeeze exercise must be practiced until you are letter perfect in it, which may take you five or ten minute periods of home practice. In fact this trigger squeeze exercise is so important that every expert shot practices it two or three times a week, exactly as you see every expert golfer practicing his swing on the lawn or on the side lines at the golf club.

Not until you have become letter perfect in this trigger squeeze exercise should you think of firing a single shot through your rifle. If you have just purchased your first rifle you should not, at this period, handle it at all except to practice the prone position with the gunsling, aiming, and the trigger squeeze exercise.

Having become fairly skilled in and familiar with the three primary essentials of Holding, Aiming, and Trigger Squeeze, which should take you never less than ten days of home practice, you are ready to proceed to the range with your rifle and cartridges. But before you start study the chapter on sight adjustment, and practice adjusting the sights a little. On the range your first efforts will be directed toward grouping your shots in a small circle on the target. When you are able to do this it is proof that you have learned the three primary essentials fairly correctly.

Next you apply what you studied in the chapter on sight adjustment and you learn to place your group of shots in the center of the bull's-eye. Now you are on the road to becoming a fair slow fire shot. At least you have a clear understanding of the essentials of slow fire. Perhaps this has taken you five afternoons on the range, perhaps less. About five more afternoons and you will be grouping all your shots in about a 2 ½ inch circle in the center of the bull's-eye at 100 yards. You will begin to see the light. You will be very much encouraged and interested. You see yourself well on the way to becoming a fine rifle shot.

All this time you are confining your shooting entirely to the prone position with the gunsling, and you should also keep up your trigger squeeze exercises daily at home. You cannot have too much of these trigger squeeze exercises. I should say that the ideal course of instruction would be to shoot on the range twice a week, or on Saturday afternoons, with 15 minutes trigger squeeze exercises every day at home. Remember what I told you above about *the good shot being the man to whom correct trigger squeeze had become a fixed habit.*

As you proceed with your slow fire shooting in the prone position, and with your perfection of the three primary essentials, you will also realize that

Other secoondary essentials

there are other secondary essentials. These are *Calling the Shot, Sight Adjustment,* and *Wind Allowance.* You will find them explained hereafter, and gradually you work them into your slow fire shooting. Now you are becoming a really good slow fire shot. You should be averaging a score of 90 to 95 points in ten shots, all however shooting in the prone position with the gunsling.

Having proceeded this far, you should then take up the sitting position. Read up on it first, then become accustomed to it by position and trigger squeeze exercises at home, and then introduce it into your range practice. It is a most valuable position for the hunter, and you should learn it well.

In the same manner precisely, you then proceed to the kneeling and standing positions. The kneeling position is a favorite one with artists, but it is distinctly out of favor with riflemen. In fact I would almost say that if you want to you can neglect it. Certainly if it does not particularly appeal to you pass it up. I have never fired a single shot at game from the kneeling position. Not so, however, with the standing position. Do not neglect it, but on the contrary from the time you take it up, put in at least half your practice in this standing position (and afterwards in rapid fire in it). It is the most important position for the hunter. From it you will fire practically all the shots at deer in forest country, and at least half the shots at big game in other countries. It is the most difficult position of all in which to learn to shoot really well because of the holding problem, and it requires a whole lot of practice, not only on the range, but in the trigger squeeze exercise as well. I do not believe a week has gone by in forty years that I have not practiced the trigger squeeze exercise in the standing position for at least five minutes.

Now you have become a good all-around slow fire shot in all four of the firing positions. You will now be able to shoot well on woodchucks, prairie dogs, hawks, crows, and also on big game at long ranges; that is when your target is standing still or practically so, and you have time to assume a steady position, and time for careful, methodical aim and trigger squeeze. But you have not yet acquired any ability in that fast shooting which is so necessary to connect with a running buck, game on the move anywhere, or animals likely to get out of sight in an instant. You still have to learn snap shooting and rapid fire to round you out as a practical rifle shot.

Snap shooting and rapid fire

The procedure in rapid fire is exactly the same as in slow fire. First you practice the prone rapid fire exercise at home until you are letter perfect in it. Then you take up range practice, starting slowly at first, and gradually speeding up your time until you are shooting your five shots in 20 seconds. Never go so fast but that you keep every shot well on the target, and the majority of them in the black bull's-eye. When fairly skilled prone, then proceed to the other positions in their order in the same way. During this period, and from now on, half your trigger squeeze exercises at home should be in rapid fire.

Snap shooting is the rapid delivery of the first shot from a position of ready with the rifle locked. It simulates the shot that you get when walking along and game suddenly appears at fairly close range. It is learned in connection with your rapid fire shooting by requiring that the rifle shall be held in the position of ready (butt below the shoulder) with the safety on, before giving the command for commence firing or before the rapid fire target appears. That is putting the rifle to the shoulder for the first shot and taking off the safety should be performed within your time limit.

Before you complete your training and start for the game fields, I should also advise some firing, both slow and rapid fire, at cardboard silhouettes cut out and painted to give the size and appearance of game, and set up on the rifle range at various distances. This is to get you accustomed to aiming at natural targets instead of the conventional bull's-eye target you have used thus far. This is particularly necessary in order that you shall learn how to aim at game, and how to adjust your sights so as to place your bullets in vital parts in the same manner and with the same ease that you have learned to place them in the center of the bull's-eye. This shooting had better be at unknown distances so you will also have the problem of trajectory and the fall of the bullet to solve. Better get a friend to place these silhouettes at distances from 100 to 350 yards while your back is turned. Estimate your distance to them, fire, and finally pace the distance to see what it actually is.

These are the essentials of your training. Sounds like a hell of a lot of work. So it would be were it not so absorbingly interesting. But it's just like playing any other interesting game—golf or tennis. Really it is a lot more absorbing to a man who is mechanically minded. There are always scientific problems to solve, demanding brains and skill rather than brawn.

Shooting is a lot more absorbing to the mechanically minded man

II
POSITIONS
FOR RIFLE SHOOTING

No aspect of effective marksmanship merits more attention than shooting positions. The hunter, for example, may need to make a split-second decision on whether to take a shot. Alternatively, he may have time to get into a specific position, and when that is the case, he obviously will want to choose the one that makes a telling shot most likely. Many types of competitive shooting actual involve different positions, and marksmen must do their best to master all of them.

The five selections that follow cover the subject in considerable detail, but for those interested in even more information, there is a fine chapter on the subject, entitled "The Shooting Positions," in Edward C. Crossman's Military and Sporting Rifle Shooting *(1932). Similarly, two chapters from Townsend Whelen's* The Hunting Rifle *(1940) — "The Prone Position" and "The Sitting, Kneeling, and Standing Positions" — are also helpful.*

●

Jack O'Connor was a skilled shooter, one who practiced every day, even if it was only dry firing. For practical advice, his "Steady Shooting Posi-

Jack
O'Connor
on steady
shooting
positions

tions," taken from the handy little booklet 7-Lesson Rifle Shooting Course (1981), is hard to beat. He also offers more detailed information in several of his books. These are listed in the bibliography at the end of the current work.

STEADY SHOOTING POSITIONS

The principles of hitting a stationary object, as we have seen, be it a bull's-eye, a woodchuck, or an antelope, are very simple. All one has to do is hold the rifle steady, align the sights correctly, and get off the shot without disturbing the aim by jerking the trigger or flinching.

One of the indications of the experienced shot and a good hunter is that he always takes the steadiest position he can manage, as he wants to place his bullet just right and kill cleanly and humanely. If he can't use a rest or a lie down, he'll settle for sitting, and if he can't sit he'll kneel. Only as a last resort will he shoot offhand. If conditions are such, however, that he can shoot prone, prone it should be, because that is the steadiest position of all.

THE PRONE POSITION

Use of the prone position in most big-game hunting is limited, but anyone who takes his shooting seriously should practice it. As you lie down on your stomach and place your elbows on the ground, place your body at an angle of about 45 degrees to the left of your line of sight. These instructions are for a right-handed person, of course; if you're left handed, place your body at 45 degrees to the right of your line of sight. Your legs should be spread apart. Place your left elbow directly under the barrel, so the rifle is supported by solid bone against solid ground, just as a pillar supports a building. Your right elbow should be sloped outward, so your upper arms and chest form a sturdy "tripod."

But, alas, much of the time prone simply cannot be used in hunting. In flat plains country, grass and low bushes are apt to get in the way. When shooting downhill the position is impossibly awkward, as no one can shoot with his legs and fanny higher than his head. The use I have found for prone is in hunting mountain game, where the animals are approached by crawling up behind a ridge, often above timberline. The hunter can slide his rifle along ahead of him in the final phases of the stalk, and quickly settle into prone position as soon as the game is in view. Often he can combine the standard prone position with a rest. Many times I have put my 10-gallon hat on a stone or over a solid clump of bunch grass. I know of nothing more comforting, nothing better calculated to head off an incipient attack of buck fever than the sight of the intersection of those crosshairs in the scope resting solid right where you want them.

THE SITTING POSITION

The queen of all shooting positions is sitting

In most of the big-game hunting I have done, the queen of all positions is sitting. It puts the line of sight high enough so that it can be used on high grass and low bushes. It can also be used on a hillside. It is much more flexible than prone and can be used nicely for running shots whereas prone generally can not. If used with a sling, sitting is a very steady and practical position.

The best way to assume this position is to sit facing to the right from the line of aim at an angle of about 45 degrees (to the left if you are left handed), lean way over, so that the flat of the upper arms is against the flat shinbones. Then there is flat against flat and no wobble. The tension of the back muscles will pull these surfaces into close contact, with a resulting steadiness that is the real key to a good sitting position.

Rest the forend of the rifle on the heel of your palm, with the elbow almost but not quite under the rifle. Brace the part of the right arm that's immediately above the elbow against the right leg just below the knee. Spread your feet well apart, for steadiness of tripod effect. On the side of a hill, dig heels into the ground, but on level ground keep feet relaxed as naturally as possible. Trying to dig the heels in on the level results — with me, at least — in a tremor, which doesn't help at all.

A variation of the sitting position is with legs crossed. I do not use it, but many good shots do.

So do teen-agers whose legs have grown faster than their bodies. At 14 I sat cross-legged; the conventional sitting position gave me cramps.

The beginner often makes two grave mistakes in the sitting position. He sits upright and puts his wobbly elbows on his wobbly kneecaps. That way, his position is no steadier than offhand. Bend way over! Get the flat of the upper arm against the flat of the shins. Get the left elbow under the forend with the rifle resting on the heel of the palm!

Sitting is a good steady position, even without a shooting gunsling. With one, and a good loop high and tight on the upper arm, it can be almost as steady as prone and can be used for a long and difficult shot under conditions when getting into prone is impossible.

THE KNEELING POSITION

Kneeling is nowhere near as steady as sitting, but it does have the virtues of being a bit faster to get into and giving a higher line of sight. It also has its advantages when sitting down would fill the shooter's pants full of thorns. To get into the kneeling position, stand facing at about 45 degrees to the right of the target. Then kneel down and sit on your right heel, resting the weight of your body on it. Some shooters like to sit on the side of their foot instead of on their heel — try it and see which you like best. Your left knee should point toward the target. As in the sitting position, avoid putting wobbly elbow on wobbly kneecap; instead, hook your upper left arm over your knee and let the tension of the back muscles do most of the work.

OFFHAND SHOOTING

Offhand is the toughest of all, but under certain conditions it must be used, and anyone who plans to hunt big game should not neglect practicing it. It is *the* position for brush and heavy woods where game is come on suddenly, mostly at close range, and often on the move.

To assume a good offhand position, your right elbow should be about level with your shoulder and the butt of your rifle against the pad of muscles formed at the shoulder joint. If the steel buttplate is farther inside against your collar bone, the recoil is apt to hurt, and if your right elbow is down toward the waist it is difficult to get your right eye in line with the sights with modern stocks. Again, for all shooting remember that the thumb of your right hand should be around the grip and not alongside it. With your thumb around the grip you will have more control over your trigger finger and over the rifle.

For fast running shooting your left hand should be moved pretty well out on the forend to give leverage for a fast swing, but for a precise offhand shot your left hand should be farther back toward the receiver and the weight should rest on the heel of the palm with your elbow almost directly underneath the barrel. In this position your left hand merely serves as a support. Your right hand should pull the rifle back against your shoulder and when the sights look right, take up your final ounce of pull.

This is the standard offhand position in military rifle shooting and from it a good shot should be able to keep the majority of his bullets in a six-inch circle at 100 yards or in a 12-inch circle at 200 yards. A bit steadier is the hip-rest position, which is permitted in the standing position in small-bore shooting. The left elbow rests inside the hip and the left hand supports the rifle just forward of the trigger guard.

The standard offhand position in military rifle shooting

Now and then a precise and difficult shot must be made from offhand. The hunter may see game suddenly and be afraid that if he moves it will be gone or he may be standing in high grass where any other position would be impossible. It is always easy to forget the misses but I'll never forget the best offhand shot I ever made on a game animal. I was hunting many years ago in northern Sonora, Mexico, when I saw a buck standing under a tree across a canyon. Since the point I was on was covered with waist-high chaparral any position but offhand was impossible. The buck was about 300 yards away, but I decided to try the shot as I had everything to gain, nothing to lose.

As I stood there the intersection of the crosshairs performed a figure 8 but finally it settled for an instant right on top of the buck's shoulder. I took up the final ounce of pull and down the buck went. But this experience was an exception. It isn't once in a blue moon that a 300-yard offhand shot would have to be taken.

But no one should neglect practice in the offhand position, as skill on the hind legs will save the hunter's bacon many a time. It is *the* position for most deer hunting in the brushy East and for the heavy forests of the Pacific Coast. In the open bush of East Africa most game is shot from the hind legs, either from straight offhand or with the aid of the steadying rest from a tree or an ant hill. The last desert sheep I shot was from offhand. I had thought a bunch of rams were on the other side of a saddle, but they had moved, and the first thing I knew I had sneaked right in their midst where they were lying in scattered boulders. The one I killed was on the run and all of 35 yards away.

Any rifleman should learn all the standard positions, how to use them efficiently, get into them quickly.

Bryce Towsley's thoughts on shooting positions in the field

This coverage of field positions by Bryce Towsley, though highly opinionated (something that is common among writers on guns and marksmanship), makes plenty of sense and gives every shooter reason to ponder positions he might use when hunting. Positions in the field come in many forms. Shooting while comfortably seated in a shooting house, on a stand with padded rails, or by a sandbag is one proposition. Taking a snap shot at a whitetail in full flight is a quite different one indeed. In this selection, which appeared in the June 2000 issue of American Rifleman, *Towsley looks at the various positions the hunter might need to take while afield and makes practical suggestions on how to shoot most accurately from each of them.*

PRACTICAL SHOOTING POSITIONS IN THE FIELD

Shooting position can make a huge difference in outcome when hunting. There are four basic shooter-supported field positions that rifle hunters will fire from: standing, sitting, kneeling and prone. As practical shooting positions for hunting, all have their place, but each also has its unique strong points and weaknesses. The key with them all is to always try to have bone rather than muscle supporting the rifle. The old adage is to "build a bridge of bones." Bone is solid and immovable, whereas muscle is soft, flexible and subject to tremors. If you are among the living, your bones are covered with soft tissue. Think of this as padding for the structural support, like the foam or sandbag on a rifle rest. Visualize a solid, internal, structural bridge of supporting bone between the rifle and the ground. Any time you interrupt that

"Build a bridge of bones"

structure with supporting muscle, you induce more movement and less control.

STANDING OR OFF-HAND

Standing up and shooting "on your hind legs" is absolutely the worst position for most hunting. But I'll wager that well over half the big game critters shot at are dodging bullets fired by a standing hunter. I'll also wager that more big game critters owe their continued existence to so many hunters' insistence on shooting from this position than to any other single aspect of shooting.

That said, often it's the only option. When the shot must be taken fast, or when vegetation or terrain prevents using other positions, the hunter must shoot off-hand. Many a still hunter or tracker has never killed a deer from any other position.

Further, standing is extremely helpful because it will teach a shooter a lot about the art of field shooting, and for that reason alone it should be practiced often. It's rare for a truly good field shot not to also be a good off-hand shot as well. To become one, a shooter must learn the discipline of trigger control, how to control sight wobble, and the relationship between the two. If a shooter can do it well from standing, he can do it very well from any other position.

One reason standing is such a poor position to shoot from is that it is almost impossible to build that bridge of bones. Competitive shooters come close by using forend extensions with palm rests or weird-looking positions that allow the left elbow (for right-hand shooters) to be wedged against the hip. None of that really works well for a hunter. In the end, you will find that the muscles of your left shoulder and arm are supporting the rifle. You can build a little tension by pulling back with that hand as you push forward with your right shoulder, and that helps steady the gun and calm your muscles. But you can't escape that it's still muscle supporting the rifle. Not only that, but you are holding the rifle at the furthest position from the ground where it is still possible to aim. As a rule of thumb, the closer to the ground you can put the rifle, the steadier the position will become.

The position is simple: stand at an angle to the target, usually close to 90 degrees, with your left shoulder facing the target. Your feet should be shoulder-width apart, with the left pointed slightly to the target. The key is to find a position that is solid and comfortable. Snug the gun butt into the pocket formed between the muscle of your shoulder and your collarbone. Do not put the rifle butt on your collarbone or on your biceps. This pocket helps steady the rifle but also puts a little meat behind it to absorb the recoil. This will vary a bit with body type, so you may have to experiment some to find what works best for you.

The standing or offhand position

Your right elbow should be about parallel with the ground. Keep your left arm under the rifle, much like a waiter carries a large tray. This again keeps bone supporting the rifle as much as possible. If the arm is held out to the side, as many shooters try to do, you are depending more on muscle to hold the weight of the rifle.

KNEELING

Kneeling is a poor way to shoot a rifle

This may be a competitive shooting position, but in my opinion, it's a poor way to shoot a rifle. In theory, it should be more stable than standing, but I have never been able to shoot well while kneeling. Because kneeling also puts your line of sight nearly as low as sitting does, and considering that sitting is a far superior shooting position, I see little use for kneeling in the field. Some say it's faster than sitting, and I suppose that may have some merit. But if you use kneeling rather than sitting because it saves you a half second, what do you have? Usually just a faster miss.

Once again, use the concept of bones supporting the rifle. Your left knee will be up, pointing at the target and supporting your left arm. Don't put your elbow directly on your knee; that's a wobbly position, and your elbow will keep slipping off. Instead, find a comfortable position where the edge of your elbow and upper forearm are against your knee. Body types vary, and each shooter will have to find what's comfortable for him.

Slump your body forward and arch your back to lower your center of gravity. It helps to build a little muscle tension between the left knee and left arm. Keep your arm under the rifle so that the bones of your arm and leg are supporting the weight.

PRONE

This is said to be the most stable position for a rifleman. I have watched the best Olympic shooters up close, and a good prone shooter can shoot almost as well as from a bench rest.

But not me. I don't like prone for several reasons. First, it rarely works in the field. It simply puts you too low to the ground, and there is always something in the way when you try to shoot. Even if you think the path is clear, remember the bullet's path is initially lower than your line of sight.

Problems with the prone position

I can easily count on one hand the big game animals I have shot from the prone position. Or I could simply count the layers of scar tissue over my right eye, because I think every one of those shots left me bleeding, from the scope hitting me in the face. The prone position puts your face forward on the rifle stock and close to the scope. That not only creates problems with the eye relief of most scopes and results in less than a full field of view, but it also shortens the distance the scope needs to travel to draw blood.

But for those who can work it, prone is steady and for that reason alone is a useful position. The traditional hunting position is for the shooter to lie on the ground with his body at about a 45-degree angle to the target. This allows the body to act like a spring and flex a little more under recoil, absorbing and dispersing the force. Many shooting coaches teach the shooter to lie more in line with the rifle, but they are usually shooting .22 rifles. The more directly behind the rifle you are, the more your body will feel the full effect of the recoil.

Keep your elbows close together and in front of you. The left one should be under the rifle, supporting it. Again, support the rifle with bone. Position your legs so they are comfortable. It sometimes helps to cock the left leg up a little and put tension on the muscles of the leg and back.

SITTING

The sitting position is the hunter's best friend

This position is the rifle hunter's best friend. It gets him up above the vegetation, steadies the rifle and allows him to absorb the recoil without lasting physical damage. It is, for all practical purposes, quick to assume and easy to move around if the animal changes positions before you can shoot. Which is an important point that is often forgotten until it's too late.

Sit at about a 45-degree angle to the target. You can cross your legs at the ankles in front of you or simply plant your feet side by side on the ground. Actually, you may find yourself using both styles as the situation dictates. Don't place the points of your elbows on the points of your knees. This is painful and as wobbly as a drunk on a Saturday night. Use the flats of your arms against the flats of your legs in any way that fits your body style well. Different body types will use slightly different positions and everybody has to work it out for themselves. But again, think bone support. Personally I like to cross my legs and hunch my back so I am low to the ground and balled up with the back of my elbows against the front of my knees. This also induces muscle tension that helps to steady the rifle. If you can get your back up against something like a tree or log it steadies you even more.

Certain types of hunting make the likelihood of taking standing shots quite high. Man drives for deer come to mind, as does traditional still hunting (it is easy to forget that the use of tree stands, tripods, elevated shooting houses, and the like belongs to the modern era). The standing shooter faces special problems, and Wayne Van Zwoll examines these in detail in the following se-lection, which was published in a 2000 issue of American Hunter.

SHOOTING STANDING

"Stand up and shoot like a man." Bad advice. You'll shoot much better sitting or kneeling be-

Wayne Van Zwoll's seven tips for good shooting from the standing position

cause your center of gravity is lower and you have more ground contact. But if you must shoot quickly or over brush, standing may be your only option. Here's how to practice a position you'll try never to use — but one that could someday put venison on the table:

1. Before you lift the rifle, point your feet properly. Place them shoulder-width apart, with your weight evenly distributed. For starters, a line through your toes should cross your rifle's shadow at roughly a 30-degree angle. That will get you close to a comfortable position. If the sights are off target, adjust your body by first moving your feet. Find your natural point of aim: the direction in which the rifle naturally points. Do not force the rifle onto the target with your arms!

2. Grasp the grip firmly and pull the rifle's butt into your shoulder. Keep your left elbow nearly under the rifle and your right elbow almost horizontal. Your right shoulder will form a nice pocket for the buttpad. Raise the stock comb to your face; drop your face as little as possible for a firm contact with the comb. Touch the trigger with the first joint of your index finger.

3. Keep your head erect so that you can look straight through the sight. Squint if you must. Scopes should be mounted so that the rear (ocular) lens extends to the rear guard screw.

If you must mount the scope so that the lens housing extends more than an inch over the grip, the stock is probably too long for you. Your eye should be about 3 inches from the ocular lens when your face is as far forward as comfort allows.

4. Take two deep breaths — one as you shoulder the rifle, the other as you let it settle on the target. Relax as you release the second breath; do not forcibly empty your lungs. Now the sight should be on the target, and your trigger finger should be taking up slack.

5. Apply pressure to the trigger when the sight is on target; hold pressure when the sight moves off target. The rifle should fire when the sight is where you want it. When you run out of air, or if the rifle starts to shake badly, do not jerk the trigger. Start over. Resist the urge to time the shot — that is, to yank the trigger as the sight bounces onto the target. Most often, you will miss.

6. Follow through, maintaining position as the rifle recoils. Call your shot — that is, before you look in the spotting scope or retrieve your target, tell yourself where the bullet hit. An accurate call means that you had your eyes on the target and knew where the sight was when the bullet left. That is very important! Calling your shots is the first step in correcting problems with position, breathing and trigger control.

7. Practice offhand more than any other position. Dry firing (empty) enables you to practice more often and without recoil. Get good before you try to get fast. Hurrying a shot teaches bad habits. When a big buck forces you to hurry, you'll be faster *and* more accurate if you've practiced proper form.

Further thoughts on the sitting position from Jack O'Connor

Another common field position — and one that is preferable to standing, when time or the situation permits — is the sitting one. Jack O'Connor looks at this position, which he describes as "the best compromise between prone and offhand," in a piece that originally appeared in Jack O'Connor's Gun Book *(1953).*

SIT AND YOU'LL HIT

On the plains and in the mountains, the sitting position is the most useful of them all when you're after big game. It isn't quite as steady as the prone, so your shooting will be a little less accurate. It isn't quite as fast as the offhand when you have an easy-to-hit target, but it's a lot faster for a *precise* shot at a difficult mark. It doesn't put the line of sight quite as high above the ground as the kneeling position, but it's a heck of a lot steadier. Finally, it can be used under a greater variety of conditions than any other reasonably steady position.

I do about three-fourths of my practicing from

the sitting position, the rest offhand. I use the kneeling position very rarely, and my prone position is usually not the conventional type — I rest the rifle's forearm on a rolled-up jacket placed on a stone, a log, or something of the sort.

In the mountain and canyon country of the Southwest, where I grew up, the usual shots at deer are across canyons that may be from 150 to 400 yd. wide. When game pops into view, the thing to do is to sit down instantly, get on, and touch her off. But *sit!* Once I sat down and got off a shot so quickly at a running buck that my companion, who was looking the other way and didn't see the deer, thought the gun had gone off accidentally. From my first sight of the deer until it lay dead three seconds may have elapsed.

On the other hand, I remember taking an offhand shot at a buck drowsing under a tree like a sleepy horse. I was in waist-high chaparral and, of course, could not have seen him if I sat down. The buck was between 250 and 300 yd. away. I assumed my best target stance but my sights wavered all over the buck and 20 or 30 ft. of the surrounding territory. It must have taken me a good minute to get off the shot. If I had been able to sit down I could have knocked off that buck within seconds.

When I used to shoot a lot of running antelope and black-tail jackrabbits, I'd sit down if the target was much more than 100 yd. away. Sitting is not as flexible as the offhand or even the kneeling position, but it is flexible enough to cope with most running game in open country. Its major hazard is that you may sit on something that wasn't meant to be sat on, but that seems of small consequence when a buck mule deer with 10 points and a 38-in. spread is on the opposite side of the canyon.

I have carried home many a bruise from sharp rocks or sticks, but my worst punishment came, not when I was after a lordly buck, but when I ran into a whole flock of jackrabbits. I came over a ridge and there, on the opposite side, were five or six big juicy antelope jacks. Automatically I went into a sit — on a pile of cholla balls. Imagine about 10,000 No. 10 fishhooks sticking out of an egg and you have it. I had 7,692 cactus thorns in my rear end and I slept on my stomach for a week.

A good position for shooting across or down a hillside

The sitting position is not only fast and fairly steady but, best of all, it can be used — unlike prone or kneeling — to shoot across or down a hillside. For mountain hunting it is the business. In plains hunting it is very useful for a steady shot when no rest is available and you can't lie prone because grass and weeds are too high or because cactus, thorns, or sharp rocks make lying down hazardous.

Just how accurately can a lightweight, scope-sighted hunting rifle be shot from the sit? A good rifleman should be able to keep three-fourths of his shots inside a 10-in. bull at 300 yd.

Now and then he'll score a possible, but ordinarily from one to three or four shots will wander out of the black. They should not, however, from that position, be *far* out.

Holding an 8 or 9 ½-lb. hunting rifle steady is harder than holding down a 10 ½ or 11 ½-lb. target rifle. At 200 yd., if our boy is holding and squeezing well, practically *all* the shots should be pretty well centered in the 10-in. black. On occasion I've shot such groups running around 4 in. And once, with a scope-sighted .270, I grouped 5 shots at 200 yd. that measured only about 2 ¾ in. across. But I don't kid myself that in these cases it wasn't about 85 percent luck.

Be that as it may, a good shot with a 4X scope on an accurate rifle will kill more jackrabbits and woodchucks at 200 yd. from the sit than he'll miss. And even at 300 yd., with a scope of 8X or 10X, he'll make a surprising proportion of one-shot kills. Since errors of aim from the sitting position tend to be horizontal rather than vertical, there is more leeway on a big-game animal than on a varmint, so it's no astounding feat to place all shots in the forward half on an elk or caribou at 400 yd.

In shooting game — be it jackrabbit, woodchuck, white-tail deer, grizzly bear, or what have you — there are no close 4's. Only the 3's count. It is better by far to get in one well-aimed, well-held, well-placed shot from the sit than to get in three or four poorly aimed, poorly held, poorly placed shots or misses offhand. No time to sit? I have seen many a man miss three or four shots at standing game that he could have killed dead if he'd taken a second to plant his posterior on the earth.

Recently I read about an African lion hunter who, when faced with a charge, always sat down if the grass was not too high. He figured on getting off one well-held, well-aimed shot and knocking the lion for a loop.

I remember one sad occasion when I elected to shoot a deer from offhand rather than take a second longer and drop into the sit. I came around a point and saw, about 200 yd. away, a beautiful buck that had apparently heard me and got out of his bed. He was poised there — alert, beautiful, his gray body outlined sharply against a dark timber background, the sun glittering on the polished points of his antlers. (The ones that get away usually look big, but I'll swear that buck had 18 points.) He saw me as I saw him, and I was afraid he'd scram into the timber before I could drop down into the sit, so I slowly lifted my rifle— and shot right over the top of his back. On the target range I'd have got a close 4 for that one, but he got away just as cleanly as if I'd shut my eyes and missed him by 50 ft.

The principal mistake of the uninstructed beginner

When the uninstructed beginner first tries the sitting position, he almost always makes one principal mistake. He sits up too straight and puts his wobbly elbows right on his wobbly kneecaps. That position is little steadier, if any, than offhand. The secret of a good sitting position is to lean forward and put the flat of the left arm, just above the elbow, against the flat of the shin just below the left knee. Feet should be well apart and feet and ankles relaxed. I have often read that "the heels should be dug into the ground." That's the poorest advice I know of, since the digging induces a tremor. The only time the rifleman should jam his heels into the ground is when he's shooting from a steep hillside and has to dig in to keep from skidding.

Everyone, I believe, has to work out the minor details of his own sitting position for himself. A man with a paunch, for instance, cannot bend forward as far as a flat-bellied youth. Some riflemen prefer crossed legs rather than outstretched ones. For me, though, the key to a good solid sitting position is the relationship of left arm and shin, as described above. What happens to the right arm is relatively unimportant, just so the position feels comfortable and *relaxed*. The natural tension of the back muscles will pull the upper arms against the shin and bring equilibrium and relative steadiness.

In no position should a rifleman try to hold by main strength. He should always feel relaxed. The harder a man tries to hold, the more tense he becomes; and the more tension, the greater the wobble.

My own besetting sin is tenseness. I often catch myself bearing down, determined to hold that damned rifle steady if I have to squeeze it in two at the grip — and when I hold like that, the old musket wobbles all over the target. Then I must *deliberately* loosen up.

I am convinced that the difference between the ordinary good rifleman and the superlative one is not that the latter has better eyes or muscles, or is smarter or better-looking, but simply that he can relax, even when picking off the biggest buck he ever saw at 350 yd. or firing the last shot in a string when a 5 will mean a win and a 4 a tie. The more relaxed the rifle shot is, the steadier he tends to be and the more he can concentrate on a gentle trigger squeeze.

The key to accuracy is relaxation

If a man misses a standing buck from the sitting position up to 250 yd., it's not because he couldn't hold properly but because he yanked his shot. Really wild shots always come from a yank. Sometimes, of course, a shot may "get away" from a shooter; that's because the rifle goes off when the squeeze is in progress but not at the precise moment the shooter wants it to. Such a shot hits out of the black on the target range, or out of the vital area on game, but the deviation won't be very wide. The lad who misses his game by feet or who knocks out 3's and 2's on a target or misses it completely does so *not* because he cannot hold steady but because he is yanking the trigger. Under any conditions, it must always be squeezed gently. A good rifleman may squeeze it *fast,* but he squeezes it, never yanks it!

Years ago another citizen and I were doing some revolver shooting. I was pretty sour. I protested that I couldn't hold the lousy roscoe steady. "That's not the trouble," quoth my companion. "You're yanking the trigger, trying to catch the 10's as they go by. You can't shoot a handgun like that. You're jerking the whole thing."

Then he demonstrated. He took the revolver and deliberately wobbled it far more than even the poorest holder would. *But he squeezed his shots off.* He didn't get all of them in the black by any means, but he had no wild shots such as I'd been getting. I learned my lesson then and there.

A good gunsling, properly adjusted, is one of the great inventions of the human race, along with fire, the wheel, and good-looking dames. Particularly wonderful is it to the sitting rifleman who wants to polish off a woodchuck perched insolently on a rock at 200 yd. or to nail a fine buck poised for flight high on some lofty ridge way out yonder. Every game shot who takes his shooting seriously owes it to himself to get a good sling, then learn how to adjust it and use it. And never forget that a sling takes the curse off toting a heavy rifle, which otherwise is one of the most awkward burdens known to man. You

The gunsling is one of the great inventions of the human race couldn't run fast enough to present me with a rifle to which a sling could not be attached, even if said rifle were done up in $20 bills.

Best type of sling for the hunter is the one-piece Whelen type, $7/8$ in. wide. It's much better for our purposes than the $1\frac{1}{4}$ in. two-piece military and target sling. Normally, the front swivel should be about 15 in. forward of the center of the trigger. Short-armed men want it farther back, and target shooters who use a low prone position want it farther forward. That's why swivels on target arms are adjustable for position.

The best sling for the hunter is the one piece 7/8" wide Whelen type

The sling can be permanently adjusted for use in the sitting position and for carrying. The one-piece sling is a single strip of leather 52 in. long, with a claw hook at one end; holes are punched into the strap to take the hook. The sling also has two keepers and a stout leather lacing.

The whole key to successful adjustment of the sling for the sitting position is the loop, which is formed when the strap is joined by the leather lacing. I place the lacing 18 in. from the base of the swivel or, with Winchester quick-detachable swivels, about 17 in. from where the sling joins the swivel bow. I put the two keepers on the loop; when both are drawn down against the arm, one helps keep the other in place. Total length of the sling for comfortable carrying is determined by the placement of the claw hook. If, for instance, you want to use both hands for climbing and carry the rifle slung over your back, you can move the claw hook into another set of holes.

No sling without a correctly adjusted loop is worth a hoot. Proper adjustment can be arrived at only by experiment. If the loop is too short or too long, it loses its value and introduces shades and tremors.

The so-called "hasty" sling, by the way, is a snare and a delusion. After years of solitary, melancholy brooding and endless experiments, I am convinced that the use of the hasty sling is a waste of time and a handicap to the shooter.

The so-called "hasty" sling is a snare and a delusion

Get into the Whelen-type sling and use it in the sitting position. Except for prone with tight sling, or prone with the fore-end of the rifle resting on some object, this is the steadiest of hunting positions and the easiest to shoot accurately from.

The rough-and-ready "practical" hunter should not sneer at it as belonging only on the target range. It's a wonderfully effective position for the game shot, one that enables him to place his bullets humanely on big game and to knock off varmints at long ranges when he cannot lie prone.

Best group I ever shot on a big-game animal from the sitting position with a tight sling was on a grizzly at about 200 yd. with a .30/06 and 180-gr. bullet. First shot caught him standing, second and third when he was trying to get out of the open and into the timber, fourth when he was lying on the ground — the last shot was for luck. All four shots could be covered by the palm of the hand. Now, luck played a big part in that shooting, but the tight sling in a good sitting position had a lot to do with it, too.

The sitting position, then, is one to cultivate, both with and without sling, if you aspire to be a good game shot. If you practice it, you'll be rewarded by shots that will warm your heart and by trophies you couldn't have otherwise got.

It's the ace of the hunting positions!

Townsend Whwlwn on position and aiming drills

No matter what the position, the old adage "Practice makes perfect" has a great deal of validity. In this piece, Townsend Whelen offers some simple drills that can be done in one's home at any time. Although it appeared the better part of a century ago, this treatment of how to aim reminds us that in many aspects of marksmanship, the more things change, the more they stay the same. The selection comes from The American Rifle *(1918).*

POSITION AND AIMING DRILLS

"The Small Arms Firing Manual" of the Army prescribes that the preliminary practice of organizations before starting the regular season's course of target practice on the rifle range shall include position and aiming drills. These drills are intended to teach the correct firing positions, to develop the muscles used in holding the rifle, to accustom one to the handling and manipulation of the rifle, to give practice in aiming, trigger squeeze, and calling the shot. They form a part of the daily instruction of all organizations for about a month prior to their going on the rifle range. No man who is really expert with the rifle neglects to practice these exercises regularly every day, and particularly for a month or so prior to, and during, the range practice season.

The rifleman or sportsman will find that a few minutes a day practice in his own room will do wonders in making him thoroughly expert in the handling of his rifle, and the novice will find that it will give him just that practice that he needs in holding, aiming, and trigger squeeze. The following suggestions regarding these drills will be found useful:

The target should subtend the same visual angle that it does in outdoor practice. For example, at 100 yards a target 2 feet square with a 5-inch bull's-eye is very satisfactory. Therefore for position and aiming drill, if the distance from the firer to the aiming target be 5 yards, the target should be one-twentieth of this size. Such a target should be made of a yellow paper, similar to wrapping paper, so that it will have the same appearance as the regular range target. In this way the rifleman in aiming will have almost exactly the same picture in his eye as he would on the outdoor range, and uniformity in aiming will result. Such targets should be suspended from the wall, in a well-lighted place, so that they are at the height of the rifleman's eye when he assumes the firing position.

The sportsman who has but one small room in which to practice, and who will desire to do most of his practice in the standing position, can get along very well with a small target made on thin, almost transparent paper, and pasted on the window pane. Such a target may be either a bull's-eye target, or it may be the silhouette of an animal, a deer, for example. A figure of a deer for use on a window pane at 3 yards should be about 1 inch long by half an inch high.

The sights should be adjusted to that range which the practice is to simulate. The rifle is to be snapped at the target without ammunition. It does no harm at all to snap a bolt-action rifle. With a lever-action rifle it is best to introduce a small piece of rubber pencil eraser between the hammer and the firing pin for hammer to strike on.

The standing and kneeling positions should be assumed the same as outdoors. In the sitting position the heels can be make secure by tacking small cleats to the floor in the correct position, or use a large door mat, large enough to both sit on and rest the heels on. In the prone position use a blanket folded to about four thicknesses to rest the elbows on.

Play the game fair. Use all the skill you are capable of to get a steady position, an accurate aim, and a clean trigger squeeze. Position and aiming drills carelessly performed are worse than useless. They teach bad habits, and are a positive detriment to good shooting. Hold the rifle as though you expected it to recoil; that is, as though it was loaded with a ball cartridge.

In practicing for target shooting hold yourself down to the same time limit you would have in competitions, and fire the same number of consecutive shots that would be required in a match. In practicing for game shooting fire slowly at first until you attain the skill to call a bull eight times out of ten, then speed your firing up to that point where you can get a good hold, good aim, and good trigger squeeze in two seconds after placing the rifle to the shoulder.

Rapid fire should be practiced also, with a view to perfecting oneself in both manipulation of the rifle, and quick aiming and trigger work. For such practice it is best to use dummy cartridges, as the feel of the working of the action is usually quite different with an empty rifle. Dummy cartridges can easily be made by taking empty shells, leaving the old primers in the shells, resizing the neck of the shells, and seating bullets. The powder is of course omitted. To distinguish such cartridges from ball ammunition, rub the shells with a little mercury which will turn them silver color. In using dummies place a folded blanket on the ground where the dummies will fall when ejected. This

Dummy cartridges are good for practice

will save the dummies from becoming badly deformed.

Dummy cartridges may also be used to practice the rapid refilling of the magazine, a most important matter, particularly to the military rifleman.

There is almost no limit to the amount of good practice one can get in his own room. After becoming skilled in the standard firing positions vary the positions slightly as one would have to in the field for quick shots where the level and precise footing could not always be looked after. A small moving target can be arranged to run along the window-sill, and this target can even be made to bound up and down like a deer. Also one can learn to shoot left handed.

Remember that all this practice is of no good unless the rifleman takes all the pains that he is capable of with each and every shot, just as though his life depended upon that very shot.

III
SIGHTING IN

*Getting the most out of a rifle requires having it
sighted with precision. Whether open iron sights
or (more commonly) a scope is involved, getting the
device zeroed at the optimal distance is a must.
That distance will vary according to the type of
hunting, the nature of the quarry and its terrain,
the ammunition being used, the rifle's caliber,
and other considerations. Some shooters, especially those my grandfather used to disparage as
"sunny day hunters," find sighting in a nuisance.*

*For most, though, it is a rewarding exercise,
whether undertaken as a prelude to the upcoming
hunting season, as one final bit of practice before
a shooting competition, as a way to fine-tune a
new rifle or new scope, or for some other reason.
Unquestionably, a target showing a tight three-
or five-shot group, especially when you find you
can shoot that group consistently, brings a quiet
sense of pleasure and satisfaction.*

*The selections included here cover most key
aspects of sighting in a rifle, and they range from
traditional wisdom to the thoughts of modern
experts.*

**Traditional
wisdom and
the thoughts
of modern
experts**

●

*Advice from Jack O'Connor is invariably wel-
come and always makes sense. Figuring out how*

to avoid misses is what every shooter has in mind. This material comes from O'Connor's work entitled Sportsman's Arms and Ammunition Manual *(1952) and presents a variety of fixes for inaccuracy as well as ways to keep rifles shooting straight.*

HOW NOT TO MISS

Jack O'Connor's sighting techniques

Nothing I know of is calculated to embarrass a citizen who is a pretty good shot more than to pull down on a relatively easy target, squeeze off — and then never touch a hair. The chap who does something like that before witnesses is in a tough spot. He has enough confidence in his shooting to feel that something is sour, yet at the same time he cannot help wondering whether he yanked that one. Being a seasoned sportsman, it doesn't seem probable that he'd have an attack of buck fever, but still he doesn't know for *sure*.

If our hero speaks up and announces to his pals that something is haywire here, he is guilty of seeking an alibi. Usually it is best to say nothing and then at the earliest opportunity to find out what cooks.

I've had the experience not once but many times, and I've seen others have it. All of a sudden a trusted rifle will change its point of impact — and can that louse up a hunt!

Not long ago I went on a modest little expedition for deer. With me I had a very fine and accurate rifle with a good scope on a quick-detachable side mount which I had never taken on horseback. Not long after my companion and I took out, and before the wedging effect of the saddle scabbard on the scope had got in its dirty work and changed the point of impact, a coyote trotted up a hillside and stopped somewhere around 228 yd. away to look us over. I pulled out Old Betsy, held the cross hairs on the purp's shoulder, and touched her off. Result — one coyote gone to his reward.

Later in the day we saw the head of a deer silhouetted against a patch of sunlight in the timber below us in a canyon, and a careful examination with binoculars revealed about six other deer, one a good four-point buck. The wind was right and the deer had not seen us. I sat myself down and missed that buck with four shots — *four well squeezed-off shots!*

My companion told me he'd seen two of the shots strike high. Later we spotted another buck lying down in a basin. I stationed my pal by my side with the binoculars and told him to call my shot. I held the horizontal cross hair of the scope even with the *bottom* of the buck's body as he lay there in the snow. My pal reported that the shot had gone over the top of the animal's back. I managed to scratch that buck down by holding well under him, but it was a sloppy performance and I did not enjoy it. A check later on a paper target showed that musket shooting 3 ft. high at 200 yds.! The front portion of the mount had been bent down, which of course made the barrel point *up* and the bullets go in the same direction.

Check sights for damage or loose screws

Any change of alignment of the sights, either iron or glass, will of course change the point of impact, often sufficiently to cause a miss on even a large and close-by target. One chap I talked to last season missed his dream buck because in pulling his rifle from the scabbard he wound the windage screw of his receiver sight out. The buck was running away from him and every shot went to one side. He found out what had happened, corrected his windage by bore sighting, then went on and got himself a trophy very nearly as good as the one he missed.

If Old Betsy starts shooting off, the first thing to examine is the sights. Have they been damaged by a fall? Have they been moved? Are they loose?

Once in Mexico I hunted with a good shot who came in one night with his face so long he was almost stepping on it. It seemed he had unaccountably missed three nice bucks. We examined his musket and found that the shaking it had got on horseback had so loosened the scope mount that it rattled like a castanet when he moved it. We tightened all the screws, put up a target on a cactus, and got on the beam again. Next day he collected his buck.

Another time, on a deer hunt, my scope-mounted rifle fell out of the scabbard and took a heck of a knock. I saw no bucks that day. On the way back in I fired three shots at a sitting jack rabbit about 100 yds. away. I might as well have been throwing rocks. On paper I found the rifle shooting way off toward the Johnson place. The reason? The fall had bent the rear end of the scope tube down.

When Ken Niles, the radio announcer, hunted antelope in Wyoming with me some years ago, his rifle had been tossed around by a railroad employee with more muscle than sense. The aluminum tube of his scope was bent perceptibly, and it would have taken some doing to hit an elephant at 50 yards. Luckily, the bend was so bad we noticed it; otherwise he'd have done some plain and fancy missing. As it was, he used my spare rifle and got a fine buck.

Saddest tale I know is of a certain movie star who showed up at a deer camp in northern Arizona with a scope-sighted rifle back in the days when the scope was spot news. All the kibitzers had to get a load of that scope, so it was passed from hand to hand. Next day, before a whole flock of open-mouthed fans, our hero hit nothing that he aimed at. Finally he found out that someone had been fiddling with the elevation dial of the scope just to see how it worked. That night he sighted in the rifle once more, and the next day he collected a fine Kaibab mule deer.

I am reminded of another tale — this time about an exhibition shooter. He was going to bust some potatoes and oranges in the air with a .351 Winchester automatic with open sights. He couldn't hit a thing. Some heel had put the rear sight up into the last notch.

How do I know? Well, I was the heel. Before the shoot he had assured me that he never saw his sights. I claimed he did. When I told him I had done the foul deed he chased me around 27 pine trees with an ax.

Another little joker to watch out for in a bolt-action rifle is the loosening up of the guard screws. You should always keep them tight, and always check the front screw *first*. It is surprising how much loose ones will change the point of impact.

Pal of mine missed a whole flock of easy shots at a big ram by overshooting. Finally the sheep stopped way out yonder where the bullet was curving down again and my friend killed him. We examined the musket that night. Guard screws were so loose that the rifle actually rattled in its stock.

Another unpredictable little item that changes point of impact is the warping of the wooden stock. A sporting-weight barrel is very flexible, by the way. Put one in a vice and you can bend it perceptibly with a finger. What a wooden fore-end that warps after you've sighted in does to it is plenty. Warped hard *against* the barrel, the fore-end makes the rifle shoot high. Warped *away* from the barrel, it makes the rifle shoot low.

Point of impact can be changed by a warped wood stock

Once I took a little jaunt down into Mexico. First, with the 180-gr. bullet in my .30/06, I killed a coyote at 325 paces. Thinking the coyote closer than that I had held dead on. I should have missed because at that distance and with my rifle sighted in for 200 yds. the bullet should have gone low. We question our misses, but we usually accept our hits with smug satisfaction.

Next I plastered a mule deer at about 35 yds. Then came the pay-off.

I was on a little hill when below me, somewhere around 200 yds. Away, I saw one of the biggest-antlered white-tails I have ever laid my eyes on. I squeezed one off with the cross hairs centered in the middle of his chest behind the shoulder. The buck went down, jumped up, and beat it. Apparently I had merely clipped him across the top of the back.

I next had an easy shot at a coyote that was standing 100 yds. away. I only took some hair off old Don Coyote's back.

When I shot my gun on paper, I found the bullets were landing 6 in. high at 100 yds. No wonder I hit that first coyote out around 300 yds. when I should have missed him! The bullet was dead on at that distance but high at intermediate ranges. No wonder I missed the white-tail; at 200 yds., on an average, the bullets would strike 7 inches high! If I'd held low instead of where he was biggest I could have got him.

In this case the answer was that the fore-end had warped up against the barrel. I took the barrel and action out of the stock and found that just back of the fore-end tip the excessive pressure had worn the barrel channel hard and black. The pressure was so great that when I loosened the front guard screw I could see the stock spring like a bow. The cure, of course, was to take a bottoming tool and rasp away some of the wood. I did it. Since then I have peddled the musket, but its new owner reports that he has had no trouble.

Stock blanks should always be cut so that the grain does not run parallel to the barrel, but at an angle. This weakens the fore-end so that it cannot exert so much upward pressure. Friend of mine had a Model 70 Winchester that shot high with the lowest adjustment of the Lyman 48 receiver sight. It was the old story of a warping fore-end. We took out some wood and cured it.

Warping stocks, I am convinced, are responsible for most of the stories one hears about rifles changing their point of impact with changes in altitude. The sportsman lives in a nice, dry, steam-heated apartment, where he keeps his rifle in the closet in the spare bedroom. He takes a trip to the mountains of British Columbia, where the base camp is beside a trout stream and just across from a muskeg meadow. Humidity is much greater than in his city apartment, and the fore-end warps up against the barrel. When be shoots his musket he finds that the bullets fly high.

"Ah!" he says. "The reason my rifle shoots high is that I am at a higher elevation!"

As far as I have been able to determine, there is nothing whatsoever to this hypothesis. For a long time I lived at an altitude of about 2,500 ft. in the Southwest. I used to hunt at sea level on the Mexican coast and at 8,000 to 9,000 ft. in the mountains. If I ever found a change in the point of impact, it was always due to one of the factors that I have mentioned. *Never* altitude.

Accuracy of point of impact is not affected by altitude or temperature

With a good rifle with a straight barrel in a well-inletted stock, even changes of temperature apparently make little if any difference. I used to sight my rifles in with the thermometer hovering up around 105 or even 110 degrees F. in the shade, then take off for the Canadian Rockies, where the natives fainted in droves and muttered about the heat wave if the temperature hit 70 degrees in the direct sunlight. One of the first things I always did was to check the sighting of my rifles, by shooting carefully at a paper target from an improvised rest; and I never found that temperature made any difference I could ascertain.

Up in Canada once, I had been shooting a pet .270 in which I had all the faith in the world, and with which I had already killed a fine ram and a moose. Coming down the mountain one evening, I saw a big black wolf strolling across a river bar. He was around 175 yds. away, unsuspecting, and a dead duck if I ever saw one. I sat myself down, put the dot low on his shoulder, and touched her off. The wolf stopped, not even scratched, and I was aware that the sand kicked up well beyond him. I couldn't believe it, so I took another pop at the wolf with the same hold. Again the sand kicked up, and away went the wolf. I swung ahead of the wolf, holding with the line of his feet, and finally managed to scratch him down. For a definite check I put another cartridge in the chamber, took aim at a rock about as far away as the wolf had been, and shot. Again the bullet flew high.

Luckily I had a spare rifle, a .30/06, with me. I finished the hunt out with it. My first guess was that the stock of the .270 had got thoroughly soaked in a rain the previous day and had warped. When I got home I took the rifle out on the range and shot It. The group at 200 yds. was way high. I turned the elevation dial down the required number of clicks. My first shot was in the 200-yd. bull, my second was at the top of the bull, and my third was up where the first group was.

The internal adjustments of the scope had gone haywire, but plenty, I removed the scope, sent it back to the maker, and had him replace the whole business.

All of this would tend to indicate that the citizen who invests important money in a hunting trip is what as known as a chumperoo if he dashes forth with but one set of sights on his artillery.

Consider two scopes for the same rifle

Another pious idea is to have two scopes for the same rifle — something which is possible with a good many mounts. There is no reason why with the Echo one could not have two detachable portions with two scopes for the same rifle. With the Griffen & Howe, the Jaeger, or the Noske this should also be possible, though in each case I believe the detachable portions would have to be especially hand-fitted at the factory to the base. With the Stith Master mount anyone can take as many scopes for the same rifle as he wants to, if each spare has internal adjustments with which it has been sighted in.

One chap I knew had an old .30/30 Winchester Model 94 with which he had killed a great many deer. For years he had used the standard 170-gr. soft point bullet at a muzzle velocity of 2,200 foot seconds. When the 110-gr. load at around 2,700 came out, he decided that it was his meat. He bought a couple of boxes and went deer hunting. Four days later he came back with no ammunition and no deer. Too late he found that his rifle was shooting about 18 inches high at 100 yds. with the stuff!

Let's lay down a few rules to take the sting out of this tendency rifles have to stop shooting where they look.

Rules for accuracy

1. Never start off on a trip without carefully sighting in.
2. Never change ammunition without checking point of impact.
3. Always keep screws tight.
4. Never let the rifle lie around where the stock can absorb moisture.
5. Always check the point of impact at the end of trip into hunting country.

6. If you have but one rifle, see that it is equipped with auxiliary sights.
7. Always take a spare rifle on a long and expensive trip.
8. If you miss an easy shot that you have called as being good, find out at once what is wrong.

Bryce Towsley discusses sighting in your rifle

In this selection from Making Shots: A Rifle Hunter's Guide *(2000), Bryce Towsley offers a no-nonsense approach to sighting in a rifle. Although he recommends sandbags, and although sand is the material most commonly used for stability, you might want to consider kitty litter as a substitute. A leaking sandbag that allows tiny grains to get into a rifle can lead to all sorts of problems.*

THE BASICS OF GUN SIGHTING

If there is anything more important to the preparation of your hunt than properly sighting in your rifle it escapes my notice. But so many hunters, either through ignorance or laziness, neglect to do it right. Why gamble on something so easily controlled?

The only way to sight a rifle is to shoot from a solid rest

The only way to sight in a rifle is to shoot from a solid rest. It's not a test of your shooting ability; it's an adjustment process for a precision instrument. You must eliminate all human error, and your skill (or lack of it) should not affect the outcome.

Use a shooting bench and sandbags or another rest that will support both the forearm of the rifle and the toe of the butt stock. This rest should be firm but have some give. It has to hold the rifle perfectly still, and often pillows or rolled-up blankets fail to do that. They are too flexible and soft, and the rifle can move on them too easily. It will be difficult to hold the gun still against the forces of your body's functions such as breathing or your heartbeat. At the same time, the support can't be hard, and it must be able to flex and move a little when the gun fires, or accuracy will be poor and your zero may not be correct for field shooting.

Sandbags are best. You can buy commercial bags or make your own. Commercial rests with dense foam between the gun and the rest are good as well, because the foam provides a solid but flexible rest. Regardless of what you use, you must support the forearm, never the barrel of the rifle. You must also support the toe of the stock near the butt. You will find that the front support must be higher than the rear. To achieve this, simply boost the front sandbag with a couple of boards, a cement block, or whatever else is handy, as long as it's stable. The key is to keep the gun as low to the bench as possible.

The bench should be shaped so that there is a "wing" along your right side (for right-handed shooters). This allows you to support the rear of the rifle while your body is positioned correctly for shooting. Snug yourself into the bench so that

Use a shooting bench and sandbags

your chest is pushing against it both in the front and on the side wing. This will wedge you into a "corner" and will make you more solid. The trick is to eliminate all movement.

Bore sight before you start

Your gun should be bore sighted before you start. If you don't have access to an optical bore sighter, you can remove the bolt and settle the gun into your rest. Look through the bore at the target, and center the bull's-eye in the bore. Without moving the rifle, look through the scope and adjust the crosshairs until they are also centered on the bull's-eye.

One trick for holding the rifle still is to cut V-shaped wedges out of opposite sides in a cardboard box to hold the rifle. Put a little weight in the box, and wedge the gun into the cuts to hold it still while you adjust the scope. Bore sighting will only get you on the target to allow you finish sighting in by shooting. You should never consider hunting with a rifle that has been only bore sighted.

Buy some decent targets designed for sighting in rifles; they are far better than anything home-made. What you pin them to is unimportant as long as it holds the target steady. I often just staple a target to a large cardboard box and throw a few rocks in the bottom to hold it down.

Put a target at 25 yards and carefully fire a shot at the center. You should be able to see the bullet hole through your scope. If you can't, mark it on the target with a piece of tape or a black marker so that you can. Lock your rifle into the sandbags, and center the crosshairs on the bull's-eye. Without moving the rifle, adjust the scope until the crosshairs move from the bull's-eye and are centered on the bullet hole. You may wish to use the slotted cardboard box you made for this as well. Fire another shot at the center of the target. You should be pretty close to dead-on at 25 yards. If not, repeat the process.

Move the target to 100 yards, and shoot from your sandbags or rest again, being careful to make sure the rifle is rock steady and your scope is on its highest power. Do not try to hold the rifle as you would when hunting; placing your left hand under the forearm will induce movement. Instead, use your left hand to move and adjust the rear sandbag until the crosshairs are on the bull's-eye. You should not be supporting the gun's weight at all; let the sandbags do that. The minute you try to hold the gun, you induce movement. The only reasons you are touching the rifle are to pull the trigger and to keep from being hit by the scope when the gun recoils.

Do not hold the rifle as you would for hunting

At this point, you and the rifle should be rock steady and the crosshairs should not be moving. If you are not and they are, you need to re-evaluate your rest and your position at the bench until everything is stable. You should feel like you are "locked in" to the bench and the rifle — almost like you are all one piece.

With the gun empty, aim at the bull's-eye and

slowly squeeze the trigger until the gun dry fires. (This will not hurt a modern center-fire rifle.) The crosshairs should not have wavered off the bull's-eye. Continue to practice this dry firing until you can do it every time without the crosshairs moving.

If the gun has any degree of recoil, it's a good idea to have a pad of some kind between it and your shoulder when you are ready to fire live ammo. Again, this is not a test of how tough you are and how much recoil you can absorb. There are some commercial pads on the market that are very good, but I often use an athletic elbow pad that I bought in a sporting goods store. Another thing that works well is a section of foam insulation made for water pipes. This not only has the foam to absorb recoil, but the hollow center acts like a shock absorber. These are inexpensive and can be found at any home supply store. If the gun is a large caliber, a small sandbag between you and the gun is a good idea.

Being careful to squeeze the trigger slowly, fire a group of three shots. Find the center of the group and make your adjustments from there according to the instructions that came with your scope. If you lack the instructions, most American scopes move ¼ inch per click at 100 yards. Be aware, though, that some move ½ inch and a few scopes move ⅓ inch per click.

After making the scope adjustments, use the soft end of a bullet to gently tap on the scope's adjustment rings. Often the internal adjustments will stick a little, and tapping on the scope will help to seat them. If you don't do this, the scope may not move until you fire the rifle again, so your next shot will not reflect the changes you made, which can be confusing.

If your target doesn't have grid lines, mark a cross with the intersection of the lines on the center of the bull's-eye. Find the center of your three-shot group, and measure straight over to the vertical line. This will give you the amount of left or right adjustment you need to make in the scope. Now measure up or down to the horizontal line and make the adjustment for that.

Allow the rifle to cool down a bit and then fire three more carefully aimed shots. Your group should now be centered on the target. If for some reason it is not, repeat the process until it is. Always fire at least a three-shot group before making adjustments. If you fire one shot and adjust from that, you can spend all your time and ammo chasing bullet holes. A group will show if you are flinching or experiencing other shooting problems or if your rifle has accuracy problems; one shot will not.

Fire at least a three-shot group

Let the rifle cool off before firing your final group, to see if there is a point of impact change from a hot barrel. Remember, you will always fire your first shot at big game from a cold barrel. Make certain that you adjust your final point of impact from the same cold barrel.

Bryce
Towsley on
the value of
a shooting
bench

As Bryce Towsley explains in this piece, taken from Making Shots: A Rifle Hunter's Guide *(2000), the beginning point for solid, consistent marksmanship is a shooting bench. Whether the focus of your desire for improved accuracy is plinking, big game hunting, or competitive shooting, this advice on what you can learn from bench shooting looms large.*

THE BEAUTY OF THE BENCH

**Even Davy
Crockett
had to
practice**

It is not an American heritage inherent to our breeding to be a crack shot. Even Davy Crockett had to practice. Back in my competitive shooting days, I had the good fortune to meet and compete with some of the best shots on earth. They did not get that way by luck. To a man, they gathered the skills by practicing. The old statement "I can't hit paper but I am deadly on game" is just not true. The really good shots hit what they shoot at no matter what the composition.

It amazes me that a hunter will spend so many days and dollars in the quest for a buck and neglect the most important aspect, the very thing he is working for: the shot. A chance at a trophy animal is too rare an opportunity to blow it for something so easily controlled, yet year after year this continues to happen. Before you go out and start blasting, you must make sure that your practice will work to improve your shooting and not just help you to get better at bad habits. It will do you no good to keep repeating the same mistakes over and over; this will only make it that much harder to unlearn them. Regardless of your present ability, it is best to start at the beginning of a shooting improvement program. If you skip a step, it may show up in problems later.

Although it is often stated that shooting from a bench has no practical benefit for the hunter, I strongly disagree. Shooting from any position is poor practice if the same mistakes are repeated over and over and you don't realize you are making them. Learn the basics of shooting from a bench, where the human factor can be minimized. Practice the fundamentals of sight picture, breath control and trigger pull from a bench with a solid rest. When you can regularly shoot groups approaching the rifle's capabilities, it is time to progress to field positions.

Learn the basics of shooting from a bench

A rifle's capabilities often remain a mystery, even to long-time owners. Determining the best groups from a rifle takes an experienced shooter, and if you have progressed to that level, you probably don't have any reason to be reading this. There will come a time when you know the rifle well enough to recite its accuracy capabilities, but for now you need something to measure by. Any factory rifle today should be able to shoot five-shot groups of 3 inches or better (usually much better) at 100 yards. Most newer bolt actions should shoot groups half that size. Until you can do that well or better with every group you fire, you should stay at the shooting bench and continue to work on the fundamentals.

Before you start, it's a good idea to take the rifle to a gunsmith or a competent gun-guy and have him make sure that all screws are tight. This should include all bedding screws as well as all the scope mounts. Then have him bore sight it. Next, go to a good 100-yard range with a solid shooting bench. If you cannot find a range with a bench, there are several portable benches on the market you can bring with you.

Follow the instructions in the section on sighting in the rifle [Editor's note: See "The Basics of Gun Sighting," earlier in this chapter.] until you have it hitting where you want it to at 100 yards. Now, fire five shots as carefully as you can. It is advisable to pad your shoulder; it won't make you a wimp, but it will improve your shooting. I use athletes' elbow pads — one for most rifles, two for the big guys. You also might consider a muzzle break. Always wear hearing protection; that too will help in the flinch department as well as preserve your hearing.

At this point, don't worry about where you are hitting as long as it's somewhere on the target. Your five holes should be relatively close together — say, 3 inches or less. If they are not, you are flinching or the gun is not accurate with the ammo you are using. Continue to try, and if you just can't make the group size shrink, try different ammo. If you still cannot find the problem, it may take another more experienced shooter trying your rifle to discover why it isn't grouping. Be forewarned, though: it's almost always the shooter!

By firing five shots, you can tell if you begin to flinch. If you do and the groups open up, it's advisable to stop shooting for the day and give it a rest, because all you will do from then on is burn shells and heat up your temper. Go back another day and start again fresh.

The best practice at this point is to continue to shoot from the bench until you can shoot to the rifle's capability on demand. It may take several weeks of shooting before you reach this point, and if you still don't know what that capability is, you haven't shot enough groups from your rest.

I can't stress enough the importance of mastering the fundamentals before you attempt to go on to practicing field positions. Don't expect to learn it all in one session. If you are starting to find your concentration wandering and your groups opening up, call it a day. You can't force yourself to overcome it, and you will only be frustrated and conditioning yourself to bad habits. Stop while you are shooting well, and end the day on a positive note; it makes it easier to maintain the mental attitude and determination needed to learn the shooting skills.

After you have mastered the fundamentals, you can progress to practicing from field positions. However, take a trip back to the shooting bench every now and then to make sure you are not picking up some bad habits or forgetting the basics of good shooting.

Many of us find it convenient, whether in shooting or in life, to have matters laid out step by step. In the following piece, which is a revised version of a chapter in his book Bolt Action Rifles *(2003), Wayne Van Zwoll offers five straightforward steps to take when zeroing in a rifle.*

Wayne Van Zwoll's five steps for zeroing in a rifle

FIVE STEPS TO ZERO

Make quick work of sighting in your rifle — and hit more often!

Zeroing, or sighting in, is simply aligning the sights (scope) on your rifle so that the bullet hits where you aim at a certain distance. Because the bullet's path is an arc and your line of sight is straight, they coincide at only two places: first, where line of sight angles beneath the arc, and next, when gravity pulls the bullet back through the sight line. That second crossing is the rifle's "zero" range. The most useful zero depends on the bullet's trajectory and on how far you intend to shoot. For most big game rifles, it's 200 yards. Zero there with a .30-06 or similar cartridge, and your bullet will stay within 3 vertical inches of point of aim out to 250 yards or so. On big game, 3-inch vertical error still gives you a killing hit in the chest. The 200-yard zero permits a dead-on aim as far as most marksmen can hit in the field.

At 300 yards, you'll have to shade high. But that's better than a long zero that causes overshooting at mid-range, where most game is shot.

Very fast, flat-shooting bullets from magnum cartridges do allow a 250-yard zero. "Woods" rounds with steep trajectories (the .30-30, for example) justify shorter zeroes — 150, maybe even 100 yards.

Here's how to zero in five easy steps:

1. Mount your scope low so that you get full cheek support when aiming. Mount it well forward to get a full field of view when your face is well forward — so that you won't have to pull your head back to find the target or to avoid getting bumped on recoil. Cinch base screws very tight, and snug ring-screws alternately as you would lug nuts on a wheel, to get firm, even pressure.

2. With the bolt removed, lay your rifle on a rest or sandbags, and center a distant object in the bore. (I use a rock on a hill a mile away.) Now, without moving the rifle, adjust the scope reticle onto the object. This bore sighting will put your first bullets near point of aim, saving time and ammo. Pump rifles, autoloaders and lever-actions can be bore sighted with a collimator* you slide into the muzzle. Just center the grid with your reticle.

*A piece of optical equipment that uses a convex lens to aid in adjusting the line of sight.

3. At the range, place your rifle on sandbags or a rest. Now shoot twice at a large paper target 100 yards away. Adjust the sight, moving it the direction you want the bullet to go. Most hunting scopes have quarter-minute clicks; each gradation of a windage or elevation dial shifts point of impact about ¼ inch at 100 yards.

4. Move the target to 200 yards, and shoot again from the rest, this time firing three-shot groups between adjustments. When the bullets hit center, clean the rifle, let it cool and fire another group. You may have to refine your zero, to put your first, cold-barrel bullet on target — the bullet you'll use on game. Don't fret if groups "walk" when the barrel heats. The first three shots matter most.

5. Now take the rifle off the rest. Fire three-shot groups from hunting positions at 200 yards. The paper will not only point up any change in point of impact but also measure your marksmanship. If you shoot often with a sling or a bipod, use it. I've found a tight sling can pull groups as much as 9 inches to 7 o'clock at 200 yards. You may be smart to adjust your scope for a zero from unsupported positions. I do.

There's a sixth step: practice. A rifle that can put all its bullets in the middle of 200-yard targets puts venison in the freezer only when you can control each shot!

Far fewer folks shoot open sights today than was once the case. For most, optics rule supreme. Yet there are situations in which you must rely on fixed sights. Some states, for example, do not allow the use of optics during traditional muzzle-loading season, but there is no reason not to use the adjustable sights found on some modern black powder rifles. Similarly, you may find yourself competing in a match where optics are not allowed. Or possibly you are old school and want to do your hunting without any of the optical accoutrements so common today. For those who use open sights, Townsend Whelen offers some timeless advice. It comes from The Hunting Rifle *(1940).*

Townsend Whelen on sight adjustment

SIGHT ADJUSTMENT

Before you start your range practice you must understand sight adjustment. If you take a new rifle to the range you may not be able to strike the target with it because the sights have not been adjusted. It is true that some attempt is made to adjust sights on rifles at the factory. The tester fires a few shots and moves the sights so that at 100 yards, or some other distance, the rifle then shoots fairly close to the center of the bull's-eye *for him,* and *for the am-*

munition he is using. But this does not necessarily mean that the rifle will then shoot very close, or close at all to where you aim it under the conditions under which you use it. Every man aims and holds a rifle slightly differently from almost all other men, and sights adjusted for one individual would be correct for another only by mere chance. Also different makes and lots of ammunition require a different adjustment of the sights to strike at the same place at a certain distance.

Adjust sights for your own peculiarities of aim and hold

The shooter must adjust his sights for himself, for his own peculiarities of aim and hold, and for the ammunition he is using, and he is up against this problem on his very first visit to the rifle range with his new rifle in order to make his bullets strike, not only in the bull's-eye, but on the target as a whole.

The problem of sight adjustment is extremely simple. There are only two short rules that need be memorized, and then you have the entire matter at your finger tips. The first of these is:

"MOVE YOUR REAR SIGHT IN THE DIRECTION IN WHICH YOU DESIRE YOUR SHOTS TO STRIKE."

That is if you desire your shots to strike higher on the target, raise your rear sight. If you desire them to strike further to the right on the target, move your rear sight to the right. That is simple, is it not?

The next rule tells you how far to move your sights to make them strike the desired amount in the desired direction. Suppose your first shots strike on an average, three inches above the center of the bull's-eye at 100 yards. You wish to lower the center of impact three inches. If the front and rear sights were 36 inches apart, and you were to lower the rear sight $1/100$ of an inch, then you would lower the center of impact $1/100$ of an inch at 1 yard, or 1 inch at 100 yards. It would be very convenient indeed if there was a scale on your rear sight like this $1/100$ of an inch which would permit you to adjust your center of impact to inches on the target. Well that is precisely what you do have on modern rifle sights. They are graduated in this manner. These graduations which have the value of inches on the target at 100 yards we call MINUTES, because one minute of angle subtends 1 inch, actually 1.047", at 100 yards. Also a change in adjustment of 1 minute will change the center of impact ½ inch at 50 yards, 2 inches at 200 yards, 5 inches at 500 yards, and so on. Therefore we have our second rule of sight adjustment:

"ONE MINUTE EQUALS ONE INCH PER HUNDRED YARDS."

memorize that too.

It now remains to see how to read a minute on the scale on your modern sight. All modern sights adjusting to minutes are constructed with scales on the micrometer principle. That is there is a slide or stem with a scale on it having graduations either 5 minutes, or 25 half minutes apart, and then there is a knurled screw with graduations around its head numbered in either 5 minute lines, 10 half minute lines, or 25 half minute lines. If we start at zero on both scales, then turning the knurled screw one complete revolution, raises the slide or stem one graduation. If we turn the knurled screw only one graduation, we raise the slide or stem only the amount of the one graduation on the screw head.

As you turn the screw around you will notice that it "clicks" as it passes each graduation. The sight is arranged thus so that you can feel the graduations as well as see them, and you can thus adjust the sight in lights that are too dim to see the graduations.

When you obtain your first rifle having a sight, operate it a little until you thoroughly understand its principle, and how to surely turn it in the right direction. Lots of beginners make the mistake of moving their sight the wrong way, that is lowering it when they wish to raise it, or turning the windage to the right when they wish to turn it to the left. Make yourself thoroughly familiar with its operation, and remember that when it is elevated the eyepiece containing the peep hole should raise, and when you adjust it to the right the eyepiece should move to the right across the scale. It is really exceedingly simple.

Besides the great convenience of being able to adjust your sights so as to be able to place your bullets just where you wish on the target, and change adjustment to quarter, half, or full minutes or inches on the target, and to record these adjustments for future reference, there is another great advantage of using sights which read to minutes. As a given cartridge will shoot with practically identically the same muzzle velocity in all normal rifles chambered for that cartridge, it follows that that cartridge in those rifles will also cause its bullet to fly with a standard trajectory, and that that cartridge will require the same elevation in all rifles that fire it in order to reach a certain range. Thus we know the elevation in minutes required for all standard cartridges at all different ranges up to 1000 yards, or to the distance at which the cartridge shoots with accuracy. These elevations are given in the Table of Angles of Elevation to be found on page 461. Having this table, and having previously shot your rifle at a certain distance and found the elevation required at that distance, by referring to the table you at once know approximately your correct elevation for all other distances. That is, having found your elevation say for 100 yards, from the table you can at once find how to set your sight in elevation for shooting at 200, 300, 400, 500, or 1000 yards.

As an example of this, suppose you are shooting a .30-06 rifle, with the .30-06 Western cartridge loaded with 180 grain open point boat tail

Techniques for setting correct elevations for all distances

bullet, which has a muzzle velocity of approximately 2700 feet per second. And suppose that after several days' practice you found that your correct elevation on the rear sight of your rifle, for shooting at 100 yards with this cartridge was 4 minutes. Then, referring to the Table of Angles of Elevation you see that the 100 yard elevation for the 180 grain Western boat tail ammunition is 2.5 minutes. The reading on your sight for each range will then be 1.5 minutes higher than the figures in the table, or you make a table as follows:

RANGE	ANGLE OF ELEVATION .30-06 B.T. 180 GR M.V. 2700 F.S.	YOUR RIFLE SAME AMMUNITION
YARDS	MINUTES	MINUTES
100	2.5	4.0
200	5.0	6.5
300	8.0	9.5
400	11.5	13.0
500	15.0	16.5

In other words the correct elevation for 400 yards on your sight and for this ammunition would be 13.0 minutes. Also, if you desired to keep your sights adjusted for 200 yards in hunting you would set the Lyman 48 rear sight at 6½ minutes.

We seldom use the wind gauge in hunting, but we do use it right along to get our rifle properly zeroed for windage and to keep it thus. As a result of two or three days' shooting on days when there is no wind, you find that the wind gauge has to be set, let us say at 2 minutes right in order to have the shots strike in a vertical line passing through the center of the bull's-eye. This then is your zero for windage.

All the above had to do only with adjusting your sights so that the rifle will shoot where it is aimed. Also keep in mind the matter of setting the sights so as to best take advantage of the trajectory of the rifle, and the way in which your sights should be adjusted for actual hunting.

Target shooting, particularly at distances over 300 yards, is really a continuous process of sight adjustment. At distances of 500 yards and over the shooter may have to change his sight adjustment two to four times during his string of 10 shots. The wind may change and make a change necessary in the windage adjustment. Or he may find that his rifle seems to gradually be shooting off towards one side of the bull, and he makes a slight change to keep his shots going more nearly in the center of the bull. But ordinarily you do not experience this difficulty in shooting at 100 yards, or in your hunting. After you have had a few days' experience on the range, and have gotten used to shooting with ammunition, you will find a certain "normal" sight adjustment which will result in your shots practically always striking close to the center of the bull when your aim and your trigger squeeze have been correct. This is then your normal elevation for 100 yards, and it is from this

Target shooting is a continuous process of sight adjustment

normal 100 yard elevation that the sight adjustment for hunting is figured. Therefore, at this stage you should record that normal elevation or zero very carefully in your score book.

Let me now in conclusion, caution you again to memorize the two rules for sight adjustment:

1. MOVE YOUR REAR SIGHT IN THE DIRECTION IN WHICH YOU WISH YOUR SHOTS TO STRIKE.

2. ONE MINUTE EQUALS ONE INCH PER HUNDRED YARDS.

IV
RIFLE BALLISTICS

The behavior of bullets in flight has always fascinated marksmen. Phrases such as "Kentucky windage" and "a good, flat-shooting rifle" spice the vocabularies of hunters and bench shooters alike. Anyone who does much shooting soon comes to realize that a host of factors, often interacting, affect the behavior of a bullet. Among these are weight, the barrel's rifling, the powder charge, wind, atmospheric conditions, and of course distance. There's no escaping the pull of gravity, and the longer any bullet is in flight, the more it drops; all shots eventually return to earth.

Ballistics is mostly science, but I would argue there is also a bit of art (or call it "gut feeling" or "instinct" if you prefer) involved as well. Buffalo hunters with Plains rifles may not have even known the word ballistics, *but you can bet your favorite gun that they had an intuitive understanding of drop. Similarly, although they lived generations before range finders and charts explaining the drop of a given load over specific distances, they knew how much elevation and wind allowance they needed to bring off a telling shot.*

We have come a long way since Plains rifles and frontier shooting matches, but collectively we are probably poorer marksmen than our prede-

cessors. *Those hardy souls had to know their guns and their guns' performance capabilities inside and out, for their livelihoods and sometimes even their lives depended on such knowledge. Accordingly, they practiced, experimented with different loads, and became intimately familiar with all aspects of shooting. We would do well to emulate them.*

One crucial issue faced by shooters in the past has basically been eliminated, thanks to the development of highly accurate, lightweight, and easily used range finders. With a click of a button, you get accurate readings (to within a yard on better range finders) at distances that certainly are as far as any ethical sportsman should shoot. Therefore, no in-depth coverage of the matter of judging distance is included here. However, for anyone who does hunting where shots are likely to involve distances of more than a hundred yards, determining distance is of vital importance. The answer to the problem, thankfully, is a simple one: get a good range finder and learn how to use it in conjunction with your rifle.

Get a good range finder

At the least, every serious marksman needs to have a basic understanding of ballistics. Here we get varied looks at the flight of the bullet from Jack O'Connor, Townsend Whelen, and Bryce Towsley.

●

This material comes from Jack O'Connor's handy little manual, Rifle and Shotgun Shooting Basics *(1986). It is the trajectory portion of a*

*chapter devoted to trajectory and range. Pre-
dictably, O'Connor's comments on range are just
as squarely on target as those on trajectory, but
range finders have pretty much rendered the
necessity for concerns about judging distance
obsolete.*

BULLET TRAJECTORY

When a bullet leaves the rifle barrel it immediately begins to fall from the *line of bore*, although
at the same time it is rising toward the *line of
sight*. All bullets are acted on by the force of gravity. A 150-grain 7 mm. Magnum bullet dropped
from the hand will hit the ground at exactly the
same time as the same bullet fired from a rifle
with a muzzle velocity approaching 3200 feet per
second, for both are free-falling bodies of the same
weight and shape. If the same 7 mm. bullet could
be speeded up to 4000 or even to 5000 fps it
would also hit the ground at the same time. However, the faster the bullet travels the farther it goes
in the interval while gravity is acting upon it. The
faster a bullet is traveling, the "flatter" the path of
travel — that is, the less it falls for every foot of
forward travel.

So the answer to the often-asked question as to
how far such-and-such a bullet will travel without
dropping is, "No distance at all." Near the muzzle
where velocity is high the drop is very slight, but it
is there just the same. "Flatness" of trajectory depends on the initial velocity coupled with the

shape and sectional density of the bullet. A long sharp-pointed bullet loses velocity more slowly than a short round-nosed bullet and hence shoots "flatter." And that last word should read "more nearly flat" or "with a less-pronounced curve."

To get down to concrete instances, Remington used to load a round-nosed 110-grain bullet in .30/06 caliber at a muzzle velocity of 3350 feet per second. In spite of its high velocity this bullet had a more curved trajectory over 300 yards than did the Remington 150-grain Bronze Point bullet which left the muzzle at a velocity of about 400 feet per second less. The latter had better shape and sectional density — or, to employ a fancy term, a better ballistic coefficient. This is why using a lighter but faster bullet of the same caliber does not always pay off. In a given caliber, the shorter the bullet is the faster it loses velocity and the more pronounced its trajectory curve is.

The shorter the bullet the faster it loses velocity

Because gravity remains constant whereas velocity is always falling off, the path of a bullet is a curve known as a parabola — NOT the arc of a circle as is often imagined. Consequently, the high point of the trajectory over any given range is not halfway but somewhat beyond. It is at about 110 yards over a 200-yard range, and at about 165 yards over 300 yards. The farther the bullet travels, the greater the drop.

This all may be on the technical side, but it shows three things: 1. Bullets are always falling. 2. Strictly speaking, no rifle is really "flat shooting."

3. High muzzle velocity is only one factor in a comparatively flat trajectory.

In order to compensate for the drop of the bullet, the rifle that's properly sighted in has the bore pointed *up*, as the rear sight is higher than the front sight. The line of sight, then, is an imaginary line running straight to the target. The line of bore is another imaginary straight line which intersects the line of sight and continues on. The trajectory curve is the path actually taken by the bullet. It crosses the line of sight once near the muzzle and once again at a considerable distance, but it never goes above the line of bore because the bullet falls continuously after it leaves the muzzle.

If a rifle is fired with its line of bore exactly horizontal, the bullet drop at 100 yards is amazing. Here are some figures: the .22 Long Rifle bullet, at a muzzle velocity of 1140 feet per second, has a drop, or total fall below the line of bore, of 15 inches. A high-velocity version of the same bullet at 1280 fps has a total fall of 13 inches. Even the 170-grain .30/30 bullet, which steps along at the much faster rate of 2200 fps, falls 4 inches. The 180-grain .30/06 bullet is traveling at 2700 fps when it leaves the muzzle and drops 3 inches. Speed the bullet up to 3110 (as in the case with the 150-grain 7 mm. Remington Magnum bullet or the 130-grain .270) and the drop is only about 2 inches. Speed it up still more, until it is traveling like the .220 Swift or the 100-grain .270, and the total fall is only about 1 inch. *The faster a bullet*

Bullet drop at 100 yards is amazing

travels the less it falls over a given range, because the less time gravity has to work on it.

Total fall
from line of
bore of var-
ious bullets
at 200
yards

Now let's look at the total fall from line of bore of those bullets over 200 yards, at which distance they are slowing up more and gravity has had more chance to get in its dirty work:

.22 Long Rifle (standard speed)	55 in.
.22 Long Rifle (high velocity)	50 in.
.30/30 (170 gr.)	18 in.
.30/06 (180 gr.)	11 in.
.270 (130 gr.)	8 in.
.220 Swift (48 gr.)	4 in.

The thing to do in sighting in a rifle, then, is to jockey these figures of total fall, line of sight, and line of bore around until we have a useful combination. We tame this trajectory business and *learn* it thoroughly.

In the case of the .22 with high-speed ammunition, for example, we learn that we tame the trajectory curve a bit by hoisting it above the line of sight, then letting it drop again. In a bore-sighted .22, at only 50 yards the total fall of the high-velocity Long Rifle bullet is 3 inches, and at that range you'd miss the head of a squirrel; but if you line up its iron sights on a point 50 yards away, the bullet will hit the point of aim — and it will rise only about ½ inch above the line of sight at 30 yards.

Even when zeroed at 75 yards, the low-velocity .22 Long Rifle bullet from an iron-sighted rifle will cross the line of aim *first* at about 10 yards, climb 1.3 inches above the line of sight at 50 yards, cross the line of aim again at 75 yards (the distance at which it is said to be sighted in or zeroed), and fall 4 inches below the line of sight at 100 yards — a far cry indeed from the fall of 12 inches at that distance, if the bore were horizontal. Anywhere from the muzzle to 85 yards, the bullet would not deviate enough to miss the head of a cottontail — or, in most cases, the head of a squirrel.

With the scope-sighted .22 the range can be stretched a bit with the same maximum trajectory height above the line of sight of 1.3 inches. In this case the low-velocity Long Rifle bullet will first cross the line of aim at 12½ yards, cross again at 85 yards, and be only 2 inches low at 100. Even with that sighting, though, the bullet, because of its low velocity, is 7 inches low at 125 yards and 15 inches low at 150 yards. All of which explains why the finest scope in the world won't make up for the shortcomings of a .22 Long Rifle on varmints at long range! Gravity simply has too much time to work on the bullet.

To me it seems sheer folly to sight in a rifle for some short distance simply because most game is killed at that range. I once read a very good hunting tale by a man who used a scope-sighted .270 which he zeroed for 100 yards because he had it doped out that he would probably shoot his deer at that distance. Now suppose our hunter had got

It is sheer folly to sight in a rifle for some short distances

a quick shot at 250 yards and he had held dead on. The 150-grain bullet would have fallen 10 inches below point of aim and he probably would have missed his buck.

On the other hand, if he had sighted in for 225 yards the bullet would have been only 3 inches high at 100 and 150 yards, and only 2 inches low at 250. Unless you plan to go around shooting deer in the eye, a 3-inch deviation from line of sight surely is not excessive!

With the standard .270 factory loads with the 130-grain bullet, I do the preliminary sighting in at 25 yards and adjust the scope to hit the point of aim at that distance. The bullet then strikes 3 inches high at 100 yards, 4 inches high at 150 and 200 yards, at point of aim the second time at 275, and only 2 inches low at 300. At 325 yards the bullet is about 4 inches below the point of aim. For shooting big game — even deer and antelope measuring from 14 to 18 inches from top of shoulder to bottom of chest — this is not excessive deviation. Sighted for 200 yards, on the other hand, the bullet falls 4 inches below point of aim at only 260 yards.

Let's apply the same formula to the scope-sighted .30/06 with the factory 150-grain load at a muzzle velocity of 2910 feet per second, sighting in so the bullet first crosses the line of aim at 25 yards and strikes 3 inches high at 100 yards. At 150 yards the bullet strikes 4 inches high; at 200 yards it's 3 inches high; at 250 yards it is at point of aim the second time; and the bullet does not fall more than 4 inches below point of aim until it has passed the 290-yard mark. Such a sighting makes the .30/06 a pretty good long-range sheep and antelope rifle!

Now let's take a look at the ordinary deer rifle — say an iron-sighted .30/30 using a 170-grain bullet with a muzzle velocity of 2200 fps. If you sight one of these in for 100 yards, at 200 yards the bullet fall below the line of bore will be about 10 inches — enough to miss even a big white-tail buck with a center-of-the-chest hold. On the other hand, if the rifle is sighted in for 150 yards the bullet will fall only 5 inches at 200 yards, and a hit with no allowance for drop is probable. What's more, at 100 yards the bullet is only 2 inches above the line of sight, and that is so little deviation as to be negligible. Substantially the same trajectory applies to any of the other so-called deer cartridges — including the .32 Special, .35 Remington, and .375 Winchester.

The iron-sighted rifle using a cartridge with a velocity of from 2400 to 2500 fps can well be sighted in for 175 yards. This will include the .30/40 Krag and .300 Savage with the 180-grain bullet; also the .358 Winchester with the 200-grain bullet, the .30/06 with the 220-grain bullet, and the 7 mm. Mauser with the 175-grain bullet. With any of these the bullet will be 2½ or 3 inches high at 100 yards, at point of aim at 175 yards, and only 2 or 3 inches low at 200 yards.

When such rifles are scope-sighted, the trajectory is apparently flattened out a bit, and they

Let's take a look at the ordinary deer rifle

can be zeroed for 200 yards. In that case the bullet will first cross the line of sight at 25 yards. At 100 yards it will be 3 inches high, and at 250 only about 5 inches low — all of which means that with the 180-grain bullet and a scope sight even the old .30/40 Krag can stretch right out there.

Acceptable mid-range trajectory height above line of sight depends upon the size of the game

How much mid-range trajectory height above line of sight can be permitted? That depends on the size of the game. The squirrel hunter, for instance, who usually aims at the head, cannot have much more than an inch. The varmint hunter too shoots at small targets, and in his case a 2½-inch deviation is the most he can work with. I prefer a mid-range trajectory of no more than 1½ inches for varmint shooting.

The hunter of big game, on the other hand, has much larger marks — from the small deer measuring 14 inches from chest to withers, to the huge moose of from 36 to 40 inches. A 4-inch deviation is peanuts even on a medium-size animal like a bighorn ram or a mule deer.

Knowledge of trajectory and the practical application of this knowledge is enormously useful. The hunter should memorize the trajectory of his rifle. If he doesn't trust his memory, he can copy off the dope from a trajectory table and tape it to the buttstock.

This look at trajectory takes a somewhat different perspective from that offered by O'Connor. It comes from Townsend Whelen's The Hunting

Rifle *(1940). The original piece also included considerable information about estimation of distance, a task that has, as I have already noted, basically been assumed by effective range finders.*

Townsend Whelen's perspective on trajectory

TRAJECTORY

On the rifle range, you know precisely what the distance is, and this distance does not vary from shot to shot. But in shooting at game you never have these conditions. Thus an intimate knowledge of the trajectory of your cartridge is necessary for success in hunting.

This knowledge of the trajectory is necessary in most hunting countries. In a thickly forested country where shots are never obtained beyond 100 yards a knowledge of the trajectory is not necessary, because you can keep your sights continually adjusted for 100 yards, and then the bullet will never strike higher than about 1 inch above the point of aim at 50 yards, and you have to make no allowance for distance in aiming, everything within 100 yards being within the point blank range of your cartridge. But in most countries you will get a few shots beyond 100 yards, and in open mountain or plains country you will get a great many at very long distances. While it is always well to stalk as close as possible to the game before shooting, on some terrain it is just impossible to get closer than 250 to 400 yards without disturbing your game. Furthermore game may offer a shot at 200 yards, you may miss that shot, and the next one you get may be at 300 yards.

All of the ammunition companies publish tables giving the trajectory of their cartridges. They will show you, taking for example, the .30-06 cartridge, 180 grain pointed bullet, fired at a muzzle velocity of 2700 feet per second, that when firing at 100 yards the height of trajectory at 50 yards is .69 inch, when firing at 200 yards the height of trajectory at 100 yards is 3.05 inches, and when firing at 300 yards the height of trajectory at 150 yards is 7.72 inches. These heights of trajectory at mid distance are pure trajectory figures. That is the height is above a line drawn from the axis of the bore at the muzzle to the center of the bullet hole in the target.

Now these figures are not at all what the hunter wants to know. What he wants to know is first the best "point blank" distance at which to set his scope. He knows that the bullet never flies absolutely flat. That the bullet starts to drop from gravity as soon as it leaves the muzzle. But he does know that it flies practically flat for a considerable distance, and he wants to know what that distance is. When we say "practically flat" we will have to qualify that a little. When shooting at small game we would hardly miss anything if at a short distance our bullet would strike an inch, or even an inch and a half above the line of aim. At what distance then, can we sight in our rifle so that at half that distance our bullet will not strike

The hunter wants to know the best "point-blank" distance at which to set his scope

more than 1 inch or 1½ inches above the line of aim? Let me give you one or two answers to that question right away to make matters clearer.

With the .22 Hornet cartridge, if we sight our rifle in to strike the exact point of aim at 150 yards, the bullet will fly approximately ⅞ inch above the line of aim at 50 yards, and 1 inch above the line of aim at 100 yards, and aiming at the exact point we wished to strike on a woodchuck, and making no allowance for distance, we would not miss that point by more than an inch because of trajectory. Furthermore, with that same aim, the bullet will drop only ½ inch below the line of aim at 175 yards, and will drop 4 inches low at 200 yards. Thus, with this sight adjustment we have to make no allowance when aiming for the distance up to 175 yards, and at 200 yards, or what we estimate to be 200 yards, if we aim just a trifle high to allow for the 4 inch drop, we will come pretty near making a good hit on every shot. Now that is more like what the hunter wants to know about his trajectory.

In shooting at big game it will make no particular difference to us if our bullet strikes as much as 2½ inches above the line of aim when the sights are set for the point blank distance. The bullet striking only 2½ inches above where we aimed it would not miss the vital part of any big game animal.

As another immediate example, if you sight in a scope sighted .30-06 rifle to strike the exact point of aim at 200 yards, the bullet will strike approximately 1¾ inches high at 100 yards, and will drop 9 inches low at 300 yards, or 23 inches low at 400 yards. Here again we have just the kind of trajectory information the hunter wants to know. Up to about 225 yards, with his rifle sighted for 200 yards, he has to make no allowance for distance in aiming. True, at 100 yards the bullet will strike about 1¾ inches high, and at 225 yards it will drop about 2 inches low, but no one is going to miss the vital parts on big game with any small errors like that. Then at longer distances, if he estimates that the distance is somewhere between 250 and 300 yards, all he has to do is to aim slightly higher on the shoulder of the animal to allow for what he thinks is about a 9 inch drop. Or, if the animal is a very long distance off, what he thinks is somewhere around 350 to 400 yards, if he will aim with the top of his front sight just barely above the top or backbone of the animal, and above the heart area, his bullet is almost certain to drop somewhere around 18 to 23 inches and still land well inside the chest cavity of the animal. Thus we have a trajectory which will give us a sure hitting range up to almost 400 yards.

After you have thoroughly tested and begin to know your rifle as your alphabet, you are ready to take it into the hunting country. You are getting a fine reliance in it and on your shooting which you could obtain in no other way. You are beginning to feel that you can absolutely command an animal at all distances up to 400 yards, and that you can put your bullet practically anywhere you wish, and insure a large proportion of clean kills on the first shot. In other words you are becoming a real hunter-rifleman.

This intriguing look at the effect wind has on a bullet's flight comes from a leading contemporary writer, Bryce Towsley. It originally appeared in the December 2002 issue of Guns & Gear *magazine. Those interested in an earlier and somewhat different perspective on the subject of wind might want to look at "The Problem of Wind Allowance" in Jack O'Connor's* Complete Book of Rifles and Shotguns *(1965), "Wind Allowance" in Townsend Whelen's* The Hunting Rifle *(1940), and "Wind" in Edward C. Crossman's* Military and Sporting Rifle Shooting *(1932).*

Bryce Towsley on the effect of wind on the bullet's flight

THE ANSWER IS
BLOWIN' IN THE WIND

The wind's effect on a bullet's flight has been a subject of heated discourse for as long as shooters have been trying to hit targets at long distances. We have developed charts and computer programs in attempts to make predictions, but at best they are only a guideline. All the mathematical theorists from Einstein to my cousin Philip can't predict exactly what a bullet will do when it is fired through a real-world moving air mass.

However, the computer programs and ballistic tables are useful in learning about the wind's effects, and it is hardly a waste of time to study them. . . . But the flaw in these tables and programs is that the predictions are built on laboratory conditions and assume a constant force and direction of wind.

Things are different in the atmosphere we shoot through. Winds gust and wane, with currents and flows affected by terrain, vegetation and a million other factors. Although the wind may be blowing at one speed where you are, your bullet can travel through wind that is moving at several different speeds, before the distant target is reached. The same with wind direction: over a given distance, wind can curl around, double back, eddy, switch and change its attitude more times than a six-year-old with a sugar buzz. If there is one constant in a wind's influence on a bullet, it is this inconsistency.

The one constant in a wind's influence on a bullet is inconsistency

The effect as predicted in the charts and computer programs uses the velocity and ballistic coefficient of the bullet to determine the time of flight, which is in effect the amount of time the wind has to act on the bullet. The more time the bullet is in flight, the more the wind will blow it off course. Other factors include the bullet's size and shape and the area available for the wind to blow against. The bullet's weight is a factor as well. It is easier to push around a light object than a heavy one. Who would you rather wrestle, Hulk Hogan or Bill Gates? Same principle.

Wind direction is another factor. A 90-degree side wind will blow against the full profile of the bullet, but a wind of any different angle will have a differing percentage of the bullet's surface to act on. A full head or tail wind will have either the point or the base of the bullet to blow against, which affects retained velocity and, consequently, bullet drop. For example, a .44 Magnum 240-grain bullet with a 20 mph tail wind will have almost 100 feet per second more retained velocity at 500 yards than the same bullet with a 20 mph head wind. This will change the bullet path, even though there is no theoretical wind drift and the difference in drop is almost 45 inches. Of course, this is an extreme example and nobody really considers the .44 Magnum a 500-yard cartridge, but every bullet from any cartridge will be affected in some way.

Now suppose the wind is gusting from a 45-degree angle, or 20 degrees or perhaps 10 degrees. Maybe it will be from all three before the bullet makes it from your gun to the target. How much will that affect the lateral wind drift? How about the bullet drop? I don't have a clue. Neither does anybody else, not with all the variables.

Shooting in the wind is far more an art than a science, and the only real way to learn about reading the wind is to get out and shoot in it. A couple of days in a prairie dog town will teach you more than all the theoretical computer programs or printed ballistic tables in the world. If there is a pronounced lack of prairie dogs where you are, simply find a windy place with some good dis-

Shooting in the wind is more an art than a science

After a few thousand rounds, you may get a hand on reading wind

tance, and shoot at rocks, clay pigeons, plastic soda bottles full of water or even paper targets, and do it with a variety of firearms. Have a pal watch your hits through a spotting scope and try to evaluate each shot. After a few thousand rounds or so, you may finally start to get a handle on reading wind.

V
ACCURACY AT
ALL DISTANCES

For hunters and competitive shooters alike, accuracy is the ultimate measure of performance. It is one thing to be able to hit a target with consistency at point-blank range. It is quite another to produce the same type of performance at distances ranging up to several hundred yards. Although the hunter should always try to get as close to his quarry as possible, shots at plains game, sheep, or any kind of animals in open country are likely to be available only at considerable distances. For example, deer hunters in my home state of South Carolina regularly talk about "bean field bucks" and "bean field rifles." With the former phrase, they are referring to whitetails that feed in vast soybean fields and that can require shots at distances as far as 500 yards. Match shooters strive for pinpoint accuracy at even greater distances: targets as far away as 1,000 yards are a part of some competitions.

Many factors enter into consistently accurate shooting at a distance. In truth, most of them also come into play on shorter shots. It is just that the shooter has a lot more room for error

Many factors enter into consistently accurate shooting at a distance

when the target is close. Among the considerations that grow in significance as the range increases are trigger control, steadiness, recoil and the shooter's ability to deal with it, the infinitesimal yet vitally important amount of time that elapses between the squeezing of the trigger and the actual firing of the gun (that factor is the essential element in the superior accuracy offered by the electronic ignition systems first introduced by the Remington Arms Company), wind, the angle of the shot, and even optical illusions.

The material presented here addresses most of these issues and offers insight on how to handle them. Ultimately, though, the keys to accurate shooting at distances are practice, understanding your rifle, being aware of the factors affecting accuracy, and doing all that lies within your physical capabilities to deal with them.

●

Whether the shot comes in open country, where chances at animals 400 or 500 yards away are commonplace, or in popular competitions involving targets at distances as great as 1,000 yards, distance shooting places special demands on the marksman. Wind effect is magnified, "barrel wiggle" and trigger jerking loom far larger than they do at shorter ranges, and an understanding of the ballistic performance of guns and bullets takes on great importance. Here Jack

O'Connor, in a piece that originally appeared in Sportsman's Arms and Ammunition Manual *(1952), takes a look at a number of key factors involved in accuracy at a distance.*

Jack
O'Connor
examines
key factors
involved in
accuracy at
distance

HITTING 'EM AT LONG RANGE

YOU CAN BEGIN TO CALL IT "LONG
RANGE" AT 250 YARDS – AND TAKE
THOSE 500-YARD KILLS WITH A GRAIN
OF SALT

There are two extreme schools of thought on the subject of long range big-game shooting. The lads in one are against it from start to finish. Its members consider a 200-yd. shot a very long one, and in their writings they intimate that anyone who tries a longer shot is a poor sportsman, if not actually a fellow who plays fast and loose with the truth. I have heard members of that school who, I am convinced, couldn't stalk a traffic sign bewail the degeneracy of the modern hunter and say that anyone who doesn't creep to within bow-and-arrow range of his game is a softy.

The lads of the other school write jauntily of shots at 500, 600, and even 800 yd. and thereby fill the heads of inexperienced riflemen with very strange notions indeed. Some years ago one of these chaps told of killing a running antelope at 500 yd. and of being shocked and bitter when he discovered that his bullet had missed the heart by

6 in. The answer, he decided, was the altitude, not human frailty.

Just what is long-range shooting? Right here a few definitions might help. For the record, let us say that *short range shooting* is at ranges of 100 yd. or less, the type of shooting that is common in brushy and heavily forested country at white-tail deer and moose. *Medium range shooting* includes all shots that require no holdover with a properly sighted modern rifle. That means shots to about 250 yd. with a weapon of the .30/06, 7mm., or .257 type of trajectory.

Definitions of short, medium, and long-range shooting

To say, then, that *long-range shooting* is any at distance of more than 250 yd. may sound modest indeed, but that is the way I look at it. At more than that distance the man behind the rifle usually has to do some pretty sharp figuring of range, and if he makes a mistake he isn't going to bring home any venison, mountain mutton, or whatever sort of game it is that he is after.

I am convinced that most of the 400-yd. shots one reads about are in reality about 250-yd. shots, and that the 500-yd. shots were made at 300 yd. Even if a guide tells the happy hunter that he has killed something at 400 or 500 yd., there is no guarantee that it is a fact. Some guides are expert riflemen and fine judges of range. Others are not.

In Wyoming, my guide on an antelope hunt assured me that a buck was 500 yd. away, and I couldn't possibly hit it. I decided the buck was between 325 and 350 yd. from the muzzle and that the shot was not too difficult. From the way the bullet landed I think the buck was actually about 300 yd. away. Another time a guide swore a ram was 400 yd. away, but I held for 250 and scored a hit on the first shot.

Some men are better at judging distance than others. No one is any too good. I have been at it for many years, but I often lay terrible eggs. The last attempt I made to hit anything at long and un-determined range was a shot at a black bear feed-ing above timberline in a spot in which he could not possibly be stalked. I missed him so far he wasn't even bothered. But more of that incident later.

With good equipment in the hands of a skillful operator, however, shots at from 250 to 350 yd. are really not too difficult. In the Southwest, where I live, the principal game animal is a small, frisky, and wary white-tail deer whose habitat is wide, partly wooded canyons. It is seldom that a hunter gets more than a hasty snapshot. If the buck is on the same side of the canyon, but be-cause he can look between the trees to the *other side*, the hunter can usually get several shots at a cross-canyon buck at from 200 to 350 yd. It may sound cockeyed to Eastern deer hunters, but I'd much rather shoot a white tail at 300 yd. where I can keep him in sight than at 50 yd. where he is out of sight in a jump or two.

For a skillful operator, shots at 250 to 300 yards are really not too difficult

In the fall of 1945, I was hunting close to the Mexican border with some friends. One was armed with a 'scope-sighted .270, the others with iron-sighted .30/30's and .30/40's. A nice white-tail buck got up at between 300 and 400 yd. away, trotted a few feet, and stopped. The lad with the .270 used his binoculars, saw antlers, then dropped into prone position, held the cross hairs on the top of the deer's shoulder, and squeezed off a shot. The buck collapsed. To the others this looked like black magic, and their opinion of 'scope sights and .270's went up about 100 per-cent.

All over the West shots of this type at deer are common. A lot of mule-deer shooting is done in very open canyon and mesa country where there is little cover and where the deer tend to move out at rather long range. In some sections elk are hunted under almost identical conditions, and an-telope are often difficult to get close to.

Rifle and bullet selections for shooting at 200 to 300 yards

For all this 200 to 300-yd. shooting, the rifle should use an accurate cartridge giving the bullet high velocity. It should be equipped with a 'scope and sighted in for the longest possible range, so as to make it unnecessary to hold over the game at medium and medium-long ranges. With the 130-gr. bullet at 3,140 foot seconds, a .270 equipped with a 'scope can be sighted in to hit the point of aim at 300 yd. The bullet will rise 4 in. above the line of sight at 150 and 200 yd. and fall 4 in. below at 350. With that trajectory, the man behind the rifle does not need to hold over unless he thinks the deer is more than 350 yd. away. Then he can hold on the backbone and get a hit up to about 450 yd. His shots will strike a little high at intermediate ranges if he does not remember to hold slightly low, but not high enough to cause a miss.

Such sighting is much more sensible for open country than the often-recommended 200-yd. zero. With a 'scope-sighted .270 zeroed for 200 yd., the bullet will land 6 in. low at 300 and about 12 in. low at 350. Its range is greatly reduced.

A .30/06 with the 150-gr. bullet at 2,960 foot seconds should be sighted in to put the bullet 3 in. above the line of 'scope sight at 100 yd. This will put it 4 in. high at 200, right on the nose at 250, and 4 in. low at 300. The same trajectory figures apply approximately for the .300 Magnum with the sporting 180-gr. bullet, the 7 mm. with the old high-speed 139-gr. load, and to other cartridges in the 2,900 to 3,000-foot-seconds class.

Using the same figure of a 4-in. deviation from line of aim, the .30/06 with the 180-gr. bullet is good for a point blank range of only about 265 yd. *Remember that for open-country shooting the rifle should always be sighted in for the longest possible range that will not give midrange misses.* The more nearly the rifleman can ignore holdover, the better off he is.

The load which gives the flattest trajectory should always be chosen — and one weight of bullet, one brand of ammunition, and preferably one lot of cartridges should be the rifleman's standard. The man who mixes up different brands of am-

The load which gives the flattest trajectory should always be chosen

munition and different bullet weights and shapes isn't going to get anywhere in precision shooting, since at 300 yd. or so the points of impact with different loads will vary enough to cause clean misses.

For big-game shooting, a 2½-'scope with a medium cross hair or a Lee Dot reticule subtending 4 minutes of angle is a good bet. Most posts cover too much territory. A 4X 'scope is ever better, since it enables the hunter to hold more precisely.

The finest rifle and the best sights in the world aren't any good for 250 to 300-yd. shots unless the man who uses the outfit makes up his mind to shoot from the steadiest possible position. Last season I saw a chap with a fine 'scope-sighted .30/06 stand up on his hind legs and fire 16 shots at a big buck that got up at 200 yd. and finally went over the skyline at about 450. If he had sat down I see no reason way he should not have killed that buck. It is better to get off one careful shot from a steady position, than a dozen sloppy shots off-hand.

Kneeling is a better position than standing, but sitting is far better, and the man who wants to excel at the longer ranges should practice it constantly. It can be used in low brush, tall grass, and on hillsides when a prone position is out of the question. In country where it can be assumed, of course, prone is the steadiest of all. It is particularly useful on the open plains where antelope are so often found, and in the Rockies above timber-line where a typical shot at stalked game is from the top of a smooth rounded ridge into a basin.

The really long-range shots are those that require holding high, even with the flattest-shooting modern rifles correctly sighted to take advantage of trajectory. Such shots should not be undertaken lightly — never if a man can avoid it. I have made relatively few such shots, as I have usually found that if the game was undisturbed, I could stalk closer. If the game is frightened and running, the best thing to do is to let it calm down and come back another day. Occasionally, however, the entire success of a trip may depend on making a very long, deliberate shot.

Even with the flattest-shooting rifles, really long-range shots require holding

As we have seen, making medium and medium-long shots requires a flat-shooting rifle, a good 'scope sight, and the ability to assume a steady position and squeeze them off. When the game is still farther away, close judgment of distance and a working knowledge of trajectory must be added.

One helpful way to judge distance is to divide the range into hundreds of yards and to become skilled in this guessing game in the off season. I constantly practice this. Out for a hike, I'll see a bush, estimate the distance, then pace it off to check. Most of the time I do fairly well at it. Now and then I pull an astounding boner. Using a reticule of known value in the 'scope and comparing it with the size of an animal is also helpful.

For instance, the average white-tail buck or antelope is about 16 in. from the top of his shoulder to the bottom of his chest. You put a 4-minute dot on him and find that it exactly covers the chest from top to bottom. You can then assume that he is about 400 yd. away and hold accordingly. The width of a post reticule can also be used as a range finder, and so can the distance between the bars of certain types at European-made telescope-sight reticules.

This system is better than nothing. It can be used to check the original estimate, but it is not absolute because game animals do not come in standard sizes. Last year I measured several Arizona white-tail bucks, all full-grown 4-pointers. The smallest was 14 in. thick and the largest 18 in. Full-grown mule deer that I have measured varied from 18 to 22 in., mountain sheep from 18 to 24. Elk will vary from 24 to 30 in., and moose from 30 to 40. The last moose I shot measured 34 in. from hump to brisket. Another measured 38.

An animal looks larger in good light than in bad

The unaided eye is not too good. An animal looks larger in good light than in bad, larger against a light background than against a dark background, smaller both uphill and downhill, larger against the skyline with the source of light behind him. As a consequence, the use of the reticule will often correct some very bad estimates.

Once I was toying with the notion of taking a pop at a bull moose. He was on the skyline and, I thought, about 400 yd. away. The dot told me he was about 800 yards from me. Needless to say, I didn't shoot.

There is no way I know of to tell a big bear from a little bear at a distance. I missed the last bear I shot at so far that I didn't even worry him. My guide thinks I underestimated the range and shot under him. I have a sneaking hunch that he was a yearling cub and that I overestimated the distance and shot above him. At any rate I missed the bear.

The longest shot I ever made at a big-game animal was at a bull elk in Wyoming. It was a case of shoot or go home without the big elk head I wanted. The bull was lying down in a place where he could not be approached. I sat on a boulder, rolled up my jacket, and rested my rifle across it on another rock. It made an almost perfect bench rest, and the rifle was as steady as the rock itself. The 4-minute dot in the 'scope almost covered the elk from top of shoulder to bottom of chest, which meant that he was about 600 yd. away. I held for 600, and elk went down. Ernest Miller, my outfitter, and Charlie Peterson, my Jackson Hole guide, helped estimate the range and deserve, along with the improvised rest, much of the credit.

On a really long shot, the use of a rest is an excellent idea. I have shot from a folded down-filled jacket many times, putting it over stones, ridges, logs, so that the shot would not fly high. The longest shot I ever made at a coyote was with the rifle resting on a 10-gallon hat on top of a barrel cactus. If no good, quick, comfortable rest is available, prone with a sling is almost as good.

The long-range rifleman should not only be able to make fairly accurate estimates of range and get into the steadiest of positions, but be should always keep the trajectory of his rifle in mind. I have known men to print out the trajectory with waterproof ink on paper and then affix it to the buttstock with Scotch tape, so it would be instantly available for reference.

Some useful range and trajectory examples

If a rifle is a .30/06, sighted to put the 180-gr. bullet at point of aim at 225 yd., such a card might read like this: 300 yd. — 9 in.; 350 yd. — 18 in.; 400 yd. — 30 in. It will come in handy. Such trajectory dope is available in handbooks put out by the ammunition companies and an especially good chart is published as part of the Western Ammunition Handbook put out by the Western Cartridge Co., East Alton, Ill.

Except in an emergency, and then only under favorable conditions, the rifleman should limit his range, I believe, to the point-blank range of his particular rifle with its particular sight-setting, plus the additional range permitted by two thirds of the animal's body depth. Then, when he estimates the range at being well beyond the point-blank range of the rifle, he can hold on the backbone at a point above where he wants to hit, and squeeze the trigger.

Suppose our animal is 18 in. thick. We can

then permit a 12-in. bullet fall. Taking that figure, a .270 sighted in for 300 yd. will produce a hit in the chest cavity up to a little more than 400 yd. A rifle of the 2,900 to 3,000-foot-seconds class such as the .257, or the .30/06 with the 180-gr. bullet at about 2,700 foot seconds, zeroed for 225, will give a hit up to a little more than 300 yd. The larger animals can be hit farther away. These figures are for average deer-size animals.

I know these figures seem long to the short-range boys and short to the long-range experts, but they have worked out pretty well for me. If things are right I can, with those various rifles, hit hard and regularly at such ranges. And by *right* I mean if I am in a good position and the game is standing or moving slowly in the open. Beyond that distance it is too much of a gamble. It is too easy to misjudge the range and either miss or wound. A slight wobble as the shot is let off makes too much difference. Furthermore, the world isn't exactly full of bullets of such construction and driven at such velocity that they can be counted on always to open up properly and kill even with a well-placed shot at much more than 400 yd. Many will not expand well at more than 300 yd.

Because I do not mind wounding and possibly losing a destructive coyote, I have shot a good many of them at far beyond these ranges. I have also missed plenty, too. I have shot very little big game at more than 400 yd., and the elk I mentioned was very much the exception. When I was young and brainless I used to try those by-guess and by-gosh shots with equipment far less good than I use now. I missed so many that I grew more conservative.

Actually there isn't much need for those long shots — even the 350 to 400-yd ones I have mentioned. Mountain sheep are traditionally shot at long range, but on remembering those I have taken, I realize that the shots averaged about 210 yd. The shortest shot was at 35 yd., the longest at about 400, but most of them were made at less than 250. In most cases sheep can be stalked to within moderate range, as can all mountain game such as caribou, goats, and the bull moose often found up above timberline.

Most of O'Connor's mountain sheep were shot at an average of 210 yards

By far the longest *average* shooting I have done has been at the little Southwestern white-tail deer, and in that case I am sure that the majority of my shots have been at more than 250 yd. Because I have used powerful cartridges like the 100 and 130-gr. .270 loads and the 150-gr. .30/06, I have, in all that time, drawn blood on only three deer that I didn't bring to camp. In every case I am sure that the deer which got away had only superficial flesh wounds from which they quickly recovered.

Now and then, however, a man will have to choose between making a long shot or going home without a trophy which he may have traveled many hundreds of miles to get. When that happens, the good shot, who can judge range, who can assume a steady position, who doesn't scorn the use of a rest, and who has a good 'scope-equipped rifle properly sighted in to minimize his errors of judgment has an excellent chance of making a good, clean, satisfying kill.

In the early fall of 1945 in the Yukon, I was still shy two Dall rams. On the last day I could hunt there I saw the two I wanted, but I couldn't get very close to them without being seen. I judged the nearest to be about 300 yd. away and the other somewhat farther. Field Johnson (my guide) and I were perched on a rugged ridge, and the rams were across a canyon slightly lower than we were.

'Scope sights and high-velocity cartridges have extended the sure-hitting range of rifles, but the human animal with his bum eyes, his habit of getting excited, and his poor judgment of distance is still the same guy.

The rifleman should get as close as he can, and if he has to shoot at long range he should figure all the angles!

Get as close as you can

Call it "pull," "squeeze," or "easing off a shot," the way the shooter handles a trigger when he fires a shot has great importance for the results he achieves. Townsend Whelen understood this, and here he addresses three kinds of pulls. They involve different types of rifles, and changes in technology and gun making have altered this situation to a certain degree. But in the final analy-

Whelen discusses trigger pull

sis, as Whelen emphasizes, consistent marks-manship (insofar as it devolves from the manner in which the shooter interacts with the trigger) primarily requires practice and concentration. The selection is from The American Rifle *(1918).*

TRIGGER PULL

It matters not how carefully the aim is taken, or how steadily the rifle is held, if, at the instant of discharging the rifle, the aim and hold are deranged by the convulsive jerk at the trigger. The trigger must release the sear from the sear notch without the least movement of the rifle, or the bullet will not fly true to the point at which it was aimed the instant before the trigger was pulled. As one concentrates his whole will power on holding steadily and aiming accurately, the body becomes immovable, frozen, as it were. It is then quite difficult to transfer the will power to the trigger finger, and to press it so as to discharge the rifle, because the finger will be found to be "frozen" also. The tendency with the untrained men is instantly to relax on the hold and aim, and give a jerk or tug at the trigger. The tendency to do this must be constantly repressed. The matter of learning how to pull the trigger without aiming and holding at the same time is a very simple matter, but the co-ordinating of the trigger pull with the aim and hold so as to insure a perfect let-off, and at the same time maintaining the aim and hold to the very

end, is a matter which requires considerable practice. In fact, an expert rifleman realizes that he
must keep at practicing this all the time if he
would maintain his ability to shoot accurately.

We find on American rifles three kinds of trigger pulls. First there is the old-fashioned, "clean"
pull seen on the best single-shot rifles, and on the
Winchester repeating rifles. When the trigger is
pressed it appears to be immovable until the required amount of pressure has been applied to
cause the hammer to fall. Then it gives away all at
once, something like the breaking of a small glass
rod. This is the best type of trigger pull. With it
one soon learns how much pressure he may place
on the trigger without danger of firing the rifle.
That is, he learns to place all but an ounce or so of
the necessary pressure to discharge the piece on
the trigger as soon as he starts to aim and hold.
Then, just as the aim seems the most accurate,
and the hold the steadiest, he very carefully
squeezes on this last ounce or so of pressure which
discharges the rifle without any movement of the
piece. Triggers of this type when they come from
the manufacturers pull off on an applied pressure
of from five to seven pounds. This is entirely too
heavy for accurate work. However, they are capable of being eased up to about 3 pounds, which is
the correct weight for all-around rifle shooting.

Triggers of the bolt-action type are slightly different. When correctly adjusted there is a safety
or preliminary pull, during which the trigger

*The three
kinds of
trigger
pulls on
American
rifles*

moves back about 1/8 inch against the tension of the sear spring. This safety pull is absolutely necessary for the safety of the rifle, preventing premature discharge, and should never be eliminated. As a rule it takes about one and one-half pounds pressure on the trigger to take it up. After it has been taken up, and the trigger has moved slightly to the rear, the remainder of the pull is clean, as in the case just described, and the trigger pulls off with a total pressure of about $3\frac{1}{2}$ pounds. In pulling a trigger of this kind one must be careful to at once take up the safety pull as soon as the rifle is placed to the shoulder. That is, learn to place enough pressure on the trigger as soon as the finger touches it, to make it move slightly to the rear against the pressure of the sear spring, and then start the *trigger pull proper*, as in the first case. One can soon become accustomed to a trigger of this kind, but it never satisfies one as well as the straight, clean pull, especially in rapid fire. With recruits in the Army it has been found that the larger percentage of failures to make good scores in rapid fire is due to not taking up the safety pull at all, but when the aim seems right, pulling the trigger the whole way back with one motion or jerk. This must be specially guarded against.

The third type of trigger pull is that usually seen on self-loading rifles, and the modern type of hammerless repeating rifles. The trigger moves back quite a little before the rifle is finally discharged, but too often this movement is attended with a rough "drag," consisting of a series of jumps and catches, so that one can scarcely ever tell when he has applied the right amount of pressure. Moreover, the number of little jumps and catches to this preliminary movement of the trigger will differ according to whether the taking up movement is made fast or slow, so that one can never learn whether he has surely taken them all up or not. The consequence is that one never dares place as much preliminary pressure on such a trigger as with the first two types, and more pressure must remain to be squeezed on when the aim and hold are perfected. This leaves a larger chance for a jerk and derangement at the vital instant of discharge. Also such a trigger is liable to produce flinching, as a decided jump to the trigger when pressure is applied under high concentration of will power is liable to make one jump. First-class accuracy of shooting can never be attained with such a trigger, and this is just one reason more why such weapons are only fit for short-range work.

One is not a finished marksman until this detail of trigger pull is learned so well that it is done instinctively and correctly, even in rapid fire or under excitement. Jerking the trigger and flinching can only be cured by learning to concentrate absolutely every atom of will power on holding, aiming, and trigger pull, so that there is no room in the brain or nervous system to permit of the forming

One is not a finished marksman until the details of trigger pull are learned well

of the act of jerking or flinching. It is all a matter of practice and concentration.

Ideally, the shooter never knows when trigger squeeze will end and the firing pin will send a bullet from the barrel. As Wayne Van Zwoll suggests in this piece, which appeared in the July/ August 2003 issue of Bugle *magazine, the shot should always come as a surprise. The shooter merely endeavors to put tension on the trigger in a slow, steady, and smooth fashion, trusting his rifle to do an accurate job when he handles the trigger properly.*

Wayne Van Zwoll on trigger pull

SURPRISE: THE BULLET'S GONE

It happened in a rifle match years ago. Squirming into position, I accidentally touched the trigger. The rifle fired.

In the long seconds that followed, two possibilities emerged. One was that the bullet had missed the paper and I'd get another chance; the shot would be dismissed as a "sighter." The more probable outcome was that I had hit the paper peripherally; the shot would be scored a miss. Peering through the spotting scope, I was astonished to see a hole in the middle of the record target. Exactly in the middle.

I've never again been that lucky. But luck was only partly responsible. If you're almost ready to shoot, the rifle should be pointing at the target more often than it's pointing anywhere else. One measure of a solid shooting position is the difficulty you have in pulling the sight *off* the target. Though I hadn't yet looked into the sight when I bumped the trigger in that match, my position had kept the muzzle very near where it should have been, even as I reloaded the single-shot rifle.

Consistently fine shooting has less to do with intrinsic rifle accuracy than most shooters think. On the range and in the field, hitting depends mostly on the shooter. Specifically, you want to do three things well: find a position that brings the rifle naturally on target, control breathing so the sight doesn't pitch like a ship on high seas, and crush the trigger as you would an egg that you didn't want to leak. Triggering the shot seems the simplest of these duties. It is in fact exasperatingly difficult.

Consistently fine shooting has less to do with intrinsic rifle accuracy than most shooters think

On my last elk hunt of last year, I crept through blowing snow toward a bull I'd spotted before the squall. As the storm cleared, the bull sensed something was amiss and rose from his bed in scattered pines. He moved into a small opening, and suddenly the last hour distilled itself into a few seconds. The window wouldn't stay open long. When the crosswire found his fifth rib, I almost jerked the trigger. My heart was hammering as if this were my first elk, and I wanted to snatch this opportunity before it escaped. . . .

You may have been coached to squeeze triggers so smoothly and gradually that every shot comes as a surprise. A great plan if the sight stays still. Alas, neither you nor I can hold it still. It dips and hops and bounces from side to side. It moves like a turbo-charged figure skater or caroms from point to point like a base runner. It is *never* still. When occasionally it pauses near the middle, quivering, we know that it will dash off again just before the last ounce comes off the trigger. Our only hope for a hit comes from a solid position. It makes the target center a pivot point, the place the reticle comes back to, if only briefly, more often than any other place in its travels. Odds are that a steady squeeze will drop the striker when the sight is near where we want it.

But often the sight wanders farther, and moves with more vigor, when we pressure the trigger than when we're simply waiting for the sight to settle. Any increase in the range of sight movement reduces the time our reticle spends in the middle. Faster sight movement makes the sight picture hard to assess.

Last fall in typical north-woods second growth, I spied a deer foraging in a small clearing. There was lots of brush between us; crunchy snow made approach impossible. From the sit, I found an alley for my bullet. Slowly I squeezed. *Too* slowly. The whitetail turned away before I finished. The buck moved off and was just about to step out of sight when it quartered to show enough rib for a shot. I completed the squeeze and called a good hit. But nearly two hours later, after a tough tracking job, I considered it a stroke of undeserved luck when the buck gave me a follow-up shot.

My first hit had been about 4 inches to the right of where I'd held. Not much, but given the steep quartering angle, enough to cause a crippling hit. The failure reminded me of an easy shot I'd blown a couple of years earlier. The elk lay 80 yards below me on a steep, timbered north face. I fired right away because the shot looked so easy. The bullet missed low. A fast second shot barely clipped the animal's spine. The elk dropped but bounced back up and thundered off with its companions, leaving no blood.

I should have done better. After all, I've botched a lot of shots the way I botched those. Take the elk that didn't hear me on their track across a crusted Montana snowscape. After a clean miss, the bull ran off. I followed him up and earned a second chance.

Moose are big animals, but you don't always get a big target, and a few seasons back my only shot was through a tiny window in thick willows. The first bullet from my .35 Whelen struck a couple of inches too low to be lethal. A couple of quick shots as the bull raced through a pond atoned for my error.

In Australia last summer, a big water buffalo quartering away should have been easy to assassinate. Instead, my bullet landed mid-cage. Again, I emptied the magazine to finish.

One last example, because it's the most recent

and in many ways the most poignant. A late-season deer hunt put me in country with lots of big bucks and plenty of elk to ogle. After several days of passing up deer with average antlers, I was down to the final hours. I slipped into heavy cover on a north slope and eased through deep snow and deadfall, looking hard for bedded bucks. In a grid of lodgepole shadow, the glistening black nose of a grizzled mule deer caught my eye. In a second, I'd found a bullet tunnel. The shot sent him away, steeply downhill in giant leaps. I followed fast, certain the bullet had been lethal. But the track suddenly cut back up the mountain. It occurred to me then that either a .280 Improved couldn't be trusted or I had bungled the shot. The chase ended on top, in a meadow more than 300 yards across. He'd almost made it to the other side when a 154-grain Hornady confirmed that there was nothing wrong with a .280 Improved.

My problem is that I don't always pull the trigger smoothly. In fact, I often yank it. When in its dance the sight hops toward center, my brain screams, "Now!" Of course, Now is not really when the rifle will fire. Now is when I *wish* it would fire. Now is a handful of milliseconds — or a bushel of milliseconds — before the bullet leaves the barrel. During that time, the sight may move smartly in another direction or stay on course but accelerate past the target. Naturally, I don't want to give it time for either option. Although I can't shorten lock time, I *can* abbreviate the trigger squeeze. This urge is as strong as sex drive; it is less choice than instinct, as compelling as the need to pull your hand from a fire. The result, however, always disappoints. Yanking the trigger moves the rifle. What you saw in the sight mattered Now, but it doesn't matter much after Now. Riflemen who hit consistently have mastered not the trick of speeding up a trigger squeeze but the trick of extending the Now by cajoling the trigger.

Triggers are a bit like teenagers. Some can be cajoled. Others require a heavy hand. A few need replacing, though that's not always possible. Unfortunately, legal concerns have prompted manufacturers to increase both sear engagement and trigger spring tension. It's unfortunate because a rifle that's hard to discharge accidentally is also hard to discharge accurately. The more muscle you must apply to the trigger, the more movement you impart to the barrel. A stiff spring (heavy trigger) or excessive sear engagement (long pull) also increases lock time, leaving Now somewhere in the distant past.

Triggers are a bit like teenagers

A trigger with a crisp 3-pound letoff is commonly considered a good trigger. It's heavy for black-bull's-eye target shooting but reasonable afield, given that your fingers might be cold or gloved. Excitement can dull senses, too, so you don't want the 2-ounce triggers popular on prone guns. Sadly, many rifles come from the factory with triggers stiff enough to lift 5-pound dumbbells. A few I've tested have scaled over 6 pounds, as much weight as is in the rifle you're trying to hold still.

The lack of perceptible movement that makes a trigger feel crisp results from keeping sear contact to a minimum. Crisp pulls are good not only because they minimize finger movement but because they tend to be more consistent than long pulls. Even if you believe that every shot should be a surprise, you'll shoot better if the surprises come at the same level of finger pressure each time you squeeze.

Adjustable triggers let you set the weight and sear engagement, as well as overtravel — the movement of the trigger after letoff. Overtravel doesn't matter much, in my view. But if a trigger is too hard to pull easily, or if sear engagement is so great that you get a mushy, gritty, or two-stage pull, either you or your gunsmith needs to tinker. If warranties matter to you, be aware that trigger work can void them.

Set triggers respond to a light touch while keeping sear engagement comfortably safe until you decide to shoot. Pulling the front trigger of a double set trigger (popular in Europe) doesn't fire the rifle. Instead, it mechanically reduces weight of pull for the rear trigger. You can fire quickly without touching the front trigger, simply by pulling the rear trigger. Single set triggers incorporate a small lever in the finger pad or are so designed that pushing forward on the pad sets the mechanism for a light pull. I don't like set triggers, because they are complex. Many are slow, ex-

Crisp trigger pulls are good because they tend to be more consistent than long pulls

tending lock time. Set triggers are also expensive, and a double set trigger requires you to shift your hand slightly between pulls.

To get better hits, look to your trigger. Some factory-installed adjustable triggers — not just types, but individual mechanisms — won't give you the light, crisp, consistent pull you need for excellent shooting. Whether you tune your own or buy an aftermarket trigger, try cajoling it. You'll probably like the results, even when the shot comes as a surprise.

One of the most common problems marksmen face — and it seems to magnify exponentially with rifles of larger caliber — is recoil. When you hear a hunter or target shooter suggest that a given gun "kicks like a cross-eyed mule," chances are pretty darn good that he will flinch every time he shoots the rifle. Here, in a piece based on a memorable personal experience and taken from Making Shots: A Rifle Hunter's Guide *(2000), veteran rifleman Bryce Towsley looks at the phenomenon we call recoil and offers some practical suggestions on how to reduce it. Doing so holds the promise of better shooting, and his message has particular application for larger-caliber rifles.*

Bryce
Towsley
looks at
recoil

RECOIL

When the sights looked right, I tickled the front trigger, and my world suddenly flashed white. My right shoulder was slammed backward so violently that my right hand was yanked from its grip and then snapped on the end of my arm behind me like a whip. My glasses flew from my face, and my hat left my head. It felt like Thor had landed a solid blow with his hammer, and the people watching said it appeared as though my 230-pound body had been physically lifted from the ground. I staggered back several steps but managed to stay on my feet. When my senses cleared, I was facing in almost the opposite direction from the target. My hat was behind me someplace, and my glasses dangled from one ear. The gun was still in my left hand, but that arm was fully extended and was pointing behind me.

Because the reaction was so violent and dramatic, my buddies assumed I was being a clown and exaggerating the recoil of the rifle to the point of absurdity, but it was as real as it gets. I was dazed and confused, and when I opened the rifle, it was not registering in my still shaken (not stirred) skull that both barrels of the double rifle had fired at the same time.

What its like to pull both triggers of a .600 Nitro Express rifle

The .600 Nitro Express shoots a 900-grain bullet with a muzzle velocity of 1,950 feet per second. When I pulled that trigger, I unleashed 189,006 foot-pounds of free recoil. In that 14-pound rifle, one .600 Nitro Express cartridge generates more than 135 foot-pounds of recoil at the butt plate. By comparison, a .30-06 in the same rifle would produce 11 foot-pounds. That heavy rifle hit my shoulder with 270 foot-pounds of recoil, or about

16 times as much as a .30-06 generates in the average sporting-weight rifle.

Now, do you still want to complain about how much your deer rifle kicks? It's a fact of life that hunting rifles kick. Some kick more than others, but unless the laws of physics have been interpreted by some Clinton-appointed judge and I missed it, a moving bullet must produce recoil. The bigger the bullet and the faster it's traveling, the more the gun will recoil.

If you shoot a magnum rifle suitable for big or dangerous game, it's going to kick, and some of these guns kick a lot. If it doesn't and you are after game that can bite or stomp you, you don't have enough gun. Even deer hunters who want to jump on the high-velocity, flat-trajectory bandwagon with a super magnum are not immune. Although they weigh less than those used in big bores, those high-velocity bullets generate a lot of recoil. But none of them will kick nearly as much as that doubling .600 Nitro Express, and I survived; so will you. With very few exceptions, rifle recoil will cause no lasting or real physical damage. The wild card, though, is how well you shoot. Big guns are easy to shoot but hard to shoot well, and recoil is the reason. Think about it: how many hard-core target shooters have you seen shooting a .460 Weatherby?

Big guns are easy to shoot but hard to shoot well. Recoil is the reason

Early the following morning, one of the best whitetail bucks I had ever seen was standing 409 laser-measured yards from my stand, with no intention of ever getting closer. With the memory of that .600 Nitro's pounding still fresh in my mind, it took every ounce of concentration I had to make the 7-millimeter Shooting Times Westerner behave. I have no doubt that if I had not worked hard for years at managing recoil, that buck would have joined a few other monsters in the "missed whitetails" section of my late-night parade of life's regrets. Instead, he fell on the tracks he had been occupying.

It's not a macho thing; don't think that just because you are tough, you are immune to recoil, because you are not. Nobody is. Flinching is an involuntary reaction, and even a Spartan will have trouble if he tries to tough it out. If you want to shoot magnum rifles and shoot them well, you need a plan. And you must pay some dues.

Nobody is immune to recoil

There are things you can do to make the perceived recoil of your rifle more manageable. The first and foremost is to buy a heavy gun. The laws of physics being what they are — "for every action there is an equal and opposite reaction" and all that — the heavier the gun, the less it reacts to the "equal and opposite reaction" part. Depending on your hunting style, a gun that weighs a pound or two more may be a better choice. A heavy gun is a necessity for the big, dangerous-game cartridges and is fine for hunting from a deer blind. However, by the end of a 10-day elk or sheep hunt in the steep mountains, you may think your bootlaces are too heavy and may hate your heavy rifle. Go heavier when you can, but keep in mind the planned use for your rifle. Any hunter knows that on most hunts, you carry a rifle a lot more than you shoot it.

Stock fit and design are very important to perceived recoil. Any stock that doesn't fit well will hurt you, but a well-designed stock will tame felt recoil, which is the only recoil that matters. I have a custom rifle chambered for the wildcat .358 UMT cartridge, which is essentially a .300 Remington Ultra Mag necked up to .35 caliber. It shoots a 250-grain bullet with a muzzle velocity over 3,100 feet per second. It's a "bad boy" cartridge by any definition of the term, yet the rifle weighs only 8 pounds scoped and ready to roll. I'd be lying to say it doesn't kick, but owing to the excellent design of the High Tech Specialties synthetic stock, it is not unpleasant to shoot. The recoil is directed to where it should go, which is important to how painful a gun is when shooting. If that same gun had a stock that beat up my cheekbone, it would probably be for sale already.

Stock fit and design are very important to perceived recoil

Length of pull is important in stock design. The correct length of pull will have about an inch of clearance between the thumb of the trigger hand and the shooter's nose, when the shooter is wearing normal hunting clothes. This should also put the forearm of the trigger arm at about a 30-degree angle to the rifle. The final determining factor, of course, is the way the stock feels to the shooter, but it's important to remember that with

Length of pull is important in stock design

a short length of pull and a hard-recoiling rifle, the shooter runs the risk of "eating the scope."

It is often the face that is beaten up more than the shoulder, usually because of a poor comb design. The stock's comb should be parallel with the bore or drop slightly to the front. This will allow the stock to transmit a lot less recoil to the shooter's face. Also, some of the rough finishes that are so popular on synthetic stocks will feel like they are sanding away facial features when they are on hard-kicking magnums. The rough texture is great on the grip and forend but doesn't belong where your cheek contacts the stock.

The recoil pad should be wide and the stock's butt angled to fit snugly against the entire shoulder so that the recoil is distributed over as much surface area as possible. The angle of the recoil pad's back edge relative to the line of the rifle bore is also important to how the shooter absorbs the recoil. The closer it is to 90 degrees, the straighter back the recoil is directed and the less the muzzle will rise. The angle of the recoil pad relative to the bore is also important, so that the rifle doesn't move vertically on the shoulder during recoil. Finally, modern, high-tech recoil pads with highly engineered materials lessen what the shoulder feels, and every "well-dressed" magnum rifle should be wearing one.

The most significant recoil reduction is obtained by using a muzzle brake

Perhaps the most significant recoil reduction is obtained through the use of a muzzle brake. These can be added to any rifle, and just about every gun company today offers them on new magnum-caliber factory guns. These brakes are amazingly effective at reducing felt recoil, but nothing is free. The trade-off is that they are loud — so loud that a big magnum rifle with a brake on might not be advisable for hunting, because hearing protection is rarely worn. Most guides and professional hunters I know hate them, and some will not allow them in camp. As loud as they are for the shooter, anybody standing beside the rifle will suffer pain and permanent hearing damage if not using ear protection when the gun is fired. Some brakes are removable so that they can be used for practice and taken off for hunting. But point of impact and even accuracy changes will usually occur when the brake is removed or replaced. As for myself, I am deaf enough. I took the brakes off all my big game rifles, including the .358 UMT wildcat I mentioned.

Most shooters who mess with magnum rifles much have scars on their eyebrows. Some of us have several. That's because we have to relearn the lesson from time to time that the scope on a magnum rifle must not only be tough but have a lot of eye relief as well. Use that eye relief, and be sure to mount it as far forward in the rings as possible.

The primary key to conquering recoil — and this can't be shortcut — is to practice shooting. A lot. But you must practice correct technique, or you will simply get good at bad habits, like flinch-

Most shooters who mess with magnum rifles have scars on their eyebrows

ing. Practice a little bit, lots of times. Don't keep shooting until it hurts, but quit while it's still fun. Just make sure you do it often enough to realize that the recoil really isn't all that bad and that shooting, even with big powerful magnum rifles, is really a lot of fun.

Practice by shooting from a bench rest

Start by shooting from a bench rest. This will give you the ability to control recoil while you familiarize yourself with the gun. It will also allow you to test your ammo for accuracy and to adjust the rifle's zero correctly.

There are several devices on the market to help control recoil at the shooting bench. Find one you like and use it. No matter how big the gun, the less it beats you up, the better you will shoot with it. This constant practice of recoil-reduction techniques will help to build "muscle memory" and will trick your body and mind into ignoring the full recoil during a hunting situation. It is often said that you never feel the recoil when shooting at game, and that is basically true. The excitement of the moment keeps your attention away from the recoil. But if you always test loads, sight in, or practice while absorbing the full recoil with every shot, your mind and body will be conditioned to expect that smashing blow and will react accordingly.

My method is to use an Uncle Bud's bench bag for the front bag. When properly used, it grips the forend of the gun and holds against the recoil. The rear of the gun is supported by a Bench Wizard bag from Ultra Light Arms (now New Ultra Light Arms). This features two 5-pound sandbags connected by webbing that fits around the rear of the gun to add the weight of the bags to the gun. Another 10-pound sandbag is placed against the rear of this bag so that to move back, it must push this weight as well. Finally, a PAST shooting pad is used between the gun and my shoulder. This controls the recoil of almost any rifle.

Using these methods, I have been able to conduct long test sessions of several hundred rounds at a time with hard-recoiling rifles such as the .375 H&H Magnum. If I am shooting the really big stuff, I add a bag of lead shot between my shoulder and the rifle. We have all read about doing this, but anybody who has actually tried it knows that unless you are built like an orangutan, a big, bulky bag of shot makes reaching the trigger awkward. Rather than use a full 25-pound bag, I drained out about one-third of the shot and shaped the bag the way I wanted it for a comfortable fit between the gun and my shoulder. Then I used duct tape to wrap the bag so it would keep this shape. It's still heavy enough to soak up recoil, but now I can actually shoot a rifle while using it, rather than just theorize about doing so.

The key to shooting any rifle well is trigger control. When we flinch, it's because we yank the trigger and time it with the flinch. If you don't know when the rifle is going to go off, you will not flinch. Concentrate on sight alignment and

Trigger control is the key to shooting any rifle well

squeeze the trigger slowly and progressively so that each shot comes as a surprise, at least at first. Later, as you become accustomed to the rifle and can mentally accept the recoil, you will find that you will know when the trigger is going to break. But you have to shoot until you arrive at that point, and any attempt at a shortcut will probably start you down the road to a flinch.

Once you have mastered the nuances of your rifle from the bench and have built a familiarity with it, take your practice shooting to field positions. You will be amazed at how much you improved simply by firing a lot of ammo under the carefully controlled conditions at the bench. Use proper field technique and keep these sessions to a minimum so that the recoil doesn't begin to reintroduce bad habits. Shoot from positions where you can yield to the recoil rather than just absorb it. Finally, be sure to go back to the bench every now and then and shoot a few groups to see if you are developing any recoil-induced bad habits.

Make sure that the rifle is correctly placed on your shoulder and that your head is correctly positioned on the stock for each shot. Be careful when wearing a lot of bulky clothing in the winter; the padding can mask the rifle's position on your shoulder. Also, when practicing fast follow-up shots, be careful that the recoil of the first shot or the motion of working the action does not cause the gun to slip out of position. The butt must be placed so that the recoil is transferred straight to your shoulder. If it is out of position, the rifle can slip and cause the scope and your face to become intimate. Also, be careful not to let your head creep forward on the stock, particularly when shooting from a prone position. You need every inch of eye relief when shooting magnum rifles. If you creep up on the stock, sooner or later you will get hit by the scope and bleed all over your shirt. Be obsessive about maintaining proper position and shooting form, and learn to roll with the recoil. With proper technique and plenty of practice, you can master any reasonable hunting rifle. Your taxi-dermist will appreciate the effort.

As any gun guy would understand, the opportunity to sample African hunting history is more important than a little (okay, a lot) of recoil-induced pain.

Shots taken at a shooting range offering a nice flat layout are one thing; those taken from a lofty deer stand or in rugged mountain country are a quite different proposition. Angles can be frustrating and confusing, but in this piece, taken from Making Shots: A Rifle Hunter's Guide *(2000), Bryce Towsley does a fine job of clearing up the issues associated with shots fired while hunting in hilly or mountainous country.*

Bryce Towsley discusses making shots at angles

SHOTS AT ANGLES

One of the most confusing aspects of long-range shooting is what happens to the bullet's path when the shot is fired at a sharp uphill or downhill angle.

I think I have heard every theory on earth, but the most common are that when you are shooting downhill, the bullet will strike higher, and when you are shooting uphill, the bullet will strike lower. Technically, both of these theories are wrong.

Gravity doesn't care if the bullet is flying up or down

Gravity doesn't care if the bullet is flying up or down; it works its magic on it in exactly the same way. That is, if we disregard air friction, gravity pulls the bullet toward the center of the earth at an acceleration of 32 feet per second per second. After one second, the bullet is falling at 32 feet per second; after two seconds, the bullet is falling at 64 feet per second; and so on.

This is what causes a trajectory curve in every bullet fired. If we could fire a bullet in space, where there is no gravity, it would not drop a bit; but here on earth, gravity is a fact of life. Gravity pulls on the bullet as it travels in relation to the center of the gravitational force, or the center of the earth. The longer gravity has to work on the bullet, the faster it will drop.

In theory, a bullet that is fired from a perfectly level rifle barrel will strike the earth at the same time as a bullet that is dropped from the end of the barrel at precisely the moment the fired bullet exits the muzzle. The difference is that one bullet will hit the ground near the rifle and the other will use the time to fly through the air and will strike the earth at some distant point.

No bullet can actually go up in defiance of the law of gravity, and all bullets begin dropping toward the earth as soon as they exit the muzzle. However, to allow for that drop, a rifle must have its muzzle pointed up a little in relation to the line of sight. Using the energy of the powder charge to propel it, the bullet moves forward in a straight line with the bore (except that it is constantly dropping because of gravity). If that forward movement is in an upward direction relative to the line of sight, the bullet will rise from below the line of sight and cross it early on its journey. It will then continue to rise (in relation to the line of sight) until reaching its apex in the trajectory curve, when it will begin dropping. The bullet will again cross the line of sight at your selected zero range and will continue dropping until it hits something and stops moving.

The distance a bullet travels from the muzzle to the target, and therefore the amount of time the bullet is exposed to gravitational pull, is what determines how far it will drop in a given time span. With a steep up or down angle, the distance to the target will be longer than the distance the bullet travels in relation to the earth's center. Rather than dropping the amount we expect for the distance traveled to the target, the bullet actually will drop for the distance it travels in relation to the earth's center. The steeper the angle, the shorter that distance becomes.

With a steep angle, the distance to the target will be longer than the distance the bullet travels in relation to the earth's center

For example, let's assume that you are shooting at a sheep that is 400 actual yards away but on a very steep angle, and that you are using a 7-mil-

limeter Remington Magnum with 140-grain factory loads, sighted for a 200-yard zero. You will
expect the bullet to hit 18 inches below the line of
sight for a 400-yard shot. However, the path of the
bullet's flight in relation to the earth's center, or
the center of gravitational pull, is in reality 300
yards, so the bullet is only 6 inches below the line
of sight when it gets to the sheep. If you hold for
400 yards, you will shoot over the ram you just
paid $10,000 to hunt.

Of course, as the distance shortens, this becomes less of a factor, because the bullet is moving
faster and has less time in flight for gravity to act.
The result: the bullet drops less, and the trajectory
curve is much flatter.

Obviously, the flatter the rifle shoots, the
smaller the difference will be. With a flat-shooting
modern rifle and a sight-in that keeps the bullet
within 3 inches of the line of sight out to a given
distance, if the target is less than that distance
from you, the bullet will always strike within 3
inches of your point of aim, regardless of the angle.
This should not cause you to miss a big game
animal.

The problem comes when you cannot close the
distance and must take a long shot, and this problem is compounded when the angle is steep. Suppose the angle is very steep and the distance to
the sheep is 300 yards, while the distance in relation to gravitational pull is 200 yards. With that
same 7-millimeter rifle, you will be expecting the

bullet to drop 6 inches from the line of sight for a 300-yard shot, when in reality it will hit right where the crosshairs are centered, because the rifle is zeroed at 200 yards, which is the actual bullet travel distance in relation to gravitational pull. With luck, if you hold for a 6-inch bullet drop, you might spine the sheep instead of shooting over his back.

But you are likely to miss this sheep because of another and perhaps more important factor. The steep angle causes you to view the sheep from a different perspective. While in your mind you are seeing a broadside profile, you are looking at a lot of the sheep's back if the angle is down; if the angle is up, you are looking at his belly. If you hold in the center, as you would for most shots, the crosshairs are likely on the intersection of his side and back (for the down shot). Because of the angle, a bullet that strikes even slightly higher than you expected will go over the sheep and, once again, miss.

I almost found that out the hard way in 1995 near Devil's Tower in northeastern Wyoming. I was hunting from a stand we had nicknamed the "Grand Canyon," although it's a long way from Arizona. The blind sits on a high bluff of rimrock that overlooks a very deep and very steep canyon. In the bottom was a food source that attracted the deer who travel the timber in the head of the canyon bottom or down the trail that traverses the steep bank on the far side. It couldn't be helped that the shot was very long and at an extremely steep downward angle. The exact distance was hard to estimate (this was before laser range finders were readily available), but most guesses put it at about 300 to 350 yards. The range and angle intimidated a lot of eastern hunters, but with my 7-millimeter Remington Magnum, I wasn't worried.

When the buck turned to quarter at me, I put a Winchester 160-grain Fail Safe bullet through him. He dropped instantly and never wiggled. Strange things can happen on a long shot, and the last time I saw a deer do that, he was hit in the antler and knocked out. That one woke up and ran off; I didn't plan to see that happen here. I jacked in another shell and kept the crosshairs on the buck until I knew for sure it was over.

When I got to the deer, I saw that I had been lucky. I remember fighting with my mind about holding the crosshairs low on the deer for such a long shot. One of us lost, and I made the mistake of centering the deer in the crosshairs, thinking that would play the odds the best. The bullet came in from above, struck his spine, and traveled down and out the off side. From that angle, had the bullet been only a few inches higher, it would have missed or, worse, wounded the buck. I knew better, but I let my fear of missing override my knowledge of shooting. It was almost the very reason I did miss, but the irony escaped me until later.

The solution to shots at steep angles is to use a very flat-shooting rifle, try to keep your shots to a reasonable range, and always force yourself to aim a little lower than you think you should, to compensate for the viewing angle.

As anyone who has ever spent much time in hot, dry country knows, your eyes can play sneaky tricks on you. Yet you do not have to be in the middle of the Sahara to encounter mirages, nor are tricks of light limited to times when the heat is quite high. Here, in a piece that originally appeared in Military and Sporting Rifle Shooting *(1932), Edward C. Crossman takes a down-to-earth look at these issues as they affect marksmen.*

Edward Crossman discusses the issues of mirage and light

MIRAGE AND LIGHT

When you, presumably an abstemious person in accordance with the laws of our nation of the free and the sober, lie down to shoot on a nice warm day, you may very possibly wonder what the pit boy is doing to your target. It will seem to dance up and down, with an occasional side-step for variety, and the bull will have all the sharpness of a piece of fluffy cotton. Of course if you have been out celebrating with "the boys" the night before, the phenomenon will not bother you, which is an argument the anti-prohibitionists have overlooked.

Assuming our model shooter (theoretical),

however, he will certainly be peeved at the dirty trick he thinks his eyes are playing him. As a matter of fact, tho, this light-footed target effect is due to mirage.

When the sun beats down on the ground between you and the target, it warms the ground more than it does the air above. The ground transmits a part of its heat to the air layer in contact with it. This decreases the density of this air, and causes it to rise, its place being taken by colder air flowing down. Light waves, such as those reflected from your target, are refracted or bent when they pass thru substances of different densities. Anyone who has ever tried to spear or shoot fish in the water is aware of this, as you have to aim considerably below the fish to hit him, this being due to the different paths of the light rays in water and in air.

A definition of mirage

The rays from your target, then, are considerably warped and bent here and there in their passage from the target to you thru all this air of varying density. This effect is called mirage, and is observable as an apparent "boiling" of the atmosphere. If there is no breeze, this plain boiling is the predominant effect, but if there is any wind, the effect is as tho a stream of clear water were flowing over a white sand bottom.

When the mirage boils straight up, that is when there is no wind, the mark appears fuzzy and won't hold still, but seems to dance around. When the wind is blowing, the mirage shows the direction, but not the velocity.

The term mirage as used in rifle shooting always means this appearance of clear moving water and the phenomenon is of importance in two ways. One of them is the difficulty under extreme conditions of obtaining a clear, sharp image of the target, and the effect, denied by some observers, of apparently lifting the image of the target, causing high shots as you follow it. In view of the clearly proved error produced by the clearest of water in the apparent position of an object immersed only a foot or two under the surface — watch the apparent bend in a stick thrust into clear water — it does not seem improbable that heavy mirage might quite alter or bend the lines of light reflected from the far-off target and produce some error in elevation.

The second phase of the importance of mirage and the most important of the two is the index to light wind travel given us by mirage travel as observed by powerful telescopes.

Mirage to the layman means that strange effect of false pictures of lakes, trees, and even cities presented by intensely heated air over desert surfaces, and at times even at sea, cause unknown.

Dictionaries say nothing as to the rifle shooting meaning of the word mirage, but refer merely to the desert illusions.

If the wind comes from 3 or 9 o'clock the mirage has a flowing effect like a stream of water, but if it comes at an angle it combines this with a straight boiling, and if it comes from 12 or 6 o'clock it seems to boil faster than usual. A lateral breeze of small velocity makes the mirage combine the vertical and horizontal movements, but it flattens out in a breeze over about 14 miles per hour.

The effect of mirage seems to be open to some doubt

The effect of mirage, aside from "fuzzing up" the target seems to be open to some doubt. The clearest exposition is that given in the U. S. Army Small Arms Firing Manual of 1909: "This mirage is more noticeable as the firer is closer to the ground; it will then be more frequently observed by the soldier when firing either kneeling or standing. As the true position of the target is below the apparent, the elevation should, if the mirage is considerable, be decreased.

This can be illustrated and the extent of its effect determined if, early in the morning, before the mirage is noticeable, a telescope is directed at the target and so adjusted that the two lower corners of the target just touch the lower arc of the circumference of the field of view; the telescope should then be clamped in position. Later in the day, before commencing firing, examine the position of the range in the field of view; if there is much mirage, the target will appear considerably raised, and in some cases also laterally displaced; the extent of this apparent movement will be shown by comparing the second with the first position of the target, and should be measured by the eye, using the entire target or the bull's-eye as a unit of measure; the elevations which would otherwise be selected by the soldier should then be decreased by the amounts corresponding to these displacements."

Just to be "different" and to keep you from thinking this problem is simple, here is a quotation from Col. Whelen's "The American Rifle", "The target appears blurred and the blurred bull's-eye looks larger than when seen in a clear atmosphere. In trying to aim the correct distance below the bullseye, the rifleman naturally aims a little lower on the blurred bull, hence when mirage is present a slightly greater elevation will be required. Ordinary mirage does not displace or "drift" the image of the target."

Here again, as in many other cases in the shooting game, we run up against a direct disagreement of authorities. If you look in other shooting books you can find supporters of both theories. It has been my observation, however, and I think you will find me backed by a majority of experienced shooters, that a boiling mirage tends to raise a shot. This is especially noticeable if you have been shooting in a strong wind and the wind suddenly dies just before you shoot. You will be off for windage, and also high.

A boiling mirage tends to raise a shot

Wind-doping with the aid of mirage seems to have been an unknown sport to the Americans previous to about 1902, for from Dr. Hudson we learn that, "It was our unfamiliarity with this method of estimating wind which lost us the international match at Ottawa, Canada, in 1902, for at the 900 yard stage very unfavorable conditions arose, which it was absolutely impossible for the best coaches to judge by the flags. But the English team, who were familiar with the mirage method did nearly as good shooting as when the weather conditions were good."

Which brings to mind another factor in using mirage; flags as indicators of wind movement seem to be far less reliable than mirage. Mirage also seems to average up the total amount of lateral deflection, and thus is much better than flags.

Contrary to the dictum of many a great authority, mirage may be picked up on quite chilly days, and some windy ones as well, by using a powerful glass on number boards or other similar locations including the top of the butt where a target happens to be missing. The reason is a mystery but may lie in the accumulation of what little sun-heat there may be diffused through the clouds, and the contrast of even this slight temperature increase of the air just over this radiating surface.

Mirage may be picked up on quite chilly and windy days

One does not look for a whole landscape full of mirage, merely a little flicker along the top of the board when the wind — if there is a stiff breeze — drops a little. But, how much better this flicker is than nothing in these days of flagless ranges.

It is for this use that I can see some excuse for telescopes of more than about 21x magnification — this and possibly that lovely pipedream, possible under some conditions, of picking up bullet-holes on the target by use of the scope.

As anybody can tell you who has been to the

top of a high mountain, the sun has practically no tendency to warm the air, else the top of the mountain would be warmer than down below, nearer the sun — a trifle it is true — and above the interference of so much moisture, smoke, dust, haze and other screening effect.

Hence mirage can come only from the sun striking the ground and transforming those mysterious lines of force into heat, which in turn warms the layer of air close to the ground which again in turn rises and is replaced by air moving in. No breeze, the effect is a boil, a gentle breeze and the boil turns into a nice running stream of clear water.

Authorities allege that 15 miles per hour of breeze is the limit to which mirage will interpret wind speed. The theory is evidently that the fast moving air picks up the mirage before it rises enough to be visible or else cools off the ground. This would not be true with some desert winds which are entirely too torrid for any ground-cooling.

If mirage proceeds from heated air-layers close to the ground, then the question arises, to what height may be the effect noted. On many western ranges including our own, the bullet flies high above the ground on most of its flight over 1,000 yards and certainly no mirage is rising high enough to show the course of light breezes blowing across the space over which the bullet is high in its course.

Where a target is set on a steep hillside, as with our own 1,000 and 600, it is to be doubted whether mirage may be seen for more than the few yards of hillside immediately in front of the target.

Under such conditions the shooter wants to be jolly well sure that he is not focused on mirage produced close to the firing point, because over this portion of the bullet's flight, any breeze light enough to let plenty of mirage show, would be inconsequential to the flight of the bullet. It would be of use only when one feels confident that the breeze blowing close to the firing point is also that breeze blowing a half mile away.

DISPLACEMENT OF TARGET IMAGE BY MIRAGE

As pointed out early in this chapter, another regrettable dispute of authorities. Dr. Mann, author of "The Bullet's Flight," once set up a transit or rather a 16x Sidle scope and made observations through it under various mirage conditions as compared with his zero observations before mirage commenced to run. He reached the conclusion that so far as the scope is concerned, mirage does not in the least move the target. One joker in his test lay in it being only over short range, 200 yards or so, the other lay in the fact that a telescope was used.

The question before the rifle shooter is whether

heavy mirage apparently moves the image of the target, causing him to follow this displac[e]ment with his front sight and so get an offshot on the real target.

My own observation is that it does. Of course a shot downwind which might be charged against following the image slightly downwind from the real target, might be due entirely to wind, hence it proves nothing.

A boiling mirage, however, in my observation does produce high shots, not low ones. On a target situated on a steep side-hill a high shot might be interpreted as being caused by an actual upward sweep of the breeze, not a target image movement, but this could not be true on a flat range such as [Camp] Perry.

Desert rifle shooters will agree that most Perry shots have never seen a real mirage. There are ranges along the southwest border, and even in California where rifle shooting much over 200 yards, and using metallic sights, is out of the question during the heat of the day. I have seen mirage so bad in the Colorado desert that a line of low willows along the customary Imperial irrigation canal raised 8 ft. or so above the desert floor, would seem to tower a hundred feet in the air from 300 yards away. Even telescopes will not cut through it.

Wherefore the average shooter discussing mirage is like the traveler reciting his marvelous experiences but who admitted to the drunken questioner that he had never experienced the D. T's.

"Hell, you ain't been nowheres and you ain't see nothin'", replied the intoxicated gent.

It is fine for the easterner to give three cheers for mirage as a fine wind-indicator but there are many days on southwest rifle ranges where the shooters would cheerfully swap their super-abundant mirage for a perfectly clear day even if they had to guess wind by gazing into a crystal ball or something.

LIGHT

Light, or rather changes in light, does affect aiming with metallic sights and will produce under some conditions considerable change in the way the front sight is seen and in the resulting location of the shot group on the target.

The one effect in which authorities and practical experience all agree is that unshaded front sights, even though smoked like a country ham, will accumulate a false center slightly away from the direction of the light and will "shoot away from the light."

Unshaded front sights will accumulate a false center slightly away from the direction of the light

The effect is much more marked with glittering sights such as gold beads, and is naturally worse with unsmoked metallic service front sight than with a well blacked one, but it exists with any naked front sight and allowance has to be made for it.

This correct allowance is particularly important for 200 and 300 yard rapid fire on the A target, and failure to watch light direction and allow for it, has put many a bullseye-sized group out into the four-ring.

Strong sunlight from the 3 o'clock side of the shooter seems to form a false center on the top of the front sight — some theories have it on the side of the peep disc aperture — and this false center forming toward the light or 3 o'clock side of the front sight, is held under the center of the bull, moving the group to the left or 9 o'clock. Hence the rear sight has to be moved slightly toward the sun, precisely as if the light were wind from the same direction. Obviously when the light comes from the opposite direction, another false center is formed and the group is formed to the right.

Hence there is a constant correction between the windage setting for an early morning light, and a late afternoon light, often as much as a half point total. So the rifle is never zero except possibly on an overcast day or with the sun directly overhead.

This lateral error produced by light would not be of much importance except for rapid fire but it is quite capable of pulling five points off a score by the very slight change necessary to move the group half the width of the bull at 300 rapid fire, or 5 inches, which is less than 2 minutes and less than a halfpoint on the windgauge.

For this reason it is important for the rapid fire shooter to go to the pit in practice whenever possible and personally interview his groups fired at rapid fire to get the rapid fire zero of the rifle, the only way to get this zero. Failing this through busy range conditions, 10 small shot spotters should always be used to indicate the bullet holes for spotting from the firing point, or else a good scope laid on the paper. Indicating the position of the group with the usual paddle waving is just about as useful as having the marker wave his handkerchief.

It is open to question whether this displacement of lateral zero takes place where a front sight cover is used and the light does not strike the sight.

Light influence in elevation changes is a moot question

Light influence in elevation changes is grievously a moot question with the heavy authorities and my own experience is precisely opposite to the more commonly accepted dictum. Said dictum is that if the target grows suddenly dark as from a cloud passing over, the average man will hold farther from the bull, naturally strike lower, and hence should raise his elevation.

I have no doubt this is true with the addicts of the "thin white line" between front sight and bull, which thin white line varies grievously with every change of light, and which is to my mind a good reason for not using it.

In my own case, holding either against the bull or at times into it — the "bullseye hold" used by some Marine teams and the Navy ten years ago, a dark target does not lower my group, but if anything raises it.

"Changes of light do not affect the flight of the bullet, they do affect the manner in which the aim is taken. As all men are not affected alike by changes of light, each man must determine for himself how changes of light affect him.

"Using the peep sight, the bullseye of a bright target is more clearly defined than the bullseye of a dark one and the firer will usually hold closer to the bright bullseye than to a dark one. If the target changes from bright to dark, the shot will usually go low." Small Arms Firing Regulations, 1913 Edition.

He probably will, hunting to see where his cute lil' white line has gone to.

On the other hand Colonel Whelen says that sunlight causes a slight glitter on the sight even if well blacked, and that it is held farther from the bull in bright light than in dull, because of this false top. He says that 1 minute more elevation is called for on a bright day, as compared to a dark day. All of which checks with my own personal reaction to light.

If we admit that light forms a false center and causes lateral errors, which is a common field of agreement with all shooting authorities, there is no logic in disputing that the same glimmer may also cause the sight to be held slightly away from the bull on a very bright day, where an over-cast day the true outline is clearly seen and it is held closer.

This is not quite the same as changing from a bright target to a dark one while the firer remains in bright light, conditions for his location unchanged, but is discussing the comparison of a bright day with an over-cast one.

Probably the best solution of this particular temporarily darkened target problem is to adopt the Firing Regulations suggestion and wait for the target to get bright again. If the shot is fired on the temporarily darkened target it seems probable that the white line holder will hold lower and get a low shot, the holder tangent to the bullseye seems little if any affected.

More effect is likely when the change is at the other end of the range, and the front sight from bright sun is suddenly thrown into shadow, when the shot is likely to strike higher. For all of which reason it is a fine idea not to fire with somebody standing back of you and shading your sight if your shooting has been with the sight in sunlight.

Generally speaking my own observation is that on an evenly overcast day the group is likely to go higher than on a bright one, and that changes from light at all times are minimized by holding "against" the bull. Errors in elevation from slipping into it now and then seem less marked than those produced by this attempt to estimate a white line, and the marked variation in white lines from variations in light.

On evenly overcast days a shot group is likely to go higher than on a bright one

A front sight with a permanent, ample clearance and sturdy front sight cover over it for all shooting, such as the Marines issue and use, held tangent to the bullseye, is a sight with changes due to light cut to the minimum.

Study should be made of lateral light effect on

rapid fire grouping, outside that it is doubtful if
light changes seriously affect the point of impact
with such a sight, well blacked, and the rear likewise blacked.

VI
MARKSMANSHIP FOR
THE HUNTER

The skilled, ethical hunter places a real premium on superior marksmanship. That means far more than a brief session at the range a week before the season opens, to zero in a new rifle or test some ammunition. The hunter or marksman knows his firearm so intimately it almost seems an extension of his arm, and he has a full grasp of its performance and capabilities under all conditions.

Hunting poses all sorts of challenges that are not encountered in range competitions. Among these are deciding, often in a split second, whether to take a shot. Once that decision has been made, another one — placement of the shot — demands equally quick and precise thinking. The margin of error between a true, telling shot that drops an animal in its tracks and one that results in hours of difficult tracking or, worse, a wounded animal that is not recovered, can be quite small.

Great hunters have always been keenly aware of these considerations. Think back to the turkey shoots and similar competitions in pioneer days, for example. Every entrant in such events firmly believed he was capable of a winning perform-

Hunting poses challenges that are not encountered in range competitions

*ance, and a subtext to the contests was the real-
ization that marksmanship could well mean the
difference between surviving and perishing.
Hunters from that era also took great pains to
shoot with precision when hunting. Think of a
buffalo hunter making a "stand" with his trusty
Sharps. A man who really knew what he was
doing could drop a dozen or more of the shaggy
beasts of the plains before the herd spooked and
thundered away. Similarly, the squirrel hunters of
the Appalachians and Blue Ridge, the Great
Smokies and the Unakas, raised "barking" bushy-
tails to a fine art. They shot so precisely that the
lead entered the tree beneath the squirrel. The
shock killed the animal without damaging the
meat and let the hunter retrieve the lead for re-
casting into another bullet.*

**Six of the
20th
century's
greatest
gun writers
discuss
hunting
marksman-
ship**

*In the selections that follow, six of the twenti-
eth century's greatest gun and hunting writers
weigh in on the issue of hunting marksmanship.
They cover shot placement, target shooting and
the way it can relate to hunting, and various aspects of accuracy faced by the hunter performing
under what many would consider the ultimate
pressure for a rifleman — the moment of truth
when a trophy animal steps into view.*

●

*Jack O'Connor hunted pretty much all over the
world. He made several trips to Asia, went on a
number of safaris in Africa, and knew the game of*

the American Southwest and the Rockies intimately. A man who could write timeless tales such as "We Shot the Tamales" and who is perhaps best remembered for his love of the .270 certainly appreciated the importance of precise shot placement. In this piece, from his Complete Book of Rifles and Shotguns *(1965), he offers a sensible overview — sprinkled with a bunch of anecdotes from his personal experiences — of where the hunter's shots need to go.*

Jack
O'Connor
on shot
placement

PLACEMENT OF SHOTS
FOR BIG GAME

The shooting ability of the hunter, not the punch of his weapon, is always the determining factor in any hunting situation, especially when he is after big game. It follows, of course, that a good shooter equipped with a good rifle presents a formidable combination. It also follows that *where* a slug is placed is more important than its ballistics. For example, it stands to reason that the hunter who drives a .25/35 bullet into a vital spot, say the heart-lung area of an animal, is more certain of having chops for the frying pan than if he only manages to break its leg with an enormously heavier and more powerful slug, such as the .470 Nitro Express.

Thus a calm, deliberate and accurate rifleman can hunt the largest and toughest of game with a relatively light rifle without ever leaving a wounded animal to bleed to death or fall prey to predators. Yet the same rifle in the hands of a less skillful and level-headed fellow may strew the woods with cripples.

It's this difference in hunters that has led to so much controversy about the adequacy of various calibers. One man, let us say, hunts everything in North America with a 7 mm. and swears by it. Another comes along and declares under oath that the 7 mm. isn't even good enough for sheep or mule deer. The difference, of course, lies not in the rifle itself, but in how it is used, by whom, and under what conditions.

The controversy about the adequacy of various calibers

I know a mining man who operates on the desert of northern Mexico. Year in and year out he kills an average of two big mule deer a month for meat. He is not particularly interested in hunting or shooting, and I wouldn't call him a crack shot by any means. When his meat gets low he takes an old Model 94 Winchester .30/30 equipped with a Lyman 1-A tang peep, puts on a pair of basketball shoes for silent stalking, and goes out to some section where deer are plentiful. He hunts with about the same emotion that you and I feel when we buy a rump roast at the corner butcher shop. He never takes a shot at more than 100 yards, and he never takes a running shot. If it is possible, he rests his rifle on the limb of a tree or drops into the kneeling position. He always aims behind the shoulder midway on the animal, giving him a circle of from 14 to 20 inches in which to place his shot. If brush is in the way, he finds an opening, or he doesn't shoot. If the animal is standing in the wrong position for his favorite shot, he either works into a better position or lets the animal shift. If the buck becomes frightened and takes off, he doesn't fire, because he knows that he'll see another deer that day or the next, and he doesn't want to chase a wounded animal or to spook all the deer in the neighborhood with a wild bombardment. When he buys one box of .30/30 cartridges, he is, in effect, buying 20 deer.

Tell that hombre the .30/30 isn't a top deer cartridge under all conditions and he'll think you've lost your mind. In his hands, under the same conditions, it would also be a good moose cartridge. Which sets up another maxim; if an animal is hit right with almost any fairly adequate cartridge, a kill is the result.

On the other hand, a great deal of vastly unrealistic stuff is written every year about the placement of shots, mostly by people who apparently assume, that nothing but undisturbed deer are hunted, and then only by cool and level headed marksmen like our miner. These articles always come complete with cutaway diagrams of bucks showing how to reach the vitals from various angles. Such pieces don't do any harm and they may do some good, but they skip lightly over the fact that bucks are often very uncooperative. They don't patiently wait around while someone plinks a bullet into them.

A great deal of vastly unrealistic stuff is written every year about shot placement

THE BRAIN AND SPINE SHOTS

These experts are fond of pointing out that even a well placed .22 rim fire will bring home the venison. With that very obvious statement no one can disagree. Consider this, though: under modern hunting conditions, the brain and spine shots which make even a .22 effective are usually almost impossible to make. And this: if those small, vital areas are missed, the result all too often is a wounded animal that escapes.

The worst place to shoot a fine game animal is in the head

There is hardly a worse place to shoot a fine game animal than in the head. If the brain is struck, the animal is, of course, killed instantly. But the brain is a small mark. If it is missed, the result may be a broken jaw that dooms the animal to slow death by starvation, And that does happen. Once I found the carcass of a fine buck with the nose and mouth shot away; it had starved to death. Even if you hit the brain and kill the animal in its tracks, the resulting sight is likely to be one to turn your stomach. I once pulled down on the head of a buck about 60 yards away and killed him. The light, high-velocity bullet blew up in the animal's skull. One look at the pulpy, shapeless head, the bulging eyes, the antlers askew — well, I was almost ready to quit hunting deer. A grand animal like a buck deserves a better end.

I cannot get enthusiastic about the neck shot, either. If the spinal vertebrae in the neck are broken, the deer dies instantly. If the spine is missed, however, the neck shot is no more deadly than a shot in any other muscular tissue. I remember seeing a big bull caribou drop after a neck hit — and then get up and run 300 yards before a lung shot brought it down. I once knocked down a fine mule deer with the same kind of shot. He got up and ran. My companion and I tracked him a full half mile. The bullet had severed a big artery, and it seemed incredible that a mule deer could contain all the blood that that one lost.

Head and neck shots are justified at short range and under favorable conditions, particularly by the man who knows his anatomy, and who has to stop dangerous game in an emergency. For ordinary hunting, though, these shots are a long, long way from ideal.

About the only time a shoulder shot is justified is when the hunter wants to disable a potentially dangerous animal like a grizzly or an Alaska brown bear. Broken shoulders will put an animal down and render it helpless without killing it; even with only one shoulder broken, even a grizzly cannot manage a charge on a hillside. For that reason veteran grizzly hunters try to break the shoulder with their first shot. Some men also try for the shoulders on other large animals, like moose, that are hard to kill in their tracks. However, the shoulder shot will wreck a lot of meat by filling it with bone fragments. If the shot goes low it means a broken leg. Then an animal can travel all day, only to be pulled down eventually by wolves.

The only justification for a shoulder shot

THE LUNG SHOT

Well, where should you aim? The best place of all is the lung area back of the shoulder. The advantages of this shot are many. A reasonably adequate bullet placed there almost always means a one-shot kill. Death is not always instantaneous, but it is usually quick. The rapid expansion of the bullet tears up the lungs, administers terrific shock to the whole nervous system and very often ruptures the heart or otherwise stops its action. As I write this, the last head of game I shot was a grizzly. He was below me, about 125 yards away, walking slowly across a big, open, timberline basin. The .300 Magnum bullet went high through the left lung behind the shoulder and emerged low through the right lung. The bear fell to the shot, got up, took two steps and fell dead. The only other grizzly I ever saw killed so quickly was one I hit in about the same body area with a 130-grain Silvertip bullet from my .270.

A lung shot usually kills quicker than a heart shot

Strangely enough, a shot through the lungs near the heart usually kills more quickly than a shot through the heart itself. The heart-shot animal almost always runs frantically 20 to 200 yards before falling dead. And if it gets out of sight, you may think you've missed completely — as I once did. I was painfully clambering down a high ridge toward camp — beat up, thirsty, and footsore — when a fine whitetail buck came out under the cliffs below and started running up the opposite side of the canyon. I just had time to throw a cartridge into the chamber of my .270, sit down and get off a shot. The buck jumped about five feet in the air, lit and disappeared over the top before I could shoot again.

Well, I knew my cross hairs had been on that buck. Still, I was inclined to believe I'd missed him, probably with a shot that hit a rock and stung him with fragments. But the more I thought about that high and frantic jump, the more convinced I became that I'd hit him. So, tired though I was, I retraced my steps, crossed the canyon and climbed to where the buck had disappeared. There he lay, dead as a mackerel. I discovered then that the bullet had gone in just behind the last rib, ranged forward and blown the heart to pieces.

The lung shot is a quick, if not instant, killer because the ruptured lungs drown the animal in its own blood. The lung area is a much easier target to hit than either the brain or spine because it's larger. Furthermore, this type of shot doesn't destroy any edible meat. If the bullet goes too high, it will break the spine; if too far forward, it may break the shoulders or land in the neck. And even if it lands in the paunch, it may still kill or disable the game if the rifle is a powerful one.

The lung shot is a quick killer

No matter which way the animal is facing, you should try to drive the bullet into this large lung area. You give yourself all the odds on a quick kill, especially if your rifle has more than average power.

AVOID GUT SHOTS

Above all, try to keep your shots out of the abdominal area. Now and then a paunch shot — particularly with a light, easily expanded bullet of very high velocity — will result in a quick kill. But all too often a gut-shot animal can run for miles, even when hit with a powerful bullet.

Often a gut-shot animal can run for miles

The heart and the lungs are vital organs. Any serious interference with the functioning of either means quick death. But the stomach, intestines, and other abdominal parts are not immediately necessary to life or movement. We have seen that an animal with a pair of broken shoulders cannot travel, and that an animal with a ruptured heart or torn-up lungs dies quickly. But animals have been known to travel a considerable distance with practically all of their paunch organs missing.

Once, in northern Arizona, I took a shot with my .30/06 at a buck running away from me down a hill. The 150-grain Bronze Point bullet struck him high in the left ham and went through, laying open the entire abdominal cavity. The buck went down, but when I got to him, he lurched to his feet and ran with his stomach bouncing along 30 feet behind him. He was practically gutted.

Another time, in Sonora, Mexico, I saw the abdomen of a desert ram ripped open by a 150-

grain bullet from a .300 Savage. That ram jumped over a barrel cactus, had its protruding stomach caught on the terrible thorns, and lost every organ in its abdomen. Yet it kept going — and the hunter tracked it a mile before he found it dead.

It is true, of course, that abdominal shots have dropped a lot of game stone-dead in its tracks. Very often, a bullet like the old 139-grain Western open point in the 7 mm. would do it. So would the 87-grain bullet in the .257 or .250/3000, the 130-grain bullet in the .270 and the 150-grain bullet in the .30/06. I have also had many reports of quick-kills with gut shots by the .220 Swift. The point is, though, that sometimes such a shot results in a quick kill, but sometimes it doesn't, even with a rifle of high velocity and rapid bullet disintegration. Dressing an animal that has been gut-shot is always a messy, disagreeable business. The good hunter tries to keep his bullets out of the abdominal cavity if he possibly can.

ADVANTAGE OF POWERFUL CALIBERS

It is fairly easy to place your shots when game is plentiful and relatively tame, but it's something else again when it is frightened, jittery, hunter-shy or on the move. Half a century ago a famous deer hunter wrote that hitting a running deer anywhere at any distance is not a bad shot. And it's true that in the course of a season, the average hunter in average country doesn't see many bucks, so he'll have to be pardoned for taking his shots as they come. The deer may be on the move, or hind-end to, or partly concealed by bullet-deflecting brush. Under these conditions how many hunters will refrain from shooting? One in ten? I'd say closer to one in 100.

I have always campaigned for the most powerful calibers

That is why I have always campaigned for the more powerful calibers for modern hunting — bullets that will knock down and disable animals even when poorly placed. You should always try to get your bullet into the heart-lung area. But you should also use a rifle with plenty of power; then, if your shot miscues, it still may kill or disable the animal.

Consider a typical shot — a frightened animal running directly away from the hunter. I have always declined such a chance at elk, moose, or grizzlies, letting these animals go their way un-shot but hoping they'll turn. These big animals are just too tough to be put down by hind-end shots with a rifle of the .270 — .30/06 class.

On deer-size animals, though, a shot aimed at the center line of the rump will usually kill or disable. I once took such a shot at a buck running away from me, at between 250 and 300 yards. The .270 bullet went right between the hams, through the abdomen and tore up the right lung. The buck traveled no more than 20 yards farther. Later on, I got an identical shot, but at shorter range. This buck — the heaviest Arizona whitetail I have ever shot — ran no more than 10 feet after the bullet connected. If a bullet goes between the hams, it will drive up through the abdomen into the lungs. If it goes high, it will break the spine above the root of the tail. The thing to do is to keep the shot high and center, because if it is low, it will disembowel the animal and the result will be a long chase. If it hits too far on either side it will mess up a ham. At best, you have a lot of spoiled meat; at worst, a wounded animal that may escape and become coyote meat.

In the case of a quartering animal at fairly close range, the hunter should shoot past the hips to drive the bullet at an angle up into the lung area. But such a shot on a running target requires a skill and coolness that I fear too many hunters do not have. Such a shot can be tried on an animal the size of deer, antelope or sheep with a .270 or a .30/06. But it should never be attempted with less powerful rifles, even though they may — under ideal conditions and with well-placed shots — lay game of that size out cold.

If a broadside running shot is offered, and the hunter feels he cannot afford to pass it up, he should swing way ahead, since it is far better to miss in front than wound in the gut. Actually, no one should attempt running shots unless he is armed with a rifle with power enough to give him a good chance of disabling the game even with a poorly-placed shot. A fast-opening bullet in the abdominal cavity — from a .270 or a .30/06, for instance — has a very good chance of knocking down the game and paralyzing it long enough for the hunter to get to it. But a shot in the same area from a .25/35, let us say, will mean a wounded animal that keeps on going and escapes to die.

Rifle power is a poor substitute for calmness and skill in shot placement

The power of the rifle is a poor substitute for calmness and skill in the placement of shot, but it is to some extent a substitute. In the Canadian Rockies, the hunter usually shoots under very favorable circumstances. The game is in the open, undisturbed, and the hunter can almost always get into a good position, wait until the animal is turned right, and take time to get over his excitement and recover his wind and steadiness.

Consequently, a .270 or .30/06 is plenty of rifle even for moose and grizzly, and, nine times out of ten, a .257 or 7 mm. will be entirely adequate. Yet the .270 and .30/06 are not any too much gun for white tail deer and antelope, which are much smaller than a moose or grizzly and have but a fraction of their vitality. Why? Simply because modern hunting conditions often make it very tough indeed to place shots properly on a buck that is bouncing through brush on the other side of a ravine, or on a spooked antelope on the opposite hillside.

The idea, then, is to place those bullets as well as you possibly can, to kill as cleanly as you can, and to take advantage of every opportunity for a one-shot kill. But your rifle must have adequate power; then, if a shot is a bit off line, the chances are still good that you'll get the game instead of letting it go away wounded.

In this selection, taken from his Rifles and Rifle Shooting (1912), Charles Askins, Sr., considers a variety of factors that can make the hunter a more effective shot. Technological advances such as accurate range finders have rendered some of his concerns pretty much obsolete, but even today, ascertaining range with the naked eye is something hunters should practice faithfully. They can then enjoy the luxury of instantaneously checking the accuracy of their judgment through use of a range finder.

Obviously, Askins' suggestion of taking pot-shots at hawks as a type of practice won't fly today. Yet it must be remembered that just two generations ago, all hawks were considered "chicken hawks" and were shot on sight. They are now federally protected, although one must wonder whether their comeback has been so complete that populations of small game such as quail are becoming overly affected by an abundance of raptors.

Such matters aside, Askins presents readers with a myriad of interesting ideas on how they can make the transition from casual plinking with a .22 to serious hunting with center-fire rifles a smooth one.

Charles Askins, Sr. presents a number of interesting ideas

OUT-DOOR TARGET SHOOTING

It is to be taken for granted, that if the rifleman has practiced assiduously, he knows considerable about shooting a rifle; can at least tell when he has held a bad shot or pulled a good one. After the amount of training he has undergone he might specialize at this time, taking up the match rifle or the army gun, but if his idea is to make an all round rifle shot of himself, especially a game shot, he will do well to continue his work.

Very fair target work can be secured at distances up to one hundred yards from the .22 long-rifle, provided the distance is measured or the sights are set exactly for the range, but we mean to go farther than that, shooting up to three hundred yards and farther. It follows that a new and more powerful rifle is in order.

Since the student has been accustomed to the .22 caliber only, it is not wise to make too radical a change, but he should be content with a weapon that, while giving a fairly flat trajectory and good accuracy up to three hundred yards, has practically no recoil. In such a weapon we have a number of cartridges to choose from.

Having our rifle, it is a foregone conclusion that we will have to get out into the woods and fields where we can use it; the man who must shoot on a measured range will have his inning later. The regulation bull'seye is two inches at fifty yards, three inches seventy-five yards, four inches, one hundred yards, six, one hundred and fifty and eight inches across at two hundred. There are finer rings inside the bull for match work, but the bull itself will do now.

Step or measure off the distance, put up a bull of a size in proportion to [the] range with a good margin of white around it, and continue the work you have previously been doing with the .22 indoors, firing from the sitting, kneeling, standing, and prone positions.

The military and match style of rifle shooting is to change the sights every time the range varies, one elevation of back sight for one hundred yards, another for two hundred, etc., the effort being to have the sights so aligned as to strike the center whatever the distance. This is the right system of course for measured ranges, and it would be well enough to practice it for a time, marking the sight for one hundred, one hundred and fifty, two hundred, and two hundred and fifty yards.

It is well to have an assistant in this kind of work to spot the shots. Change positions frequently, firing a few shots off-hand and then sitting, kneeling, or prone, carefully noting the needed changes in elevation if any. When tired of shooting from a fixed spot, take the target from some other angle, estimate the distance, and then use the rifle to verify the judgment. The man who can keep in the eight-inch bull at two hundred yards, firing one shot standing, the next kneeling, the third sitting, fourth prone, keeping it up in rotation until ten shots have landed in the bull, has a very high order of skill so far as holding and pulling are concerned.

Attempting to elevate the sights and set them

for the exact range will not do for the game shooter. In the first place it frequently happens there is no time; the shot must be taken instantly when opportunity occurs. Also the system of setting sights for unknown distance is the essence of guesswork.

First we guess at the distance, next we guess at the proper elevation, then when we miss, we guess which of the previous guesses was wrong. Of course, there are times when we might note the impact of the bullet from its striking sand or water, but this happens rarely and is generally seen too late to do us any good.

In game shooting as in actual war what must be depended upon is "danger zone." The danger zone for the soldier is taken at the height of a man, sixty-eight inches, for it doesn't make any difference whether we hit him in the head or in the foot, but the danger zone for a deer is only eight inches since we must kill him outright. The problem of the game shot then is to set his sight so as to keep his bullet in this eight-inch [zone] without any further adjustment. The limits of the danger zone are about the maximum distance at which game can be killed with any certainty, and in order to strike center the rifleman must study the path of the bullet's flight or its trajectory curve, and so hold as to correct errors.

Not everything is unknown or guessed at in this case. For example, if his rifle has a four-inch trajectory at two hundred yards, he knows that it will shoot four inches high at a hundred and about two inches high at fifty or a hundred and fifty, which he must make allowance for by his holding. He cannot make this allowance, however, unless he can very closely estimate the distance and this is the present task of our rifle student.

Now is the time to begin a long and patient schooling in judging distance within sporting ranges, say up to three hundred yards. Select a variety of targets, now a knot on a tree, again a patch of moss on a bare rock. Estimate the range and hold for it. Fire several shots so as to be sure one badly held missile will not deceive you, and then go up to the target, carefully counting steps so as to verify your judgment of distance.

Ascertaining range with the naked eye

There are certain principles bearing on the estimation of distances which it is well to fix in the mind. On perfectly level ground with no prominent intervening objects the chances are the distance is underestimated. In rough, broken country the tendency is to overestimate. In heavy timber the probability is the range will be overestimated despite every allowance. Familiar ground will be underestimated, whereas unfamiliar lands are nearly certain to be overestimated.

The novice will shortly learn that he can hold better than he can judge the distance. A diagram of shots in an eight-inch target at some unknown distance, which he decides is about one hundred and fifty yards, is as creditable as a like target at two hundred measured yards with a spotter to mark the shots. A half dozen shots, all well held, but all missing the target owing to bad judgment of distance, will prove a lesson not easily forgotten. By and by the student will come to know both his rifle and himself, realizing that for work at unknown ranges there are well fixed limitations.

Hawks, crows, jack rabbits, wildfowl, etc., are all legitimate targets for this kind of practice. Pretty soon it will dawn upon the observant youngster that holding is not half his problem. For instance he can kill a bird the size of a hen hawk very frequently at two hundred yards if he knows the exact range, but not knowing it, his best judgment will only permit him to shoot with a good prospect of success at about one hundred and twenty-five yards. The man who can kill a crow with one bullet in three at a hundred yards (estimated) is a good shot, or a hawk at one hundred and twenty-five, or a jackrabbit at one hundred and fifty. Striking the hawk is about equivalent to hitting a four-inch, the crow a three, and the jack a six.

A hawk sitting on the dead limb of a tree with the sky for a background is a beautiful target, but hitting him at an unknown range is not so easy as it looks. I have shot at one half a dozen times, finally cutting the limb in two upon which he was sitting without touching a feather — every ball was held close enough to kill had I known the elevation.

The practice with the lightly charged, high velocity rifle should be persisted in until the marksman will be able to estimate a distance in the neighborhood of two hundred yards with such certainty that he will rarely make a mistake of greater than twenty to thirty yards whatever the circumstance of light, cover, and ground. His object is to so ground himself in this art that he can call shots fired over unknown ranges with the same certainty as the known. When he misses then he will know instantly whether it was due to a poor aim or the wrong elevation.

Half the shots which miss game and most of those that merely cripple are due to a bad estimate of the range. No man ever did or ever will judge distances perfectly when on strange ground, but the clever game shot will always be found far superior to others in this respect. Other things being equal, as shooting skill, one sportsman will still be able to take his deer with as much certainty at two hundred yards as another would at a hundred and fifty, solely because of superiority in calculating the range.

Half the shots that miss game are due to bad range estimating

It should be remembered that the object of all this study of distance and bullet path is to enable the marksman to center his game, not land somewhere within the eight-inch. There are enough other factors tending to throw him out without willfully permitting trajectory to do it. As an example, the hunter might fire at a deer one hundred yards away. He knows that his rifle will shoot four inches high, but does not make allowance for that knowing that the bullet will still strike within the circle. However, inadvertently he pulls the shot four inches high, and the result is a ball eight inches from center and a lost buck. On the other hand, had he aimed low, as he should, the bullet would still have proved fatal.

Having thoroughly learned to handle our rifle up to the limits of the eight-inch danger zone, it would be well now to elevate one notch, sighting to center at three hundred yards. With the Springfield '06 ammunition this would give a trajectory height of a trifle over seven inches at one hundred and fifty yards, with a .30-30 the height would be fifteen inches. Practice with this new elevation until you know it thoroughly all up and down the line. Of course the object of the three hundred yard sight is to shoot only at ranges beyond two hundred yards, but it is well to know the bullet's path both inside and beyond the distance for which it is sighted. Of course, the ballistics of the rifle would govern its danger zone and when I mention sighting for two and three hundred yards, it might be taken as having reference only to rifles with a muzzle velocity of 2,500 feet or better.

DIFFICULTY OF KILLING GAME AT LONG RANGE

All of us have heard of the man who can regularly kill his game at extreme ranges. Sir Samuel Baker tells of dropping a Cape buffalo at eight hundred yards with one ball from a muzzle loading eight bore. Another writer speaks of shooting antelope on the run at seven hundred yards, evidently a customary occurrence with him. The Boers are popularly believed to have made a common practice of shooting game at distances of from five hundred to one thousand yards. I have recently been reading of a great game shot who could strike his quarry with fair certainty at fifteen hundred yards.

Now I do not wish to maintain that such performances are impossible nor to reflect on the veracity of the narrators, but I have a suspicion that all work of this kind is sheer, bull luck, absolutely dependent on chance. With his huge, round bullet of low velocity Sir Samuel must have held a hundred feet above the buffalo's back. Shooting a running antelope at seven hundred yards requires a lead of about seventy-five feet. As for the fifteen hundred yard man it has been calculated that with our highest velocity rifle, the Springfield '06, the ball at fifteen hundred yards would be dropping one foot for every eighteen feet of forward movement [and] consequently would fall below a twelve-inch circle in traveling nine extra feet. Estimating fifteen hundred yards to within nine feet is close work — many men could not come within nine feet in judging fifty.

Occasionally large game like elk and caribou has undoubtedly been killed at very long range. Our military experts do not regard a highest possible score at a thousand yards as anything won-

> Killing animals at extremely long range is sheer, bull luck

derful, and the inference is natural that game can be shot at a like distance. However, shooting game at the moderate range of five hundred yards is not so easy as it might seem. Kindly keep in mind that, no matter what the distance, we have to land our bullet in that fatal eight-inch circle.

No matter what the distance, we have to land the bullet in the fatal eight-inch circle

It is a question in the first place of having a rifle accurate enough to do it when fired from a machine rest. The Springfield is said to be our most accurate rifle, and Government tests show its mean deviation at that range to be 5.9 inches. This is not saying that all shots would go into an eleven- or twelve-inch for we have only the *average* deviation, and plenty of shots would go outside. Granted that it would stay in a fifteen-inch, that is considerably wider than an eight, and wouldn't do. The ordinary sporting rifle with soft-point bullets would require a twenty-four inch circle to contain the shots, with possibly not a single ball landing in the eight-inch.

As we see, not one of our rifles is accurate enough to shoot game at five hundreds yards. But even if they were, accuracy is not the only thing we have to consider. On the contrary when shooting over such a range we have to take into our calculation judgment of distance and correct elevation of sights, windage must not be neglected, light can by no means be overlooked, and the barometer, hygrometer, and thermometer must be read carefully; lastly we will have to get our projectile into the game with power enough to kill.

Tests by the Government show that the danger zone for infantry, with the five hundred yard alignment of sights, '06 cartridge, extends for only 128 yards back of the target. Infantry height is taken at sixty-eight inches, but our game danger zone is only eight inches across which reduces the distance to sixteen yards or thereabouts, hence if we underestimate the range sixteen yards in five hundred the result must be a miss or a crippling shot. Naturally the average game cartridge would be much inferior to the '06, an error in judging distances of more than twenty-five feet being hardly permissible.

A good stiff wind blowing across the range would easily drift a .30 caliber bullet two feet and the lightest breeze that could be felt would send it out of the eight-inch. The most moderate head wind would drop our bullet beneath the circle or if coming from the rear would drive it over the top.

Light might vary the elevation a foot or two, and the man who failed to read his thermometer would make a fatal oversight. Referring to the Government cartridge, a change in temperature from zero to 100 would increase the initial velocity one hundred and fifty feet, with a change in trajectory that would throw us wide of the eight-inch. Changes in air pressure and air moisture would do so, too, with like certainty.

From the foregoing it is to be concluded that the hunter who would kill his game at five hundred yards must have a more accurate rifle than any we now possess, must be able to estimate the distance to within a few feet, must have a wind-gauge and elevating back sight, micrometer adjusted, and must carry with him a barometer, thermometer, and hygrometer. Additionally he will have to be a mighty good shot. The average hunter is supposed to have skill enough to place half his shots in an eight-inch bullseye at two hundred yards, and at five hundred he would do well to strike a thirty-inch with some of the bullets scattered over a five-foot circle — this wouldn't do.

However, we will say, just for the sake of argument, that the shooter could *hit* his game, how about killing it? It is generally considered that a striking energy of about 1,500 foot pounds is necessary to prove regularly effective on such game as might be shot at long range, moose for instance. Now how many rifles have this striking force at five hundred yards?

The Springfield '06 wouldn't do, having but a remaining energy of 927 foot pounds, considerably less than a .25-35 at short range, and the latter is not thought to be powerful enough even for deer. A .30-30 at five hundred yards would have no more effect on game than a .32 caliber pistol bullet. Indeed, of American cartridges I consider that the .405 Winchester is the only one that would retain sufficient energy at five hundred yards to be fairly effective on big game.

In the light of what has been said above, it is only reasonable to limit the range at which the

Striking energy of 1,500 foot pounds is necessary to kill large animals at long range

largest game should be shot at to three hundred yards. Shots should be taken at a longer distance than this only when it is absolutely impossible to get closer, and then the rifleman is guilty of wanton cruelty to animals. Roosevelt thoroughly proved this, when in Africa, by pumping a magazine full of cartridges at a buffalo with no result other than the assurance that it would go off and die a lingering death. Van Dyke states that a deer at two hundred yards is an extremely long shot, with which I fully agree. Moreover, shooting at any game at five hundred yards is an unsportsmanlike act.

For most of us, our introduction to rifle marksmanship came with a .22. Here, in a selection from his enduring book .22 Caliber Rifle Shooting *(1932), C. S. Landis looks at use of the little rimfires as a way to improve one's shooting accuracy. He tenders some sound advice for dealing with small game, along with some appropriate reminders on safety and other issues.*

C.S. Landis on .22 caliber rifle accuracy

ACCURACY AND RANGE

Sportsmen differ widely in their views as to the accuracy needed for various forms of small game shooting with light or small caliber rifles. Accuracy ample for shooting opossums for instance, one of the more common small animals shot after being trapped, or killed at night by being shaken or shot out of trees after being treed by dogs, would not be sufficient for long range squirrel shooting.

Lethal shot circle sizes on small game

Such game as opossums, raccoons, skunks, rabbits, and the like usually require a shot in a 3 or 4-inch circle at 25 or 30 yards. That could be attained with any rifle cartridge on the market and any type of arm which would fire it. Even a fair pistol shot would expect to hit a 4-inch bullseye at 25 yards one half or more of the times, he shot at it. For any real rifleman, such shooting is as a rule, comparatively easy.

Squirrels will require a shot in a 1½ to 3 inch circle. The same holds true of gophers, and of woodchucks. Of course you can kill a chuck by striking an area a foot or so long by four or five inches across, but not always is such a hit a clean kill. In squirrel hunting you often have an area 2 inches or so wide or high by 4 to 6 inches long — measuring down the spine, in which a shot will stop the game. The same holds true of both cottontail and jack rabbits and of hares.

But, if you expect to hit the point of aim, and have that point of aim cover only a vital area, then seldom on squirrels, grouse, ducks, and cottontail rabbits can you have that area much more than about 1½ x 3 inches in area. On wild turkeys and geese it can be 6 to 10 inches in diameter, through the butts of the wings, and in the case of a woodchuck about 4 x 6 inches in neck and shoulder, but only 1½ inches high by 2½ inches long in the head.

Sage hens, prairie chickens, and blue grouse would come along with a 3 to 4 inch vital area—plus head and neck; the latter high but by no means wide. Merton Robinson, for many years past Ballistic Engineer of Winchester Repeating Arms Company, who has supervised the testing of many rifles and cartridges, advises that normal average groups (not selected groups, but average groups) made by the different cartridges of .22 rim fire caliber and the different styles of rifles and ammunition are about as follows:

.22 Short Automatic — at 33⅓ yards or 100 feet, 1¼ inches: at 50 yards 1¾ inches.

Shooting with Winchester Model 1890 rifle, or similar. This rifle is rifled and chambered only for the .22 short cartridge, when made in this caliber. Other rifles of like weight but chambered for the .22 short, long and long rifle cartridge would very likely give somewhat larger groups with the .22 short cartridges. Heavier match rifles, would cut possibly a quarter inch off the groups at 50 yards. But not more than that with the short cartridge.

.22 Long Cartridges (not long rifle, but .22 long). 1 inch groups at 100 feet, 1.6" groups at 50 yards.

.22 Long Rifle 1¼ inch groups at 50 yards or 2½ inch groups at 100 yards.

From this you can see that most small game ammunition, to which you can add ¼ to ½ inch increase in groups at 50 yards, and ¾ to 1½ inch increase in groups size for 100 yards for hollow point bullets — will kill the smallest of ordinary small game consistently at 50 yards, and most of the time at 100 yards, so far as accuracy alone is concerned, and at 150 to 200 yards it will be pretty certain on chucks (shoulder shots) turkeys or geese, in a match rifle and to 150 yards in a sporting rifle, so far as accuracy alone is considered. But accuracy alone is not the *only* thing to be thought of. Trajectory and not accuracy is the part which decides as a rule whether you hit or whether you miss. Trajectory, and at long range, wind drift.

An expert would expect to hit a 3 to 4-inch circle at 100 yards

A real, expert rifleman would expect to hit within a 1½-inch circle at 50 yards, and a 3 to 4-inch circle at 100 yards — approximately, if he had a good steady shooting position and first class .22 long rifle ammunition. He would expect to do this on game and somewhat better than this at a paper target but — he could be very badly fooled by a mistake in estimating the range or weather — and could therefore miss more often than desirable.

However, not all hunters, nor in fact not all target shots remember at all times that about 70% of hunting ammunition, and 85 or 90% of selected match ammunition groups into a circle about 60% the area of the normal average groups at that range. In other words, if at 100 yards, a rifle and lot of ammunition was shooting 1¾ inch groups, more than 75% of the shots would be grouping into one-inch groups and this is what the expert small game shot depends upon to make his kills.

In other words, he has 75% or more of his shots driving into one-inch groups at 100 yards with the best combinations of ammunition and rifle of .22 rim fire caliber and if he can place this group anywhere in a 2 to 3-inch circle at that range, naturally he will kill more than half his shots and that is how he makes consistent long range kills.

Most of his shots therefore, do not deviate more than half an inch from center with the best combination, and an inch from center with the ordinary rifle and ammunition, so far as ammunition and rifle 10-shot group deviation is concerned.

Anything more than this is error of aim, error of delivery of the shot—mechanical aiming and pulling, and error of misjudgment of range, plus error of daily variation due to light, temperature and wind.

Obviously, a first class shot, shooting offhand at 50 yards, or from a prone or sitting position, or an arm or body rest at 100 yards, should make reasonably good groups, granted he has a good shooting combination and can hold.

Any first class match shot in this country, can take a squirrel-outline target at 100 yards, the head and shoulders of a wood-chuck at 150 yards, or the life size photograph of a goose or turkey at 200 yards, and riddle that mark once he is sighted in.

In fact he can pick his spot on that game-outline target and place his shots on that spot until he wonders how in the world he ever misses game at that range with the same rifle.

Match shooting records by the hundred will confirm these statements. Long runs of 20 to 60 consecutive bullseyes on a 7⅕-inch bull at 200 yards are so common they no longer excite comment. Men are now shooting 99's and 100's on a *4-inch* ten ring at 200 yards so frequently that has become fairly common.

Of course these men are shooting prone, with a sling, using a scope sighted rifle, and they have sighting shots before they begin shooting for record most of the time, but the fact that is hammered home daily on our big rifle ranges is that a 4-inch circle has now become the unit of scoring and measurement of accuracy for the .22-long rifle match cartridge and it is making good. It is making good every reasonably calm day the thing is tried at Sea Girt, Camp Perry, and the other nationally known small bore rifle ranges.

Personal opinion, — yours, mine, some company's, has not a thing to do with this, it is a matter of definite public record that this is occurring. The evidence is beyond question. — It cannot be disputed successfully.

Therefore, thousands, yes, tens of thousands of high power rifle and shotgun shooters and as many spare time users of light .22's want to very definitely, positively and permanently disabuse themselves of the belief that a .22 is good for about 50 or 60 feet and not much danger beyond 50 yards. The bullet will carry nearly a mile at 25° to 30° elevation and is superbly accurate at 300 yards — two scores of 99 x 100 for 20 consecutive shots at 300 yards on the Military A target with 10-inch bull were made at the Eastern Small Bore Tournament at Sea Girt, N. J., July, 1931. And the match was won with that score. Yes, a contestant hit a 10-inch bullseye 19 times in 20 shots at 300 yards measured, in a public competition— the 300-Yard Small Bore Championship, with about 72 men, including the East's best long range shots most all entered. There were several 98's. A 98 means that 18 shots in the 20 struck the 10-inch center.

At 500 yards the same cartridge is also quite accurate on a calm evening. Capt. Richard made a 48 x 50 at 500 yards on the military target possibly twenty years or more ago. At a range of a third of a mile a modern .22 long rifle bullet will penetrate an inch or two of pine so don't use a .22 rifle for promiscuous shooting at the moon, at apples on a high tree, and the like in settled country because one of them might come down on someone's face and that would be quite unfortunate for two people, — you would be one of them.

A 10-inch bullseye would, if superposed, just about cover the body area of a goose or a wild turkey or the upper half of the body of a chuck — a large one standing at the mouth of his den, so don't show your wisdom in future by telling your friends that a .22 is "no good beyond 50 or 100 yards." It is with the right party pulling or pressing the trigger.

Don't worry about being outclassed on a long shot when you have a good .22 in your hands. It is a case of judging the range, then of setting the sights properly for that distance and delivering the shot. Inside of 75 yards there is so little excuse for missing any small game with a .22 that a bomb-proof alibi is merely a waste of time. Don't spring it on your fellow shooter — he'll not believe it. It's up to you to place that group on the target. The rifle and ammunition of today will do the business.

The .22 rifle is no toy. Every year its accuracy, and occasionally its power and range, are increased, and today it occupies a rank as a small caliber target and game shooting cartridge that a few years ago was given only to much larger metallic ammunition. When I say that the .22 rifle is a real hunting rifle capable of much effectiveness when properly sighted and expertly handled I speak both from personal experience and the observation of the work of most of the better small bore rifle shots of this country who have competed publicly during the last 15 years. No small bore rim fire commercial rifle and ammunition will shoot more accurately at 50, 100 and 200 yards, than the accurate .22 match rifle of today and its equally efficient and deadly ammunition. The light .22 repeater or single shot is so little behind the .22 match rifle in accuracy and effectiveness

A .22 is a real hunting rifle when properly sighted and expertly handled

that its possibilities and power should never be underestimated.

John "Pondoro" Taylor wrote two classics on African hunting: the book that used his nickname for its title, Pondoro *(1955), and the work from which this selection is taken,* African Rifles & Cartridges *(1948) (only a portion of his chapter on marksmanship is included; the portion dealing primarily with dangerous animals has been omitted). I realize that the vast majority of those who read these pages will never enjoy the privilege of making an African safari, but the advice given here, though focused on hunting in the Dark Continent, actually transcends geographic boundaries. Taylor offers all sorts of shrewd insight, and his reminder that "steadiness and patience are of far greater importance than actual marksmanship" should be a mantra for hunters. Haste and nerves have been the undoing of many a hunt.*

John "Pondoro" Taylor on bush marksmanship

MARKSMANSHIP IN THE BUSH

You do not need to be a crack shot to be a successful African big game hunter. Steadiness and patience are of far greater importance than actual marksmanship. Naturally, you've gotta know how to shoot, how to aim and how to squeeze your trigger instead of yanking at it, but you don't have to get discouraged and postpone your proposed African expedition just because you can't put them all in the black at 600 yards on your home range. I've never done any target shooting in my life, other than zeroing a batch of service rifles at 25 yards but I always manage to keep the pot boiling and, given a decent rifle, seldom need more than the one cartridge to do it. I'd probably look the veriest tyro on the range but there's many a fine target shooter who's quite useless in the bush. Big game shooting is an utterly different sport from target shooting — as different as baseball from cricket. And just as you use entirely different tools in those two games, so do you require entirely different tools for the two different types of shooting — different weapons and different sights — whilst the methods employed are also quite different.

There's many a fine target shooter who's quite useless in the bush

There's a certain type of imaginative man who likes to give the impression that he knows a hell of a lot more about hunting than he actually does, and who almost invariably starts his book with a foreword or preface in which he disparages every other writer on the subject with the idea of conveying the impression that the reader is at last going to get the real inside dope on the business from a genuine hunter, someone who really knows. That done, he then goes ahead, giving his imagination full play, and spins any kind of goddam yarn he fancies, feeling pretty sure it will be swallowed. Almost invariably, sooner or later, you will come to where this hero has dropped some animal stone dead in its tracks with a clean brain shot at some incredible range like 750 yards. You will meet others who will try to tell you the same thing. Well, we all know that the most extraordinary flukes will occasionally come off — particularly where the vagaries of stray bullets are concerned — but the point is, what the hell was the fella doing shooting at an animal 750 yards away? If he was the hunter he would like to have you believe he was, how come he couldn't get any closer than that?

Then there is the question of judging ranges. African hunting takes place under such a wide variety of totally different conditions — from the wide open plains thru different types of scrub and bush to light forest and then into heavy forest with or without dense undergrowth — that I defy any man to be able to estimate correctly the distance away that an animal may be standing under each and all of these conditions. A man who does most of his shooting on the open plains may in course of time become fairly proficient in judging distances in the districts with which he is familiar, but that same fella would be quite lost if taken to light timber country, and vice-versa. Open country generally makes an animal look much farther away than he really is, especially in the early morning, but it can be extremely difficult when there is nothing to give you a comparison. For instance, you can see the line of an animal's back as he passes thru some kind of scrub growth where the plains are slightly undulating; it might be a rhino

Open country generally makes an animal look much farther away than he really is

passing thru fairly high stuff, or it might be a lion slouching along thru quite short stuff. The line of the back of these two animals is almost identical; they each carry the head low; they each have high withers and hips and a hollow back. But altho the difference in size is considerable, it can be very difficult to say just which it is when there is nothing around to give you an idea of the height of the stuff thru which the animal is walking. There are certain types of timber which seem to magnify an animal, either giving the impression that it's a much larger beast than you at first thought, or else that he's very much closer than he really is. There are other types of bush which seem to act like telescopes looked thru from the wrong end — and they are by far the commonest.

But the fact to be remembered is, that provided you have your rifles sighted-in, you do not need to worry about range — no matter what you may think the distance is, it's a hundred to one that it's well under 200 yards. I have repeatedly stated that the average range at which animals are shot in Africa — in any part of Africa — will average between 75 and 175 yards, with just an occasional, very occasional, shot at 200. Let those boastful individuals shout all they like about killing at 650 and 750 yards; you think in terms of actual facts — and the actual facts are that the range practically never exceeds 200 or at the very most 250 yards.

The average range at which animals are shot in Africa is between 75 and 175 yards

The only parts of Africa I know where a slightly longer shot might have to be taken is when hunting that somewhat rare desert antelope — its name eludes me for the moment — which is found to the south-east of Malakal in the Sudan. It's a white beast with long, straight horns not unlike a small oryx. From the nature of its habitat it's not too easy to approach, but to compensate for that, it's not hunted to any extent. A 250-yd. shot *might* be called for here. Then there's the giant eland, also found in the Sudan. It's also very rare and, I think, strictly protected. It's generally found in somewhat undulating country inclined to be stony, with open scattered timber and not too much undergrowth. The big fellow is very shy and generally on the alert. It's very difficult country in which to make a close approach: the small stones, more or less concealed in the short grass, are all loose and persist in rolling whenever a foot is placed on the ground. I seem to remember Selous, describing his assignment to collect specimens of these eland for the British Museum, saying it was the toughest he had ever undertaken. A scope-sighted Magnum would undoubtedly be a great help to you here. However, I do not think you are likely to get permission to shoot one of these animals.

The only other place I can think of at the moment where you may be called upon to fire at upwards of 200 yards, is if you are trying for one of the scarce variety of gemsbok that are found in the desert country to the south of Mossamedes in Angola, Portuguese West Africa. Even there, however, it is extremely improbable that it will be necessary to shoot beyond 250 yards. And the same applies to that weird, semi-amphibious beast, the sittatunga. The swamps of Lake Bangueolo are *the* place for them, but owing to their habit of living in the sudd, your only chance of getting a shot is to try and catch them on the firmer ground around the edge of the swamp at first crack of dawn. The going is so difficult for you, that a close approach is practically impossible if they are any distance away when you first spot them. Under these conditions a longish shot may be necessary but 250 or thereabouts should be far enough. Here again you will find a scope-sighted Magnum a real help — the light can be very tricky at earliest dawn, and there is usually considerable mist rising from the swamps at that hour. You will find it very deceptive, and will appreciate a low-powered scope.

So you see, even for these, the most difficult of African shots on the most difficult of African game to approach, as far as my experience carries me the statement I made a little while ago — that the range practically never exceeds 200 yards, or at the very most 250 — still holds good.

I am by no means alone in stating this so emphatically. Let me quote from Major H. C. Maydon, a very keen and observant amateur who has been hunting whenever he could get the opportunity for the last 30 or more years, and who amongst various other books edited the *Big Game Shooting in Africa* volume in the Lonsdale

Library. Speaking of range etc., he writes:

"Choose a carbine or short rifle since it is easier to carry in thick bush and you will not need long shots. Try to get a rifle with a flat trajectory up to 200 yards and tear off all other sighting leaves. They only put you off or get pushed up by accident at the wrong moment, or persuade you that you can kill further than you ought. The best range is the nearest possible, with 200 yards as your limit. Never farther than 200 yards? Well, almost never. When you must break that golden rule, take a full sight and pin your faith in Nimrod. He'll play up if you are playing fair. . . . Shoot as much ordinary game as you can with the magazine rifle until you have learnt something of stalking, of judging distances, of native guides, of fatal shots, and, above all, of your own self-confidence. Then, and only then, collect your heavy rifle and go for the heavy game."

Now there is genuine advice from a real hunter who honestly wants to assist those with less experience than he has had, and who is not concerned with any boastful claims anent his own prowess or skill. Compare that with the claim made by another writer whose book is in front of me right now and in which he states that on one occasion, thanks to knowing the trajectory curve of his rifle, he was able to kill a stampeding elephant at upwards of 600 yards with a brain shot, by aiming some three feet above his head and three feet in front of him! True, he mentions that such shots could not always be brought off to order, but the impression given is, nevertheless, that such shots are by no means unusual for a man of his skill and experience. It does not occur to him to tell us anything about trajectories. You will frequently see game at considerably more than 200 yards range but why open fire right away? If you are anything of a hunter you will be able to get very much closer. If you can't be bothered doing so, then the veldt is no place for you. You are here to hunt — if long range target shooting appeals to you more than hunting, then surely the rifle range will suit you better than the African veldt.

Mirage, that bug-bear of the target shot, will not worry you under ordinary hunting conditions out here. In hot dry open country, such as you will find in the North-West Frontier province of Kenya, for instance, the mirage is considerable, and you will see a herd of zebra or other game apparently standing up to their hocks in a shimmering lake of water; but it would seem as tho the mirage acted both ways and prevented the animals getting a clear view of you as you approach, because under such conditions you will have little difficulty in getting within your 250 yards altho there is no cover at all, and you will then find that the lake has either disappeared entirely or else is now beyond your quarry. Doubtless, if you were to try a shot from the prone position, you would be bothered by mirage still, as well as being well grilled by the scorching hot ground but if you shoot

In dry, open country mirage is considerable

from either the squatting position or take a standing shot, as I always do, steadying your rifle on
your gun-bearer's shoulder, you will have no difficulty in killing clean. In all similar districts, where
the temperatures run around 120 or more in the
shade — if you can find a bit of shade! — you will
find the same thing; but generally speaking mirage
would only begin to worry you beyond the ranges
at which you should shoot.

Many men, shooting in the East African highlands, complain that their rifles shoot from a foot
to eighteen inches high, particularly in the early
morning when most shooting takes place. They
blame it on the rarefied atmosphere. Now the
Highlands of East Africa vary between 4,000 and
9,000 feet above sea level, and altho the difference in atmospheric pressure will be quite apparent to those unaccustomed to such altitudes, they
could not possibly affect the velocity of a bullet to
the extent of throwing it three feet high, as I once
heard a man state. He said that the lowering of atmospheric pressure spelt a corresponding increase
in velocity. As a matter of fact a lowering of atmospheric pressure actually means a slight *decrease* in velocity, since the bullet meets with
somewhat less resistance during its passage up the
bore and therefore gets ahead of the expanding
powder gasses, as it were, which causes a slight reduction in barrel pressure and therefore a reduction in muzzle velocity. But this is entirely theoretical; in actual practice the change in velocity is

so slight at the altitudes at which shooting takes place, that it can be ignored. Admittedly, after the bullet has left the muzzle it then meets with less resistance, and consequently retains better its initial velocity. Accordingly, the only effect a high altitude can have is to slightly flatten the trajectory, and even there the difference will be hardly noticeable — certainly not at African altitudes.

In the Himalayas in India it is quite usual for sportsmen to hunt at altitudes ranging between 14,000 and 18,000 feet above sea level. Burrard mentions doing so with a pal of his who was using a .375 and a .303; Burrard was using a .280 and a .400. They were most careful to observe all shots so as to check theory by actual practice over this question of altitude. Burrard states that neither of them noticed any change in sighting being necessary, and reckoned that his .280 gave him a slightly flatter trajectory at ranges between 300 and 350 yards. Now such altitudes are very much higher than any found in Africa, at least as far as the hunter is concerned, and therefore the rarity of the atmosphere cannot be the answer to those men's trouble who find their rifles apparently shooting high in East Africa.

The effect of refraction Personally, I have little doubt that refraction of light is to blame. In the early mornings and late evenings there must be layers of air lying at different heights above the ground all at different temperatures, because it cools quickly and considerably in the Highlands in Africa when the sun drops, and begins to heat up again pretty rapidly next morning after the sun is up. An animal seen under such conditions will have its position distorted until it appears to be standing a foot or more higher than it actually is — just as a fish seen in water will probably not be within a foot of where you stab a spear in unless you are looking practically straight down on him.

Speaking generally, and this is borne out by every other hunter with whom I have ever discussed such matters, it can safely be stated that one always over-estimates the range in Africa. In my early days, before I knew anything about trajectories, I used to be fascinated by those little leaf sights, each marked for an additional 100 yards or meters, with which almost all British and Continental rifles are fitted in addition to the fixed standard backsight. I used to carefully estimate the range and then flip up one of these little leaves, aim most carefully, and then — have my bullet skim over the animal's back. Again and again it happened, but for long it didn't occur to me that the fault was mine — that I was over-estimating the range.

One always over-estimates the range in Africa

Sometimes, if the animals haven't been shot at much, and a wild shot is fired, they will just stand there looking around and wondering what on earth is happening. I remember on one occasion, when I was very new to the game, I was trying to kill some wretched little beast for the pot. He and a companion were standing in an almost dry water course with a high perpendicular bank immediately behind them. I judged the range at slightly under 300 yards, put up the 300-yd. leaf — I was using a brand-new .303 sporter, "Mark VI" ammo — aimed a bit low and let drive. My bullet hit the bank feet above the little buck and knocked some dirt and small stones down. The little beast looked round at the bank and then looked round towards me, but otherwise didn't move. Realizing that I had overestimated the range, I put down the 300-yd. leaf and flipped up the one for 200 yards. Again I fired, and again the bullet smacked into the bank above the little buck. He decided it was no place for him and with his companion headed for more peaceful pastures. On another occasion I was given either four or five shots at a reed-buck and missed them all in exactly the same way. I can think of yet another similar occasion with a wart hog. Misled by the ground mist in the very early morning which enormously magnified the animal, I at first thought it was a buffalo. I crept up closer, however, and then saw it was only a hog. But I again overestimated the range and clean missed him with my first shot. That was the last time I ever used leaf sights or any other kind of adjustable sight. And what misses I have had since then are at any rate not due to overestimating the range.

The last time I used an adjustable sight

Nevertheless, one's eyes can play one strange tricks at times. There are two occasions, that come immediately to mind. I was hunting for meat for my men and spotted a kudu bull with his harem. I had no difficulty in getting within about 80 yards of him. I was using a 9mm Mauser by Churchill. I saw the bull standing broadside on to me, and not having learnt the shoulder shot at that time, I placed my bullet close up behind his left shoulder. The cows cleared off and the bull took a wild gallop around in a circle that would probably have taken him some fifty yards or so had he been running straight. He then collapsed. I was quite confident of the shot and just waited for him to fall. However, I was always anxious to see if my bullet had indeed taken the animal where I had intended it to, because I was mighty keen to become a good game shot, so I went along to examine him. He was lying on his right side, which was unusual, as animals generally fall on the wounded side when shot with "ordinary" rifles — not so with the Magnums — and I was astonished to see no bullet hole behind his shoulder. I told my men to turn him over, and there sure enough was the bullet hole behind his right shoulder. His *right* shoulder, mark you; yet I could have sworn I placed the bullet behind his left shoulder. How can you account for that? "Optical illusion" jumps immediately to the lips; but that's altogether too easy. I could readily believe that my eyes had been deceived so that I imagined the bull to be looking towards my left when in point of actual fact he was looking towards my right; but I cannot believe that my rifle was also deceived.

Because in that case my bullet should have taken him thru the flank just in front of the right hip, surely? The answer? I haven't the remotest idea.

The second occasion was very similar and took place some two or three years later. I was again hunting for meat for my men, and this time it was sable antelope I spotted. I took the shot at about 90 or 100 paces. I had by now learnt the shoulder shot and the bull dropped in his tracks with, as I supposed, my bullet thru his left shoulder. But it wasn't thru his left shoulder — it was thru his right shoulder. My rifle that time was a Farquharson-actioned falling-block single-loader by Greener built to handle Rigby's 400/.350 shell.

My eyes? I've never had any trouble with them; it's only within the last few years that I've taken to wearing glasses for reading. Hooch? No; I'd learnt my lesson by that time. So what? To this day I can't answer. There have only been those two times in all the years I've been hunting but they are as vividly before me today as they were when they happened.

Always take plenty shells

There's one word of advice I might slip in here: Always take plenty shells with you when you go hunting. There is nothing more infuriating than to have a wounded animal in front of you and not a single shell left with which to finish him off. It happened to me once, and I've taken darned good care that it never happened again. I went out with a Martini-Henry carbine (577/.450) to shoot something for my own pot. This is, of course, a sin-

MARKSMANSHIP FOR THE HUNTER   225

gle-shot weapon, and a killer at close ranges. I
spotted a klipspringer — a small antelope — up
on the side of a rocky kopje. I fired for his shoulder, but the smoke prevented me seeing clearly
what had happened altho pretty sure of my shot.
However, I saw a klipspringer leaping in its char-
acteristic way from rock to rock, and naturally
imagined that it was my little beast because I
could see that he was wounded. I scrambled up
the side of the kopje and then realized that my
bullet had gone thru the animal at which I had
fired and then into a companion. I didn't know
there were two of them there. My little fella was
stone dead but there was now the wounded one
which must be put out of its misery, and I had not
bothered to bring any extra shells along. It was a
horrible business, because the light was failing and
it was impossible to go back to camp, get some
cartridges, and return again before dark. My boy
found the wretched little beast dead a couple of
hundred yards away next morning. Maybe it was
as well I didn't attempt to follow that evening, or
it might have gone much farther. But it taught me
never again to go out without plenty shells.

I knew a fella who lost a mighty elephant bull
in the same way. He didn't go out with only one
cartridge but he only had what were in the magazine of his rifle, and he was one of those idiots who
believed in "filling him full of lead." He took a
head shot which went a trifle too high, and then
emptied his magazine into the elephant as he

cleared off. One shot wounded him slightly in the lungs, and another in the hindquarters. The remainder were apparently misses. The bull was pretty sick both from the head shot which had passed close to the brain, and also from the lung shot. He ran about half a mile, and then pulled up. The hunter followed in the hope that he might find him dead but had to return to camp as he had no more ammunition with him and the light was failing. He knew his men could never run there and back before dark; accordingly, there was nothing to do but quit. He went out next day but the bull had moved off during the night and he failed to find him. He quit the district a day or so following and when out hunting myself a day later, I came on this magnificent tusker, looking fairly sick but still very much alive, and killed him without any difficulty.

It's better to bring back a belt or bag of shells unfired than to run short — you can always use them later — and anyway you won't be carrying them yourself.

In East Africa more shots are fired from the squatting position than any other

In East Africa I suppose more shots are fired from the squatting position than from any other. Personally, I do not like that squatting position — maybe it's an acquired taste. In bush, scrub and forest, of course, it's out of the question. Fully 96% of my shots are fired from the standing off-hand position and by that I do not mean any of those weird positions and attitudes adopted by small-bore marksmen in competition shooting. You hold your rifle in the most natural and comfortable position, not only with the shot in view, but also in such a manner that you can reload with ease, speed and the least possible amount of movement and noise on your part, and so that you have complete control over your weapon at all times. In a word, you handle it as you would handle your pet shot gun. When hunting game you can forget pretty well your target-shooting lore — at least as far as African shooting is concerned. Your trigger-squeeze is about the only thing that remains the same. Forget all about your rifle — you know it's a good'un; you know your shells are okeh; right, forget about 'em; above all, *forget all you've ever heard about muzzle-blast and recoil.* Concentrate on placing your bullet where it will do the most good and you won't even notice the recoil or report.

By "squatting" position, I mean sitting down on the ground, both feet flat, knees drawn up, and elbows resting on the knees. It's very popular on the open Kenya plains where the grass is seldom more than a foot high, if that. But as I say, I very much prefer to drop on one knee, *with my backside well down on that heel*, and steady my barrels against the outside of my gun-bearer's thigh, he bracing his leg firmly against the ground. You get a beautifully steady shot like that.

And don't, I beg of you, DON'T, do as this guy did I'm going to tell you about. He was very nervous of buffalo, but very keen to shoot one. His

An excellent example of how it should *not* be done

own account of how he went about it is an excellent illustration of how it should *not* be done; but also an equally excellent illustration, I'm afraid, of how it is done all too often. He finally got his chance when he struck fresh spoor coming out of a dense patch of bush known to be a refuge for buffalo.   Here is how he describes it:

". . . . Everything went in my favour. When within approximately one hundred and fifty yards, I singled out the largest animal, took a standing aim just behind the left shoulder and away sped the bullet on which my cherished hopes rested. Instantly the herd, which proved to be seven bulls, came thundering down along the track they had previously made — instinctively, I presume, taking the shortest cut back to the safety of their beloved Jassie.

"It seemed that I was in imminent danger of being trampled into oblivion. This, however, did not at the time cause me the least anxiety — *I simply rammed clip after clip of cartridges into the magazine and fired into the herd*. When within fifteen or twenty yards they swerved slightly and thundered past, heads down in a cloud of dust. I caught sight of a spurt of blood from the shoulder of one, evidently the one first fired at. . .

"Now wild with excitement I tore after the vanishing herd, shouting and cursing at Mondoropuma for not lending a hand.

"This gentleman was safely up a tree. . . . He implored me not to go any farther, but all fear of buffalo had left me, and I plunged on as hard as I could go. A child could have followed the splashes of blood left by the herd; goodness only knows how many I had wounded in my desperate endeavor to bring one down.

". . . . A short time was spent following up fresh blood spoor left by the other buffalo I had wounded, but these were abandoned the edge of the Jassie where they had taken refuge. Why no trouble was experienced from following *at least four or five of these wounded animals* I cannot attempt to explain. Perhaps some other unfortunate hunter reaped the benefit." (The italics are mine.)

Well there it is. And he is so proud of it that he has written it all in a book so as to tell the world. If I had ever behaved in such an outrageously unsportsmanlike manner, far from telling the world about it, I should hide it away in the depths of my evil past and sincerely hope that the world would never get to hear about it.

Did he do a single thing right? He was scared and yet used a totally unsuitable rifle — a .303 magazine (215-gr. bullet, M.V. 2,060, M.E. 2,030, K-O value 19.2); he opened fire from the comparatively long range of 150 yards; he planked himself on the track made by the troop when they emerged from their sanctuary and along which his common-sense, if he had any, ought to have told him they would very likely return; in a frantic mixture of panic and anxiety to get at least one, he blazed off wildly into the brown of the herd — unaimed shots. He admits wounding "at least" four or five apart from the one he killed — the first one at which he fired. If he was anything of a rifleman he ought to have known exactly where his bullet had taken the bull, and therefore, since he had been hunting for some years, he ought to have known that the beast was mortally wounded and therefore his without any more shots having to be fired. He then admits tearing after the wounded animals as hard as he could go, in spite of his tracker's warnings — (I certainly don't blame that hero for seeking the safety of a tree, since he had been with this man some considerable time and must have had his own opinion of him as a hunter!).

Now I have seen and heard of this sort of thing again and again, not only with buffalo but also with elephant and rhino and on countless occasions have heard men describing exactly similar occurrences. They don't seem to realize that such accounts of their ineffableness are merely nauseating to the real, genuine hunter. But men who could behave like that are beyond shame and would readily find specious excuses for themselves.

I headed this chapter *Marksmanship in the Bush* but really there's precious little to say on that aspect of African shooting — as I find now that I've come to discuss it. Marksmanship, as such, is really of secondary importance in view of the size of the animals shot and the comparatively short ranges at which they are shot. The great thing is to pick your spot and put your bullet there — not just anywhere at all into the "brown" of the beast.

You can fill these African beasts with lead and still lose them if your first shot was badly placed. I can give you an example of what one of them can stand: I was shaking and rotten with malaria once upon a time, and my men had absolutely nothing left to eat — I simply had to go out and try to get them something. Now malaria plays the devil and all with your vision whilst the fever is on you. I first of all mistook two or three wart hogs for as many lions and then clean missed a sable bull antelope at barely 60 yards. I reeled along and presently came across a roan antelope bull at about 90 paces. I had two rifles with me — a 9mm and a 10.75mm. I used the 9mm and hit but didn't know where. We followed the roan and I got another shot shortly afterwards. And then another, and another. And still the wretched animal wouldn't fall. I was pretty nearly blind by now, but simply had to get that meat. I exchanged the 9 for the 10.75 but it didn't seem to be much better. However, after several more shots, we found the unfortunate roan's stomach and the greater part of his intestines lying on the veldt, so I perked up a bit; I guessed he couldn't get much further without that lot. Still, it took another two or three shots from my shaky and nearly blind state to finish him. Now that's not a nice story, and I don't like telling it but the malaria was directly to blame and the absolute necessity for getting my men something to eat. Altogether, I fired 13 shots into that wretched roan before killing him — simply because the first was badly placed.

The South African Dutchman, the "back-veldter," is taught to shoot the hard way. His father hands him a rifle, probably an 8mm relic of the Boer war, almost as soon as he is big enough to carry it, and two shells. He is told that he is to go out and bring back some meat; the second cartridge is to enable him to finish off a beast if he is unlucky enough to only wound with his first shot. If he fires his rifle and fails to bring home the bacon, he will get the daylights walloped out of him with the rifle's own steel cleaning rod. And that's not merely a threat — it's one of the few promises the youngster can be perfectly certain his father will keep!   If he kills clean with his first shot, he can do what he likes with the other — no questions are asked concerning it. Numerous backveldters have told me that this is how they all learn to shoot. It makes them good meat-getters from the very beginning; and if they were permitted to use only single-loaders all would be well. The trouble is that they all use Mausers and are never satisfied until they've had a shot at everything in sight with hair on it.

With reference to placing your bullet in the right spot, not merely for humanitarian reasons for the sake of killing the animal with the least possible infliction of pain and suffering, as well as to save yourself needless tramping, it also ensures that you do at least know at what you are firing. At first glance that may sound like the wanderings of delirium, but I can assure you it is nothing of the sort; more than one gay hunting party has ended tragically thru one member of it shooting and killing a companion by accident. A party of four guns was beating thru a patch of grass and low bush into which a lion had been seen to make his way. They couldn't keep in sight of one another, and one excitable sportsman, seeing a movement in the bush on his half-right front, let drive and shot his own brother dead. Another similar case was that of a party driving wild hogs in the same way, and one of them not waiting to see what it was that moved, blew off a pal's face with a soft-nose bullet from his 9.3mm Mauser. Yet another, which comes nearer home, was that of a professional guide and hunter taking a very keen but excitable visitor around. They were hunting in a patch of thick bush known to contain rhino. The guide was in front. Suddenly the visitor thought he saw something, swung up his rifle and blazed off — shattering his guide's right elbow with a .470-caliber slug. And there were many, many more.

There is one type of shooting that appears to beat hunters in all parts of the world and that is when they are shooting steeply downhill. They either don't give a thought to it at all — until after they've missed! — or else they give too darned

The shot that beats hunters in all parts of the world — shooting steeply downhill

much thought to it in the light of all they've heard and read about the difficulties of such a shot, and all the different theories that have been forwarded from time to time concerning it. Such shots are few and far between in African hunting; but they occur occasionally.

My own explanation is the awkward and strained position you are compelled to adopt to get your eye in line with your sights. The almost inevitable result being that you take too much foresight and so shoot high. Try aiming at a mark on the carpet a few feet in front of you, and then aim at a picture on the wall. You will find the latter much easier, simply because your sights come up and level themselves up in line with your eye; whereas, when aiming downwards you have to force your head and neck forward and downward to bring your eye to the line of the sights. Don't bother your head with questions of gravity and bullet-drop at various angles, or any other theoretical explanations. Just remember that you are firing from an infernally uncomfortable position and that if you aren't careful your bullet will pass over the animal's back — and make the necessary allowances. That is, when shooting downhill aim low, and the steeper the angle the lower you must aim.

Auctor: When you gave us Major Maydon's advice to beginners, you may remember he said something about taking a full sight if you are shooting beyond 200 yards. I know there are many men who vary the amount of foresight they take for different ranges, and you frequently hear the expression, "I took a very fine sight," or "I took a full sight," or something of the sort; and there are some gunsmiths who actually recommend this method of aiming in their catalogs. What is your reaction to that?

Lector: I'm afraid that was an unfortunate choice of wording on Maydon's part tho I agree that there are a great many men who say they aim in that manner. The whole object of a bead foresight is to enable and help you to always take the same amount of foresight when aiming — the bead, the whole bead, and nothing but the bead. Those who advocate altering the amount of foresight for different ranges forget that by doing so they are violating one of the first principles of aiming. Bring a little common sense to bear, son. Since judging distances accurately was one of the greatest difficulties the big game hunter had to overcome prior to the introduction of the high velocity rifle, and since the slightest variation in the amount of foresight can throw your bullet hopelessly out, how in the name of all reason can you expect to be able to estimate the correct amount to take for any given range? Besides, you will have two guesses to make instead of only one — you will have first to guess the range, no easy matter and then guess the amount of foresight to take for that guessed range! Well? Don't you think you'll have a better chance of putting your bullet where

The whole object of a bead foresight

you want it if you follow my advice? If you have your rifle sighted as I suggest you have nothing to guess at all — you just take a normal aim for all ordinary shots, and if the animal seems to be standing much farther away than usual, why, you merely hold a mite higher on his shoulder, that's all. There is no guessing called for.

And anyway, always bear in mind that the old-timer's maxim holds as good today as ever it did in the days of black powder, especially where dangerous game is concerned: "Git as close as y' can, laddie; an' then *git ten yards closer*." Get as close as ever you possibly can, and then make dead certain of your shot. The shoulder shot is by far the best for all animals, particularly dangerous game, (and incidentally the biggest target). Do not think in terms of behind the shoulder — the vital spots lie *between* the shoulders. Slam your bullet thru the bone and the animal will drop instantly — I am, of course, assuming that you are suitably armed — with spinal concussion and will die of rapid internal hemorrhage owing to the bullet and particles of broken bone tearing their way in thru the main arteries situated at the top of the heart. He will not get to his feet again.

Now practically without exception all beginners are imbued with the idea of "behind the shoulder." This is undoubtedly because the old-timers invariably spoke and wrote of aiming in that manner. But then, when you get back to the days of muzzle-loaders and black powder breech-loaders with their lead balls, this was the only

"Git as close as y' can laddie; an' then *git ten yards closer.*"

place where there was reasonable certainty of the
ball penetrating sufficiently to kill. A spherical
lead ball on the shoulder might break the bone but
would certainly fail to get thru it, unless you were
using an enormously powerful and unwieldy
weapon on small animals. The black powder Express breech-loaders were not much better in this
respect. Accordingly, right up to the end of the
last century, when John Rigby pioneered the modern nitro-express back in '98 by introducing the
.450 cordite, men were still speaking in terms of
"behind the shoulder." (The old buffalo-hunters of
the '60s in the States invariably went for the lungs
or the "armpit.")

But with modern rifles and ammunition things
are different. The metal-jacketed bullet will have
no difficulty in getting thru the bone of the shoul-
der-blade provided you are using a suitable weight
of bullet for the animals you are shooting. There is
no need to mash up both shoulders. A solid will
probably drill a neat little hole thru both, with or
without stunning but a soft-nose will set-up on the
first shoulder, inflicting a terrific punch which *will*
stun, and will then tear thru those vital arteries
and usually stop against the opposite shoulder,
with or without breaking it. The animal will rarely
regain consciousness before death overtakes him;
if he does, he certainly will not get to his feet. In
other words, the animal is yours the instant you
squeeze your trigger, and you know it — there is
no doubt.

When hunters realized the penetrative power

of the metal-jacketed bullet they at once took to this shoulder shot so as to be certain of definitely anchoring their beast. Because where dangerous game are concerned it is not the original stalk and shot, but the following of a wounded beast that is so dangerous. A brain or neck shot will, of course, drop an animal in his tracks but an animal moves his head and neck much more than his shoulder, and these targets are very much smaller. The shoulder is the largest, steadiest and most vulnerable of all targets and just as instantaneous, for all practical purposes, as either head or neck.

Townsend Whelen's great tips on woodcraft and other hunting skills

When it comes to woodcraft and mastery of all the skills that collectively make up the complete hunter — stealth, patience, marksmanship, knowledge of habits and favored habitats of the quarry — Townsend Whelen may well be reckoned as fine a writer as this country has produced. The dean of American campers, Horace Kephart, might vie with him, but "Kep" wrote far less on hunting than Whelen. This piece comes from what many consider Whelen's finest opus, The Hunting Rifle *(1940). It is replete with the practical, readily applicable wisdom familiar to readers of the author's work.*

IN THE GAME FIELDS

If you have never shot at game before, never drawn a bead on anything animate, then you may have trouble at first when you graduate from the rifle range and start to hunt. Everything will probably be strange, and very different from what you pictured it. You may have trouble in seeing game, and when you do see it you may become so excited, get "buck fever," that you cannot hold your rifle steady on it to save your life — that is unless you can get into the prone position with the gunsling which is an almost sure cure for buck fever when you have previously shot in that position long enough to have mastered it.

Buck fever is exactly the same thing as stage fright. It comes from lack of confidence and overeagerness. Only the restoration of confidence in yourself will cure it, and if you have been shooting prone on the range as much as I have advised, that confidence will come as soon as you get on your belly with the sling on your arm.

Only a restoration of confidence will cure buck fever

It is for this reason that I think varmint shooting, particularly woodchuck and prairie dog shooting, is the best introduction of all to big game shooting. You do most of this shooting in the reliable prone position. The mark is small, but not smaller than the 8 ring of the 100 yard target. You have to shoot carefully and close, and you learn to aim, not at the animal as a whole, but at some particularly vital part of it. You also learn what game looks like in its natural surroundings and over your sights, and you absorb something about stalking game — that is approaching under cover, noiselessly, and up wind.

If you are a city man you may have great difficulty in seeing game. Those who have been brought up on a farm are usually excellent at it. So too are some few urbanites who have unusual powers of observation. If you have difficulty in this respect it can be overcome by practice and experience. You must learn where to look for game, and what it looks like. Learn to "eliminate the obvious" as Stewart Edward White puts it — that is pay no attention to what is obviously not game.

Do not expect game to appear as the artist delights to depict it. It hardly ever stands out so distinctly as it does in a picture. Often it is only a more or less indistinct bit of color or shadow in the landscape, very much camouflaged but nevertheless distinctly different from the usual rocks, stumps, shrubs, and shadows which may be of rather similar size and shape to game.

Game never stands out so distinctly as it does in a picture

Of course if the game is moving you will likely pick it up quickly enough. But if it is stationary its protective coloration may blend into the background, and it will likely not have that regular, distinctive, and clear outline that will make it look like an animal. Its hind quarters may be towards you, with its head hidden, or any portion of it may be hidden by leaves, grass, a tree, or shadow. But nevertheless it is decidedly different from ordinary inanimate objects, as you will realize after a little experience, and keen eyesight or the binoculars will gradually cause what was at first a queer smudge in the landscape, to resolve itself into an animal.

If you are poor at this game, and live in a city, then I think the best way to improve is to walk in the park and practice picking up and watching squirrels and birds. No amount of book learning or theory will help you to see game. You have to have practice and lots of it. Keen eyesight accustomed to looking at things at a distance is a great asset. My eyesight has never been very keen, and so I have had to use every aid of science to overcome my handicap. I have always patronized the best oculists to have my spectacles fitted, and use excellent binoculars. As an example, many years ago I was hunting in British Columbia with two friends, and we had along an Indian cook named Judge. One day, traveling with the pack train, we had to traverse a ridge at least 10 miles long, and all of it above timberline. A blizzard was raging which made it very unpleasant as there was no break to the wind. Towards evening we were able to drop down into a little sheltered valley, where we made camp, and almost at once the weather began to clear up, the snow stopped, and the clouds began to lift. Judge ran up on a little knoll where he could get a view down the valley, and almost at once he came back whispering excitedly "Skookem mowitch!" (Rams!) I went up on the knoll and looked where he pointed, but I could see nothing with my naked eye. With my binoculars, however, I could make out a bunch of four animals but could not determine either their species or sex. So I went back to camp and got a 33-power Bardou telescope that I had along, and resting that steadily, I was finally able to identify four rams. Judge had not only found them at once, but

Use excellent binoculars

had recognized them as rams with his naked eyes. What I would not give for a pair of eyes like that!

Of course game is a far differently appearing target from the black bull's-eye and white paper affair that you used on the rifle range. You may see the animal quite clearly when you view it with the naked eye, but when you come to aim at it through iron sights it may appear very indistinct, or you may not be able to make it out at all, although you would never have this trouble if you were using telescope sights. I am here considering the most difficult cases at long ranges and in poor lights. Most of the time things will be far easier, often not difficult at all, because the range is short, light good, no vegetation in the way, a more or less contrasting background, and the animal in clear view. But under very difficult conditions do not expect that you will always be able to aim distinctly at game with iron sights, — that is where the advantage of a good scope comes in. Anything that you can make out at all with your naked eye you can always see far more distinctly through the scope, and can aim at it with surety. And usually the scope will give you clear aim at anything that you can pick up with an 8 power binocular.

Never aim at the game as a whole

Never aim at the game as a whole. Merely aiming at the outline of animals will give you many clean misses. You should pick out a spot on the animal — a vital spot — and aim at it as you did on the bull's-eye, trying to make a ten. As I have already described, usually the best spot to aim at is the heart region, well forward in and almost at the bottom of the chest. The heart in all four-footed animals lies practically on top of the lowest point of the breast bone. Aim at this spot no matter in what direction the animal is facing. Even if the animal is facing directly away from you aim just where you would estimate the heart to be in a line through the hind quarters. If the bullet is not capable of driving through the hind quarters to the heart, it will at least smash through a lot of vital tissues and organs part way thereto. If your bullet strikes a little higher than the heart it still demolishes the lungs, and likely some of the large blood vessels leading from the heart, and usually makes a clean kill. And if you go low you miss the animal which is far better than making a superficial wound and having the animal escape.

If you talk to old hunters the chances are they will warn you against overshooting — tell you to hold low. You will read this warning many times in older big game shooting literature. Pay no attention to it. It is a relic of the old days when hunters used open rear sights. If you were to use such an obsolete, cheap rear sight (and I sincerely hope you will not) then when you shoot hurriedly or in a poor light, you will not draw the bead of the front sight down fine enough in the notch of the rear sight, but most likely will aline it much higher where it can be seen easier, and the result is you overshoot. But you never do this with the Lyman type of aperture rear sight. The natural tendency is to aim correctly with the Lyman sight. Indeed if you do miss with this sight the chances are that

Pay no attention to advice that you should hold low

244 THE MARKSMANSHIP PRIMER

the miss will go low or to the right because the miss will probably be due to a jerk or flinch on the trigger, and not to your aim, and jerking or flinching usually results in your pulling the muzzle down or to the right.

Perhaps I am over apprehensive in my cautions. I have a tendency to describe the pitfalls to steer you away from them. But the fact is that if you have been training yourself as I have advised, it will not be many days before you have become accustomed to the conditions in the game fields, and then you are going to find that hitting game under usual conditions is ridiculously easy compared to getting a 9 or 10 on the 100 yard N.R.A. target. Occasionally a shot will be extremely difficult, requiring all your skill to accomplish it successfully. This is particularly true on deer bounding through the forest, or a shot at a woodchuck at over 250 yards, or a deer or ram at 350 yards or further.

Hitting game under usual conditions is ridiculously easy

I have never been much of a believer in shooting at the running deer target we occasionally see rigged up on a rifle range. It runs smoothly at a steady speed, and straight across, whereas a deer in its natural habitat bounds up and down, at varying speed, usually dead away or quartering away from you. Also it continually dodges right or left to avoid trees, stumps, and rocks. Furthermore it may be running either up or down hill. Every shot at deer will be different, whereas every shot at the running deer target is almost exactly the same.

We often hear it said that shotgun shooting is not good practice for the rifleman, but I can by no means subscribe to this. I think that bird and skeet shooting are most valuable training to teach skill in shooting at running game with the rifle. Shotgun shooting teaches lead, and swing, and keeping the gun moving-things you have to do just as much with the rifle as with the shotgun if you want to hit running game. The only radical difference between the two weapons lies in the velocity or time of flight of the charge of shot and the bullet, and the longer distance you usually shoot at with the rifle. While the eye, nerves, and brain are telegraphing the impulse to the trigger finger to pull, while the lock is working, the firing pin falling, the bullet passing up the bore, and finally the bullet flying from the muzzle to the target, the game is moving; and if it is running it will move a very considerable distance in this interval, and it must be lead accordingly.

Bird and skeet shooting are valuable training for shooting at running game

It will be well for you to consider the lead necessary on running game, because it will differ materially from the lead the shotgun shooter takes on birds or skeet targets. The time of flight from muzzle to target of a .30 caliber pointed bullet at M.V. 2700 f.s. is approximately as follows:

Over 100 yards	.116 second
Over 200 yards	.243 second
Over 300 yards	.384 second
Over 400 yards	.540 second
Over 500 yards	.709 second

These figures will also answer fairly well for other pointed bullets at about the same velocity. To them must be added the unknown lag for the eye, nerves, brain, nerves again, and muscles to squeeze off the trigger after the eye has started the impulse. This is much more with some men than others, and always is a very appreciable interval of time. Its effect is very much less for men who have been shotgun trained, and who continue to swing right through with their target even after squeezing the trigger, than for those who stop the gun when they squeeze. Don't stop the rifle when you squeeze on running game, but try to swing right along with your lead on the target.

We must also add to the above figures the time for the lock to function, the fall of the firing pin, the ignition of the powder, and the time it takes for the bullet to pass up and out of the barrel.

I should say that the human element and these intervals of time will never amount to less than .05 second, and this must be added to the time of flight. Thus at 100 yards the time from when you start to will your squeeze on the trigger until the bullet reaches the target is not less than .166 second.

Antelope on level plains have been known to run at a rate of 40 miles per hour, but I do not think that a deer bounding through a forest ever exceeds 20 miles per hour. Let us assume that speed which amounts to 29.3 feet per second, or 4.86 feet in the .166 second that it takes the bullet to cover 100 yards.

Thus in leading a deer bounding rapidly straight across your front at 100 yards you would theoretically have to lead and will to pull when the front sight was about four feet in front of its chest. If it was bounding off at an angle of 45 degrees a lead that appeared to subtend 2 feet would be approximately correct, at 22½ degrees approximately a foot, while if the deer was bounding straight away no lead at all would be necessary.

This is all pure theory of course, approximately correct as far as it goes. But the distance is never just 100 yards, but usually is very much shorter. The deer is liable to change direction any instant much like a snipe. Moreover it is bounding up and down, possibly five or more feet at every jump. Trees and bushes are continually intervening. Old hunters will tell you to fire when the deer is at the height of a bound, and aim for where the deer will be when it strikes the ground. Will the ground that the deer lands on be a hollow or a rise in the uneven forest floor? Frankly I don't know about all these matters, and I don't believe anyone else does. I have not had enough experience. The few running and bounding deer that I have connected with were at quite short range, and so far as I can tell I just swung onto the front part of the animal and pulled.

Mule deer take much shorter and higher bounds than do white tailed deer. Often they seem to bound up and down like a rubber ball. Hunting around timberline one day I ascended a little knoll and sat down. The country was very open and I

Mule deer take much shorter and higher bounds than white tail deer

could see back along my trail for several hundred yards. As I sat there I saw a mule deer doe wandering along from the left about 150 yards away. As it crossed and smelled my tracks up went its head and away it sailed in high, short bounds. Of course I did not desire to shoot it, but I tried to keep my sights on it. It was absolutely impossible to do so. The doe was bouncing up and down all the time, apparently having as much vertical as horizontal progress. No one could have made that shot with any surety. Many times a bounding deer is just too difficult a shot, and many more times it gets completely out of sight in the woods before you can even get your rifle up to your shoulder. The best of riflemen can be excused for missing or not taking shots like these.

Many times a bounding deer is just too difficult a shot

Trotting or walking deer are a very different matter. The lead necessary is very small. If you will pull when your front sight, or the reticule of your scope is on the point of the chest, you will usually be successful at moderate distances.

Shots at stationary game at very long ranges, such as at a woodchuck or coyote at 250 yards or over, or at a sheep or caribou at 350 yards or more, call for a lot of skill and care. But the problem is not very different from some you will have encountered on the target range. Such shots call for a very steady firing position, prone or sitting with the gunsling, a careful estimate of the distance, an estimate of the direction and velocity of the wind, a hold over to allow for the drop of the bullet, perhaps a hold to one side to allow for the wind, and finally, and as important as anything, a very careful coordination of aim and trigger squeeze. And when you hear that peculiar hollow thump which denotes a hit you feel pretty good.

Usually in firing at stationary game at a considerable distance you have plenty of time for your shot. Ten or fifteen seconds should suffice for all the above preliminaries, and you usually have at least that much time. Frequently you will have all the time you want. Many times I have been able to make holes for my elbows or heels. If the animal is walking around slowly and feeding there will be intervals when it is stationary or practically so, and the shot does not differ from that at a stationary beast. Sometimes when the animal is apparently not disturbed at all you can afford to wait for it to get into a better position for the shot, such as to walk out from behind a bush, or to turn broadside. But don't wait too long because everyone occasionally misses a shot by waiting too long, the animal going into its hole or out of sight behind something. Often the animal may be lying down and partly concealed, and if you whistle it will stand up and offer you a better shot. It is also sometimes possible to cause walking or trotting animals to stop long enough to give you a standing shot by whistling at them, provided that they were not previously aware of your presence.

When you have fired at an animal, and it does not drop to the shot, operate your rifle and get in

Continue to fire at an animal as long as it stands on its feet

another shot as quickly as possible. It is a good rule to continue to fire at any animal as long as it stands on its feet. Often when an animal is shot at and not hit, it will take a couple of jumps and stand still, offering you another fairly easy shot. But in such a case you have no time to spare — get the second shot in as quickly as you can.

If you shoot, and the animal starts off into a dead run, do not be too sure that you have missed it. Deer shot through the heart often act in this way, starting off in a wild, headlong race, and then dropping stone dead after they have run 25 to 200 yards. Or they may rush or stagger along a few yards and then go down. Moose may act in a similar manner, or they may walk off quietly as though they had not been hit, and collapse in a couple of hundred yards from a vital wound. Bear have been known to travel long distances, sometimes several miles, when shot through the heart. Twice I have had rams with their hearts blown to pieces, stand on their feet immovable for ten to fifteen seconds before they toppled over dead. Woodchucks or prairie dogs, blown to pieces, will sometimes crawl into their holes. Coyotes are noted for running long distances after receiving absolutely killing wounds.

So when you have shot at an animal and it has gone off, do not take it for granted that you have missed it. Stand perfectly still and note just where the animal was standing when you shot at it. Go to that spot and search carefully. When a bullet strikes a hoofed animal having brittle hair (deer, sheep, caribou, and moose), it cuts off quite a bunch of the hair, and this falls to the ground or onto a bush. Look carefully where the animal was standing for the hair that would denote a hit. Also follow up the animal's trail for a few yards and look for blood on the bushes or the ground. But even if you do not find any of these indications do not be too sure you have not hit. Some vital wounds do not emit any blood. The chances are that if you have been training yourself in marksmanship you did make a sure killing hit.

Some vital wounds do not emit any blood

Never follow the trail of any animal that you have shot at for more than 25 yards or so immediately, unless you are certain that it went off in a wild death race from a heart shot. Instead sit down, smoke a pipe, and wait for an hour or more. Then track the animal up very slowly, carefully and noiselessly, with your rifle unlocked and ready to fire at any instant. Do not keep your eyes continually on the trail, but watch the ground in front sharply, and keep very alert, watching for any movement in your front, or any slight noise. The chances are you will either find the animal lying dead, or it will be so stiffened up and numbed from its wound that it will not notice you until you get fairly close to it, will then get up slowly from its bed, and offer you another easy shot.

If you had followed it at once, presuming that feeling very sick from its wound it had bedded down in a few hundred yards, it would still be very much on the alert, would hear or see you coming before you got anywhere near it, and it would run or sneak off again without your knowledge, and you never would come up with it. It would probably die later, and if you are a sportsman you want to avoid losing any wounded game because of the suffering it entails.

When approaching a presumably dead animal always do so with extreme caution. Always approach from the animal's rear, and when fairly close throw a stick or stone at it to be sure it is dead. Many hunters have been seriously injured and few killed from approaching too close to the front of an animal that they thought was dead. The beast has jumped up and charged them. Animals of the deer tribe can inflict terrible wounds with both antlers and hoofs.

Occasionally we hear of a hunter being seriously attacked as he stooped over to cut the throat of an animal he had presumably killed. And right here it might be well to speak of this matter of cutting throats. I heard little of this practice until I began to mingle more or less with comparatively inexperienced hunters in the East. The experienced hunter never cuts an animal's throat. The amount of blood that might escape from a throat cut is too small to have effect whatever on the meat, and besides a throat cut spoils the neck skin for mounting. The proper thing to do when you have killed a large animal is to gut and dress it at once. Then if it is too large and heavy for you to carry back to camp, or you do not have a horse or

The experienced hunter never cuts an animal's throat

canoe handy, prop open the belly cut with a stick so it will air and cool inside, cover over very heavily with spruce boughs to keep the whiskey jacks, magpies, and other birds away, and go for assistance, blazing your trail back from the animal if you apprehend any difficulty in finding it again.

There are many other hints and cautions that I might give about the hunting of game, but they belong more properly in a book devoted to hunting than to one on the rifle. I have space here to mention only a few other matters connected with the use of the rifle in the game fields.

When you have seen game never for an instant take your eyes off of it. Don't look at your rifle, or at your feet, or at the ground. It is amazing how long it often takes to find game again if you lose sight of it for an instant. It may not have moved at all, but when you look again you may have forgotten the exact point where it was, and it may take you some time to find it again. Or it may move only behind a bush or bunch of grass while you were not looking, and then when you look again it may be as invisible as though it had gone off several miles, but if you had seen it move you could probably still see a part of it or a dim outline which would tell you precisely where it is.

When you have seen game never for an instant take your eyes off of it

Don't forget about the safety on your rifle. Normally when hunting you should carry your rifle loaded and with the safety set on "SAFE." Don't carry it unloaded and with cartridges in the magazine only with the fancied idea that it is safer that way. Any good rifle is entirely safe when the safety is on. If you had to stop to pump a cartridge from the magazine into the chamber when game appeared quickly you would lose many shots. And besides the noise of pumping cartridges into the chamber will almost always alarm game and send it off. The only exception to this is that when getting on horseback with a lever action rifle having a hammer you should take the cartridge out of the chamber.

Learn to function your safety without noise

Learn to function your safety without noise, and always do it that way. When game suddenly appears in view, or when you expect you will get a shot in a few seconds, throw the safety off at once, and then all the while the safety is off hold the rifle entirely in the ready position, across your chest, right forefinger through the trigger guard, left hand grasping the forearm for a shot, ready to fire instantly. Never take the rifle from this ready position without putting the safety on again. If you have thrown it off, and you feel that you are not going to get a shot in the immediate future, put the safety on again. A lot of accidents have occurred because the hunter forgot to put the safety on again.

And likewise a lot of shots have been missed because the hunter forgot to take the safety off, put the rifle to his shoulder, aimed, and then tried to pull the trigger. This usually so disconcerts one that although he may immediately throw the safety off, he makes a miss on that shot.

When in camp in the game country, always

leave your rifle, loaded and locked, where you can get at it quickly in an emergency. Game has often been known to wander into camp, and you want your rifle where you can get at it right off, and in condition for instant use. Don't lay it on the ground in camp where it is liable to be stepped on or to get dirty. Also a rifle lying on the ground will get damp on the under side, and if it also gets hot on the upper side from the sun you have all the stage set for quickly warping the stock and that may alter the zero and shooting of the rifle.

A very convenient and safe disposal of the rifle in camp is to cut two forked stakes about a foot long. Drive them into the ground, about two feet apart, alongside your bed. Lay the rifle in the forks where it will be up off the ground and where you can get at it instantly day or night. Don't leave it outside the tent at night where it would get wet from dew or rain. When traveling with a pack train, and you halt at your evening camp site, remember that the horses will wander all over the ground in the vicinity. Take your rifle out of your saddle scabbard at once, and hang it high up in a tree where horses will not walk on it or bump against it, and leave it there while you are making camp, and until your tent is up.

When traveling by canoe, and going into rough water or on wind swept lakes, always unbuckle one end of the sling of the rifle and pass it around one of the thwarts of the canoe. Do likewise with the shoulder strap of your rucksack in which you

When in camp in game country, leave your rifle loaded and locked

always carry a small supply of ammunition and a waterproof match box. Then if you are so unlucky or incompetent as to have a canoe upset, at least you have saved your rifle, ammunition, and matches, and incidentally perhaps your life which may depend on these articles. It was Stefansson, the arctic explorer, a hunter-rifleman who lived by his rifle alone for twelve years, who declared that an accident or adventure was always an indication of incompetence.

An accident was always an indication of incompetence

If you are hunting deer in thick forest country where you will never get a shot except in the standing position, take the sling off your rifle and leave it in camp. Otherwise always carry the rifle with the tail-piece of the sling loose, ready to place the sling on your arm in an instant.

In hunting with a scope sighted rifle, take the leather dust caps off and place them in your pocket as soon as you leave camp for the hunt. You should hunt with the dust caps off, except perhaps when it is snowing or raining. It would delay you a lot to have to take them off just prior to the shot. In heavy snow, if you do not have a breech cover or case, wrap your handkerchief around the breech mechanism and scope. Do the same in a dust storm. In snow watch particularly that you do not get snow in the muzzle as that might cause the barrel to burst when fired. Mud in the muzzle would do the same. If unduly apprehensive about snow or mud in the muzzle, carry a small, short jointed cleaning rod in your rucksack or in the butt of the rifle. A field cleaner would not do to clear an obstruction from the bore. In the lodge pole pine forests of the Northwest you may often have to clean the breech mechanism free from the fine pine needles which often fall almost as continuously as snow.

Every evening when the camp work has been done, I always wipe my rifle outside with an oily chamois, and if the rifle has been fired that day I clean the bore as well. To make this cleaning easier and more convenient so I will not neglect it when tired, I have the cleaning kit always convenient in the top of my camp pack. However, to my mind the greatest advantage of the modern non-corrosive primer is that if you are dead tired when you get back to camp you can safely put off cleaning the bore until the next morning, but no longer. If your ammunition contains chlorate primers of course you have to clean with water that night to avoid rust in the bore.

In a first rate game country it is wise not to have your rifle out of reach even for an instant. I have occasionally been lucky enough to have hunted in countries where I took my rifle along even when I went to the spring for a kettle of water, or down to the brook to catch a mess of trout for breakfast or supper. How I love such a country, not so much for the opportunity it offers for shooting, as for its wilderness, beauty, and the thrill of finding one's way through it alone and unaided.

In first rate game country never leave your rifle out of reach even for an instant

From time to time, the hunter faces situations that do not allow him the luxury of taking time to draw a careful bead, get his breath under control, and squeeze off a careful shot. A whitetail spooked from its bed does not wait for a second opinion; it knows beyond any doubt that there is urgent business a county away demanding immediate attention. Such situations require what we normally call a snap shot, and that shot has to be based on a snap decision about whether it is feasible. In the following selection, which appeared in a 1999 issue of Field & Stream, *Wayne Van Zwoll looks at such shots in a practical fashion.*

Wayne Van Zwoll discusses snap shooting

SNAP SHOOTING

The buck catapults through the opening and is gone. You play it again in your mind, slow motion. Your niece could parallel park a Greyhound where that deer crossed. Why didn't you shoot? If the buck had been a ruffed grouse, you could have easily fired both barrels.

The difference between pointing a shotgun and aiming a rifle isn't that great. In both cases, you must align the barrel with the target. Sights on a rifle simply help you align it more precisely. Up close, however, precision becomes less important than speed. Hitting the watermelon-size vitals of a deer far away takes time. At 20 yards, you should be able to hit a watermelon in no time at all. In fact, you do it with a shotgun routinely. When you really clobber a grouse or a clay target, the center of your pattern passes within a few inches of the mark.

Snap shooting a rifle is part art, part science. It is not merely throwing bullets at game and hoping for a hit. It is a high form of marksmanship, fluid but orchestrated, the equivalent of a smooth give-and-go in basketball. Snap shooting means taking quick aim, sometimes with a moving rifle, and ticking off a few carefully rehearsed procedures in rapid succession — or perhaps in the wink of an eye. Some tips:

Your rifle: Short, lightweight rifles come up quickly, but if you pare too many ounces the rifle won't swing smoothly. Balance matters. A slight tilt to the muzzle is what you want. The right balance is easier to feel than to describe. You won't use a sling for snap shooting, so the best kind is slender and lightweight, adjusted to hang loose. Wide, heavy carrying straps disturb your aim when they swing, and tight straps interfere with your forward hand.

Stock fit is crucial. Your eye must center the sights right away. Take this test: Put a thumbtack in the wall. Rifle in hand, step back and focus on the tack. Now close your eyes, quickly shoulder your rifle, and open your eyes as soon as the comb hits your cheek. The sights should be on target. If not, the stock comb may need work or the sight a repositioning. Sometimes you can speed up your shot by shortening the stock, especially if you wear heavy hunting clothes.

Use a low-powered scope for a wide field of

Snap shooting is part art, part science

view. Mount it low and well forward. High scope mounts slow you down by forcing you to raise your head to search for the target. A scope too far back makes you too careful in cheeking the stock. Attack the comb! You should see the scope's full field with your head as far forward as is comfortable. Experiment with scope placement, starting with the ocular lens directly over the rear guard screw.

Attack the comb!

Your technique: Fast shooting starts with good footwork. Keep your feet shoulder-width apart but your left foot advanced a few inches toward the target. Keep your weight on the balls of your feet, knees and hips relaxed. Think of how you'd shoot a grouse. Keep your right elbow high (to form a pocket in your shoulder), your left hand well forward, about in the middle of the forend (to better control the muzzle).

When still hunting through the woods, stop where you can shoot. Bucks often break cover during a pause in your movement. Pick places where your feet can be quickly placed for a shot and where you have shot alleys in several directions. Have your rifle in hand, not slung on your shoulder. Keep an elastic chest strap on your binoculars so that there's no interference when you bring the rifle up quickly. In cold weather, wear slitted mitts that free the fingers of your right hand. Keep that hand in a large jacket pocket if the day is especially bitter. You won't have time to shuck a glove when a buck streaks away.

Remember that a snap shot is still an aimed shot. If your sights aren't on target (or aren't properly leading the target), you will miss. Rehearse your shooting routine, releasing the safety, shouldering, aiming and dry firing at the thumbtack. Do it over and over, with hunting clothes on, beginning a smooth trigger squeeze as soon as you cheek the stock.

The snap shot is still an aimed shot

Snap shooting is really a quick recital of learned procedures. Practice them, and come deer season, all the openings in the woods will be just a little wider.

Part II

THE HANDGUN

Handguns have always enjoyed great popularity with American marksmen. They may not have been the firearm of choice among settlers in pioneer days, nor did they come first with hardy frontiersmen or the intrepid adventurers known as mountain men. Yet well before the Civil War, sidearms (as handguns were commonly called) enjoyed favored status with officers. Even enlisted men carried sidearms (when they could afford them; they were not standard issue at the time). The role of the revolver on the Western frontier is well known, although it should be noted that Hollywood has given us a bit of a distorted image of frontier days and firearm ways. It was long guns, not handguns, that won the West.

By the turn of the last century, handguns had become a standard part of armament in military circles, and most competitive shooting with pistols and revolvers focused on the military. For example, it is little short of amazing just how many of the great gun writers of yesteryear, and especially those who specialized in handguns,

By the turn of the century, handguns became a standard part of military armament

carried officer-rank military titles. Many of them were career military men.

Although competitive shooting with handguns has been well established for more than a century, serious interest in handguns as hunting firearms is of more recent origin. Elmer Keith did a great deal to popularize their use in the hunting fields, and today's hunters relish the challenge of hunting big game and small game alike with handguns. Indeed, it is not at all unusual to see a handgun topped with telescopic sights, something that would have been unheard of two generations ago. Whether it be plinking at rabbits with a .22 or dealing with whitetails with a large-caliber pistol, handgunning adds a dimension and an extra degree of challenge to hunting that many enjoy. In such situations, as in competitive shooting, marksmanship is at a premium.

Handgunning adds a dimension to hunting that many enjoy

In this section of the book, we look at handguns from a variety of perspectives. These range from material that is currently an integral part of the U.S. Army's training procedures, to more traditional coverage that retains all its applicability despite advances in technology and in the performance of firearms.

VII
HANDGUN BASICS

With handguns, to an even greater extent than with long guns, mastery of marksmanship begins with the basics. Arguments on the best grip and stance will endure as long as the sport itself, but no matter what the individual handgunner's preferences when it comes to these and related matters, getting them right and performing them in a consistent fashion is of paramount importance. Those of us who have watched too many shoot-'em-up westerns may be inclined to think that accuracy with a handgun goes right along with lightning-fast draws and revolvers fanned so rapidly they might be mistaken for semiautomatics.

In truth, sure and steady wins the marksman's prize in most cases, and anyone who has doubts in that regard needs to visit the site of the famed shootout at the OK Corral. How anyone came out of the tight quarters — almost point-blank range — of that gun battle is amazing. Or, to put matters in another perspective, the gunslingers who were present proved beyond doubt that they were anything but superb marksmen.

Here the incomparable Jack O'Connor (first and foremost a rifleman, but an individual who knew a great deal about all types of firearms) and four noted authorities on handgun marksmanship look at some of the key factors in accurate shooting with pistols and revolvers.

●

Expert Julian S. Hatcher examines the pros and cons of pistols and revolvers

In this piece from his Textbook of Pistols and Revolvers *(1935), Julian S. Hatcher takes a careful, considered look at the pros and cons of the two basic types of handguns. It should be noted that his use of the word* automatic *to describe pistols that used clips or magazines was commonplace in the era during which he wrote. In today's parlance, the proper description would be "semiautomatic" (meaning a new squeeze of the trigger is required to fire each round). Hatcher's evaluation of types of handguns is a sensible one, and shooters contemplating purchase of such a firearm would be well advised, before spending their hard-earned cash, to consider what he has to say about the merits of each type.*

REVOLVER VS. AUTOMATIC PISTOL

In late years there has been a great deal of discussion as to the relative merits of the revolver and the automatic pistol. A great host of automatic pistols have been invented and manufactured with varying degrees of success. In military sizes the automatics have reached the greatest perfection, and have been adopted by the United States Army, and by many other important armies. In pocket sizes automatic pistols are sold throughout the world in very large numbers. Nevertheless, the revolver has been holding its own during all this period, and is now manufactured in quantities apparently as large as ever. It is difficult to say which is actually better, the revolver or the automatic pistol. Each has its own distinct advantages and. disadvantages, which the reader must decide for himself. I will enumerate some of the advantages and disadvantages of each type of weapon.

The revolver has the following advantages:

Advantages of the revolver

1. It is an old standard weapon, everyone is used to it, and most everyone knows something about how to handle it.
2. The revolver is safer for inexperienced people to handle and to carry than the automatic pistol.
3. The mechanism of a revolver allows the trigger pull to be better than that of the average automatic.
4. A misfire does not put a revolver out of action.
5. A revolver will handle satisfactorily old or partly deteriorated ammunition which gives reduced velocities that would jam an automatic.

Among the principal disadvantages of a revolver as compared to an automatic are the following:

Disadvantages of the revolver

1. It is more bulky to carry.
2. The grip is generally not as good.
3. It is slower to load.
4. It is hard to clean after firing.
5. It is harder to replace worn or broken parts on a revolver than on an automatic.
6. Replacement of a worn or corroded barrel is a factory job.
7. Worn or poorly made weapons are subject to variable accuracy, due to improperly lining up cylinder or due to not locking cylinder properly in line with barrel.

Advantages of the pistol

The advantages of the automatic pistol are:

1. It has a better grip — fits the hand and points naturally.
2. It is more compact for the same power.
3. It is easier to load than a revolver.
4. It is easier to clean.
5. In case of a worn or corroded barrel a new one can be put in at small expense without sending the gun to the factory.
6. It gives a greater number of shots for one loading than a revolver.
7. It gives greater rapidity of fire and greater ease of rapid fire.
8. There is no gas leakage or shaving of bullets.

The automatic pistol, on the other hand, has some serious disadvantages, among which are the following:

1. The ammunition must be perfect. Old and deteriorated ammunition will cause a jam.

2. A misfire stops the functioning of the gun.

3. When the gun is kept loaded for long periods of time the magazine spring is under a tension and may deteriorate, causing trouble.

4. The automatic can not use blanks or reduced loads.

5. It has a poorer trigger pull than the revolver.

6. The magazine action requires a jacketed bullet which is not as good for practical use as a lead bullet.

7. The automatic pistol is more dangerous to handle, especially for inexperienced people, owing to the fact that after one shot it is always cocked and loaded.

8. It is not well adapted to reloading. It throws away the empty shells at each shot.

9. Many automatics eject empty cartridges toward the face, causing flinching.

10. It can not be fired from the hip as it throws cartridges into the shooter's face.

11. It throws out empty cases on the ground to remain as evidence.

12. It can not be fired from the pocket without jamming.

13. In some makes the hammer bites the hand or the slide strikes the hand and causes injury.

Disadvantages of the pistol

By far the most serious of all these disadvantages of the automatic pistol is its inability to use ammunition that is not up to the mark. For a weapon to use under any and all conditions where failure to function may be fatal, and where any and all kinds of ammunition may have to be used, the revolver is still far and away ahead of the automatic pistol, and is likely to remain so indefinitely. It is, therefore, still the choice of explorers and others to whom the possession of a hand arm in functioning condition is of paramount importance.

On the other hand, the automatic pistol is generally considered superior to the revolver for military use, where the ammunition supply is of known quality and spare parts are available.

The .45 Army automatic became extremely popular during the World War, and the experience with this arm at that time thoroughly justified the judgment of the Army authorities in adopting this as the service side arm for all branches of the Army.

For home defense use the small pocket automatic, which is usually hammerless, has the disadvantage of frequently lying for long periods of time with the magazine full of cartridges and the safety on. The magazine spring and mainspring may thus be kept under compression for perhaps years at a time. If at the same time the ammunition deteriorates from age, the result may be that the arm will not function when needed. Moreover, these small automatics always have safeties, which are an excellent thing for one who uses these guns enough to know all about how they function; but if one of these weapons becomes needed in an emergency by some member of the household who does not know much about using hand arms, it may very well occur, and has occurred, that the user was not familiar with the method of manipulating the safety and therefore could not fire the gun. These disadvantages are not shared by the revolver.

When it comes to readily understandable, to-the-point advice on handling a firearm, Jack O'Connor stands in a class by himself. Here, in a selection from The Hunter's Shooting Guide *(1978), he offers a fairly detailed look at establishing intimacy with a handgun. His thoughts on flinching, the value of dry firing, and the value of getting started with a .22 are all of particular note.*

Jack O'Connor on getting started with the handgun

BEGINNING WITH A HANDGUN

When the average American picks up a handgun and attempts to fire a shot he is about as much at home with it as he would be with a pair of chopsticks. Usually he couldn't hit the southern exposure of a northbound elephant at 30 yards. How come?

Possibly it's the influence of horse operas American kids have been seeing for the past 50 years. Unconsciously the impressionable lads absorb the technique of movie revolver shooting and imitate it. The heroes and likewise the villains grasp the pistol far over to the side. Before they cut a shot loose, they bring their revolvers back as far as the right ear. Then throw them forward in the general direction of what they plan to hit. Bang! go the revolvers. Down go the redskins, the villains, or whatever they are shooting at.

All this is excellent entertainment. The movements are fluid, the effect dramatic; but as a system of shooting a handgun it is enough to make a strong man wring his hands in anguish. The young moviegoers eat it up, not realizing that what they are seeing is not handgun shooting at all but instead a formal figure in a ballet. Watch a group of children playing cowboys and Indians some day and you'll find they handle their cap pistols just like the cowboys in the oat operas. Then when the time comes for them to shoot a real sure-enough handgun, they try their cap-pistol technique and can't hit anything. Often their beginning interest in handguns is killed because of their initial failures.

The handgun is the most difficult of all firearms to learn to shoot well

It is true that the handgun is the most difficult of all firearms to learn to shoot well, but if anyone starts right it isn't nearly as difficult as many believe. The lad who gets a suitable handgun, who starts using good form, and who practices will be shooting well before he knows it.

What sort of a handgun should the beginner select to start out with? The first fairly serious handgun shooting I ever did was with, of all things, a

.38 Special, but I wouldn't advise most beginners to tee off with a gun having that much blast and recoil. I do not think there is much argument but that the beginner's gun should be a .22. The little rimfire cartridge has many advantages. It is inexpensive, and can be obtained about anywhere in the world that ammunition is sold. But even more important is the fact that the .22 has a mild report and very little recoil. As we shall see, this is of prime importance, since flinching and yanking the trigger are the major reasons for poor handgun shooting.

What type should this .22 be, automatic or revolver? You have me there! For whatever the reason, I shoot somewhat better with a revolver than I do with an automatic. Possibly that's just one of my oddball notions, like my notion that I can do better shooting out in the field with a double-barrel shotgun than I can with a pump or automatic. Actually a very high percentage of crack handgun shots prefer the automatic because of its superiority in timed and rapid fire. Probably the revolver is somewhat *safer* because it is so much easier to see quickly if the weapon is loaded or not. The revolver also has the advantage of being able to handle .22 Shorts, Longs, or Long Rifle cartridges as the shooter chooses.

A high percentage of crack handgun shots prefer the automatic pistol

On the other hand, a .22 automatic with a fairly short barrel and good sights is an excellent supplementary weapon for the sportsman — short, flat, more convenient to carry than the bulkier revolver. The .22 automatic is a fine little weapon to pick up small game with, probably better than the revolver. Often I have seen grouse sit in a tree while a man with an automatic missed three or four times. The birds seem frightened less by the noise than they do by the movement of the shooter's thumb in the recocking of the revolver. Run-of-the-mine handgun shot though I am, I have eaten a lot of grouse and rabbits that I have plucked off with handguns. They tasted nice indeed. On one abortive sheep and elk hunt when my companions and I didn't get any real meat until the trip was almost over, we would have had to live on pancakes and oatmeal if one of my companions hadn't taken along a Colt Woodsman. As it was, we very largely subsisted on blue grouse and biscuits — and biscuits are a lot better with blue grouse than they are without. A rugged character I knew once walked 600 miles across the mountains and tundra of the subarctic in the dead of winter on snowshoes with a Hudson Bay blanket and a Smith & Wesson .22 target revolver. Mostly he ate ptarmigan and snowshoe rabbits, but he also killed a Dall sheep and four caribou with that little handgun.

The beginner should choose a handgun with adjustable sights

Whatever sort of a .22 our beginner selects, though, it should have adjustable sights. It is often said that no one can do an exact job of sighting in a rifle for another. It is even more true of a handgun. A revolver that is laying them in the middle of a 10-ring for one shooter may be clear out of the black for another. People see their sights differently. They hold differently. Because of different ways of holding, the handgun recoils differently and gives an entirely different point of impact. The same gun will shoot two different bullet weights to different points of impact and the same bullet at different velocities to different points of impact.

Nonadjustable sights are all right for close-range self-defense and military work, but the person who wants to do target shooting, who wants to knock over small game, or who wants to astonish the girl friend by making a tin can roll along the ground at a respectable distance wants a handgun sighted so precisely that he can hit a fairly small mark.

For target shooting, the common practice is to sight in a handgun with what is known as the "6 o'clock hold." Aim is taken at the bottom of the bulls eye, so that a thin white line can be seen between the top of the front sight and the bottom of the bull. The sights are then adjusted so that the bullet strikes in the center of the bull. Such a system is by no means universal even among competitive target shots. Some of the very best hold right into the bull—or sight in to put the bullet right where the top of the front sight rests. This is the way the plinker, tin-can roller, and small-game shooter should sight in, since obviously it would be fatal to have the bullet striking 3 inches high at 25 yards, let us say.

Tenseness is probably the principal enemy of precision

As in most shooting, tenseness on the part of the handgun shot is probably the principal enemy of precision. Take a look at a crack shot and he usually looks at ease, relaxed, almost sloppy. If he is going to be a topflight shooter he has to be, since tense muscles produce tremors and tremors make for poor shooting.

The first step then in learning to handle a handgun is to take an easy relaxed stance with the weight distributed evenly on both feet. Most good shots face half away from the target. I have seen many, though, who face the target and some who face away from the target at a right angle. The main thing is to feel comfortable and relaxed. The left hand can be put in the trousers pocket, hooked in the belt anywhere so it feels natural.

The handgun should be an extension of the arm

The handgun itself should be an extension of the arm, and a line drawn from the point of the shoulder to the V formed by the thumb and trigger finger should pass right through the sights. The arm, of course, should be straight, not bent.

The shooter should have a feeling of holding the gun with the pad of muscles at the base of his thumb and behind the large joint of his trigger finger while the gun rests on his fourth finger. If he does this and gets this feel, he should be grasping his handgun lightly but firmly. Depending on the size of his hand and length of his index finger, he will squeeze off his shot with the end of his index finger, somewhere between the last joint and the tip. He will *not* stick his whole finger through and squeeze with the second joint as the cowboys in the horse operas do. His object is to hit something and not simply to make a noise and look picturesque.

Holding a fairly heavy handgun out at the end of a straight arm is not the easiest or most natural thing in the world, and anyone who wants to become a fairly good handgun shot can well practice strengthening those muscles. He can do dry firing, of which more later, or he can hold a milk bottle at full length.

The ideal way to learn to shoot a handgun would be to go through a course of dry firing for a couple of weeks before buying any powder. Possibly that is asking too much, because beginners like noise and action. However, 75 percent of what can be learned by actual shooting can also be learned cheaper and easier by dry firing.

Most accurate handgun sights are of the Patridge type, with square notch in the rear sight and square blade front sight. With such sights elevation is controlled by seeing that the front sight is on the level with the rear sight and windage by seeing that the front sight is in the middle of the square cut of the rear sight — by seeing the same amount of light on each side of the front sight.

Good shotgun shots see the end of the barrel only vaguely. Instead they concentrate on the bird or clay target they are trying to hit. The handgun shot is exactly the opposite. If he is to hit much he must pay more attention to his sights than he does

Good shotgun shots see the end of the barrel only vaguely

to his target. Actually very high scores have been fired by turning the paper around and aligning the sights simply on the middle of the target. The bull's-eye would not be seen at all, yet in many cases scores would be better than the same shooter could fire by aiming at the bull! *It is absolutely fatal to let the target distract the shooter's attention from his sights!*

The beginner with the handgun is shocked and disillusioned when be discovers that he cannot hold his weapon still. Instead the doggoned front sight wiggles around in a manner to drive one nuts. Unless he is carefully coached or has read and followed some sort of elementary instructions like these, he almost always falls into the bad habit of trying to grab off a bull when the sights look just right. He thus gets into the habit of trigger jerking — and no trigger jerker can ever hit much with a handgun.

There is only one way to begin shooting a handgun

There is but one way for anyone to begin shooting a handgun and that is to keep the sights looking as good as possible and then to keep increasing pressure on the trigger until the gun goes off. Anyone who can get that through his noggin and who has enough will power to practice it is already a pretty good shot. *The wild shots come not because one cannot hold the gun steady but because of jerks and flinches.*

The handgun shooter must concentrate on his sight picture, squeeze easily and steadily, and forget when the gun is going off. If he does that he can rapidly become a pretty good handgun shot.

I am just a catch-as-catch-can handgun shot. There is absolutely but one way for me to do fairly well with any handgun — and that's it. When I begin to think about when the gun is going off, I am sunk. If I ever try to catch 10 as it rides by I am likewise sunk. I have *got* to let the gun go off by itself.

But what about genuinely good handgun shots? One told me that he knew just about when his gun was going off. Another told me he knew exactly when his gun was going off. Another assured me that he could hold his handgun rock-steady for a moment while he squeezed. But no matter what the hotshots say, the average shooter becomes pretty good only by being relaxed and comfortable, by paying more attention to his sight picture than he does to the target, and by squeezing and forgetting that his gun is ever going to go off. This business of steady holding takes care of itself, as the longer one practices, the more one shoots, the more nearly steady he can hold a handgun. He never will hold it absolutely steady and should not expect to.

The average shooter becomes good only by being relaxed

The man who starts right with a handgun and does not form a lot of bad habits he has to break is lucky indeed. The man who knows how to stand, who holds his handgun properly, and who has learned to relax, who knows the sight pictures is all important, and who has convinced himself that the way to shoot properly is to keep squeezing and let the hold take care of itself is already a better shot than the average casual plinker. Then with a moderate amount of practice, this person will soon become good.

To some people accurate shooting with a handgun becomes a genuine challenge simply because it is the most difficult of all shooting skills to master. The shotgun shooter can give quite a flinch and the spread of the pattern will cover up for him. Flinching is much more serious with a rifle, but the great weight and inertia of the rifle cut down the penalties for flinching and jerking the trigger, although at that they are serious enough. With the handgun, jerking and flinching are absolutely fatal.

With the handgun, jerking and flinching are absolutely fatal

Not long ago I was amusing myself by shooting from 50 yards at clay trap targets set up in a sandbank with a .44 Special. Of course, I missed a lot, but when I hit one I got a genuine thrill of achievement. Even greater was my feeling of satisfaction because I didn't ever miss one very far. Another time I had a Smith & Wesson K-22 with me on a big game hunt. One night we were on a jack camp, reduced to flour, butter, jam, and a few cans of vegetables. We had a 20-gauge shotgun along for grouse but that day we were afraid of the noise it would make since we had located two banks of rams which we planned to stalk in the morning. With .22 shorts I knocked over a half-dozen big tender and trusting blues. We cut them up, floured them, and fried them in deep fat. Never have I eaten a better meal. It put strength in my legs, ambition in my head, and next day my companion and I went up and got those two big rams. A little ability with a pistol or revolver comes in pretty handy at times.

I know of no type of shooting which lends itself any better to dry firing than the handgun. Anyone who wants to get good should do a lot of it. A miniature target on the wall of a room is all anyone needs. If he practices squeezing off dry shots at this for fifteen minutes a day, he'll be surprised at how much his scores will improve on the range.

A. L. A. Himmelwright discusses essentially the same subject that Jack O'Connor does in the previous selection, but his perspective is a quite different one. His in-depth look at pulling the trigger addresses in a timeless fashion one of the two most common reasons for inaccurate handgun shooting (flinching being the other one). Similarly, his thoughts on target practice, though written generations ago, remain just as valid today as they were when the ink was drying on the first print run of Pistol and Revolver Shooting *(1915), from which this selection is taken.*

A. L. A. Himmelwright discusses trigger pulling and target practice

HINTS TO BEGINNERS

FIRING

With the pistol or revolver in the right hand cock the hammer with the thumb, making sure that the trigger finger is free from the trigger and resting against the forward inner surface of the trigger guard. In cocking the piece have the barrel pointing upward. Then extend the arm upward and forward, so that when you assume your firing position the piece will point about twenty degrees above the bull's-eye. With your eyes fixed on the bull's-eye at VI o'clock inhale enough air to fill the lungs comfortably and lower the piece gradually until the line of the sights comes a short distance below the bull's-eye. At the same time gradually increase the pressure on the trigger directly backward, so that when the sights are pointing at the bull's-eye the hammer will fall.

Be careful not to pull the trigger with a jerk, but ease it off with a gentle squeeze, so as not disturb the arm. Accustom yourself not to close the eye when the hammer falls, but note carefully where the line of the sights actually points at the instant that the hammer falls. You will, no doubt, find it almost impossible to pull the trigger at the moment the sights are just right. The hammer will fall when the line of sights may point a little too high or too low, or to one side or the other of the bull's-eye; but patient practice will correct this, and in time you will be able to let off the arm at the right moment.

Pulling of the trigger is a very delicate operation

The pulling of the trigger is a very delicate operation; it is, in fact, the most important detail to master — the secret of pistol and revolver shooting. If the trigger is pulled suddenly, in the usual way, at the instant when the sights appear to be

properly aligned, the aim is so seriously disturbed
that a wild shot will result. To avoid this, the pressure on the trigger must always be steadily applied, and while the sights are in line with the
bull's-eye. It is, of course, impossible to hold the
arm absolutely still, and aim steadily at one point
while the pressure is being applied to the trigger;
but, in aiming, the unsteadiness of the shooter will
cause the line of the sights to point above the
bull's-eye, then below it, to one side of it, and then
to the other, back and forth and around it. Each
time the line of the sights passes over the bull's-
eye the smallest possible increment of additional
pressure is successively applied to the trigger until
the piece is finally discharged at one of the moments that the sights are in correct alignment.
Long and regular practice alone will give the necessary training of the senses and muscles to act in
sufficient harmony to enable one to pull the trigger
in this way at the right moment for a long series of
shots. A "fine sympathy" must be established between the hand, the eye, and the brain, rendering
them capable of instant cooperation.

After obtaining a fair idea of aiming, etc.,
watch carefully when the hammer falls, and note
if it jars the piece and disturbs the aim. If not, you
are holding the arm properly. If the aim is disturbed, you must grip the arm tighter or more
loosely, or move your hand up or down on the
handle, or otherwise change your method of holding the piece until your "hold" is such that you can

A "fine
sympathy"
must be
established
between
the hand,
eye, and
brain

snap the hammer and the aim remain undisturbed. This aiming and snapping drill is largely practised by expert shots indoors, when they do not have the opportunity to practise regularly out-of-doors.

TARGET PRACTICE

If your first actual shooting is done at the range of a club, it is best to ask one of the members to coach you until you get accustomed to the rules, etc. A target will be assigned to you, and you will repair to the firing point and load your arm. It is well to let your coach fire the first shot or two, to see if your piece is sighted approximately right. If so, you are ready to begin shooting. If, after several shots, you are convinced that the bullet does not strike where it should, the arm is not properly sighted for you.

In adjusting the sights you will find it an advantage to remember a very simple rule: To correct the rear sight, move it in the same direction as you would the shots on the target to correct them, or move the front sight in the opposite direction. Most target arms have the front sight non-adjustable, and the rear sight adjustable for both windage and elevation. A few arms have interchangeable or adjustable front sights for elevation. Move the sights a little at a time, according to the foregoing rules, until they are properly aligned. A few ten-shot scores should then be fired for record. As you become accustomed to the range, rules, etc., you will feel more at ease. This will inspire confidence, and your shooting will improve correspondingly.

Do not have your sights too fine. Fine sights are much more straining on the eyes, and have no advantage over moderately coarse sights. The rear sights as generally furnished are purposely made with very small notches, so as to enable individuals to make them any desired size.

Do not have your sights too fine

It is well to have the trigger pull at least ¼ of a pound greater than the minimum allowed by the rules. If much used, the pull sometimes wears lighter; and if there is little or no margin, you run the risk of having your arm disqualified when you wish to enter an important match.

Never use other ammunition in your arm than that for which it is chambered. A number of accidents and much difficulty have resulted from wrong ammunition. In the same caliber the actual diameter of the bullets frequently varies considerably, and a few shots, even if they should not prove dangerous, may lead the barrel, and thus cause much delay and annoyance. When a barrel is "leaded" from any cause it will become inaccurate. In such cases, particles of lead usually adhere to the inside of the barrel at or near the breech. A brass wire brush, of suitable size to fit the barrel, will generally remove it. When this fails, carefully remove all oil, cork up the opposite end of the barrel and fill it with mercury, letting the latter remain in the barrel until the lead is removed.

Occasionally the powder is accidentally omitted in loading a cartridge. When the primer explodes, the bullet may be driven partly through the barrel and remain in it. When this happens, whether from this cause or any other, always be careful to push the bullet out of the barrel before firing another shot. If the bullet is not removed, and another shot is fired, the barrel will be bulged and ruined. This may occur with a light gallery charge.

When shooting the .22-caliber long rifle cartridge, there will be an occasional misfire. In withdrawing the cartridge the bullet will stick in the barrel and the powder spill into the action. To prevent this, hold the barrel vertically, with the muzzle up, and withdraw the shell carefully. Then remove the bullet in the barrel with a cleaning rod; or extract bullet from a new cartridge, inserting the shell filled with powder into the chamber back of the bullet and fire it in the usual manner.

Do not use BB caps in any pistol that you value. They are loaded with a composition of fulminate of mercury in combination with other substances that cause rusting and the bullets have no lubrication. These caps will ruin a barrel in a very short time. The .22-caliber conical ball caps are loaded with black powder, and the bullets are lubricated, making this a much better cartridge; but it is best to adhere to the regular .22 ammunition for which the arm is chambered.

Never, under any circumstances, shoot at objects on the heads or in the hands of persons. There is always a possibility of something going wrong, and such risk to human life is unjustifiable, no matter how skilful you may be.

It is necessary to exercise extreme care in practising with the pocket revolver. Some persons delight in practising quick drawing from the pocket and firing one or more shots. This is dangerous work for the novice to attempt. Most of the pocket weapons are double action. If the finger is on the trigger and the arm catches in the pocket when drawing, a premature discharge is likely to result, which is always unpleasant and sometimes disastrous. Practice in drawing the revolver from the pocket or holster should always be begun with the arm unloaded. Only after a fair degree of skill is acquired should actual shooting be attempted. For quick drawing from the pocket the only double-action revolvers that are fairly safe to handle are the S. & W. Safety Hammerless, and the Colt "Double Action," which has a safety notch for the hammer to rest on.

Exercise extreme care in practising with the pocket revolver

Drawing a revolver from a holster is easier and much less dangerous than drawing it from the pocket. Larger and more practical arms are generally carried in holsters, and such arms should be single action in all cases. In practicing with a holster weapon, fasten the holster on the belt, and anchor the belt so that the holster will always be at the same relative position. The holster should be cut out so that the forefinger can be placed on the trigger in drawing. Always carry a loaded revolver with the hammer resting on an empty chamber or between two cartridges.

In the woods, or in localities where such shooting would not be likely to do any harm, it is good practice to shoot at a block of wood drifting down in the current of a swift-flowing stream, at a block of wood or a tin can swinging like a pendulum, from horseback at stationary and moving objects, and from a moving boat at similar objects. Such practice is largely indulged in by cowboys, ranchmen, and others in the western part of the United States. The shooting is generally rapid-fire work with heavy charges at short range, and is to be commended as being extremely practical.

Many reports of wonderful shooting are gross exaggerations

Many of the published reports of wonderful shooting are gross exaggerations. The prowess of the so-called "Gun Men" of New York and other large cities is greatly over-estimated. These criminals do not practice shooting with the fire arms they use but operate by stealth and intrigue which makes them dangerous. They are, in fact, very poor marksmen, few of them being able to hit an object the size of a man more than 15 or 20 feet away.

In shooting a long series of shots with black powder ammunition, when the rules allow it, the barrel should be cleaned and examined every six or ten shots, depending upon the clean-shooting qualities of the ammunition used. It is well to examine the shells, also, and note if the primers have been struck in the center. If not, then some of the mechanism is out of line, and the parts likely to have caused the trouble must be cleaned.

After securing good, reliable arms, stick to them. Much time and progress is frequently lost by buying and trying different arms, ammunition, etc. If in any of your shooting, you should get results that are peculiar and unsatisfactory, make it your business to find out the cause of the difficulty, and remedy it as soon as possible.

"Blazing away" a large quantity of ammunition carelessly and recklessly is absolutely valueless as practice, and is a waste of time. Give your whole attention to your work, and try your very best to place every shot in the center of the bull's-eye.

It is very important to keep a full, detailed record of all your shooting, for comparison, study, etc. A suitable book should be provided for this purpose. Do not fall into the habit of preserving only a few of the best scores; but make it a rule to keep a record of *every shot*, and figure out the average of each day's work. The more painstaking and systematic you are, the more rapid will be your progress. By careful, intelligent work, it is possible to become a fair shot in three or four months, and a first-rate shot in a year.

It is possible to become a first-rate shot in a year

Charles Askins, Jr., had a great deal of practical experience with handguns. They were an integral part of his years as a lawman, he taught

Charles
Askins, Jr.
on starting
out as a
handgun
shooter

their use to military recruits, and he was a top-level competitive shooter. In this piece, "The First Training," taken from Colonel Askins on Pistols & Revolvers *(1980), he looks at putting the proper foot forward (both figuratively and literally) when one starts out.*

THE FIRST TRAINING

Anyone can be a pistol shooter — and a good one — if he can master the trigger pull. That is, if he can mash the trigger at that precise instant when the sights are aligned perfectly on the mark he will be an overnight success. It does not matter whether he grips the gun perfectly, stands perfectly, holds his breath perfectly, and has made a perfect choice of firearm and caliber; all are subordinate to the squash on the trigger.

The great bugaboo to successful trigger manipulation is an overpowering prediliction on the part of the gunner to jerk the trigger and not press it evenly and softly. These flinches are uneven and violent and swing the muzzle wide of the mark. It is my contention that sooner or later some enterprising handgunner is going to find a way to jerk the trigger uniformly. When he does he is going to have the battle won! It takes literally years to achieve a smooth, even balanced trigger squeeze. The laddy-o who will finally stagger onto a system whereby he can make his shots hit dead center and do it with a consistent and uniform trigger

It takes
years to
achieve a
smooth
trigger

yank will show all of us the way! This oracle
hasn't bowed onto the stage as yet and until he
does we must labor along with the only system
we know. A long and hard course of sprouts which
produces results slowly and grudgingly.

The trigger releases the hammer through, usually, the design of a simple sear. To force the trigger out of its notch in the hammer requires a force
of, generally, about 3 to 4 pounds force. This pressure is applied by the index finger of the shooting
hand. On the face of it nothing could appear more
simple than to tighten the first finger just ever so
slightly and thus set the hammer in motion. However, a number of factors are involved which com-
plicate the equation.

To begin with the pistol weighs only 2½
pounds, and when a force of this magnitude is
applied against the gun it is bound to move. If
that force is applied suddenly and violently
as when the trigger is jerked the movement of
the piece is exaggerated. This is only one of the
problems.

While the trigger is being pressed ever so deli-
cately the shooter must keep the sights in precise
alignment with the mark and this requires some
doing. When the gun is extended to full arm's
length from the body it moves, wobbles, trembles
and gyrates. As a matter of fact it is never entirely still. The business then is terribly complicated by the necessity for keeping the sights
trained, one with the other, and the both with the

At full
arm's
length, the
handgun is
never
entirely still

bullseye, meanwhile struggling mightily to control the tendency of arm, hand and firearm to sway, and all the time essaying to press the trigger only during those brief intervals when the gun is bearing dead on.

To be a really first-rate marksman, with the ability to press on the trigger smoothly, evenly, and gently, meanwhile maintaining a proper sight picture, and all the time holding the pistol with such good control as to keep the sights in alignment and press away the last few ounces of force required to set off the hammer necessitates, at a very minimum of not less than two years of constant practice.

If this is discouraging let me remind you that there are an infinite variety of skills in the pistol game. A marksman may be a going-hell-for-leather shooter or he may be just a dub. And as a helter-skelter sort of handgunner maybe gets more fun out of the sport than the bucko who is determined to be nothing less than a champion. It all depends on the *aficion*.

There are an infinite variety of skills in the pistol game

A good trigger should not have a weight of more than 3 to 4 pounds and that one which is nearer the three-pound breaking point is the better. It must be absolutely motionless, that is, when force is placed against it there can be no perceptible movement. Not in the slightest. When the pressure of the trigger finger comes up to 3 pounds the sear should let go cleanly and abruptly, there can be no feeling of sponginess.

There must be a trigger stop so that the very instant the sear is released the trigger comes abruptly against its stop.

To manhandle a trigger the shooter grips the pistol with a very hard grasp, straightens his arms completely, locking both at the elbow, and then he lines the sights one with the other. The only reliable sights for the handgun are the patridge type, i.e. a one-eighth-inch post in front and a square notch behind. The post completely fills the notch and the very top of the front sight is held precisely where the gunner wants the bullet to strike.

The only reliable sights for the handgun are the patridge type

With the sights in good alignment the marksman maneuvers the front post into the very center of his target. As the sight touches this point he places a little pressure on the trigger. Not a great deal of force for if he adds all the 3 pounds needed to fire the gun it will be violently diverted. Only a little force is applied, if it could be measured it would probably not amount to more than three or four ounces. In doing this the pistol is moved off the mark. The gun is never really still and the marksman only puts pressure on the trigger during those all too brief periods when the sights hang dead over the target center.

Once the 4-oz of force is pressed against the trigger the shooter does not relax this force as the sights swing off the center. He holds this and as he carefully works the front post back into the center of the target once more he tightens another 3-4 ounces. Again the gun moves and as at first he holds his accumulated pressure and slowly and patiently swings the sights back to the target's middle again.

This is kept up, never relaxing the pressure on the trigger, being careful not to inadvertently increase it while the sight is off the center, and finally after maybe as many as a half-dozen tries — squeezing only when the sights are dead center, holding the pressure while they are wide of the target, he finally forces the pistol to fire. The hit will be a fairly good one. This may take a full minute, with some slow-pokes it requires two or three minutes; with the experts it uses up only 2 or 3 seconds. And yet the squeeze of the latter is quite as precise as that of the meticulous one. It is all a matter of practice.

There is a school which advocates that the marksman squeezes and squeezes and is never certain just when the gun is going to fire. This is a bunch of hogwash. The shooter must know his gun and his pull so intimately as to be certain within a fraction of an ounce exactly when the sear will release. Don't ever put any stock in the joker who tells you "just squeeze when the sights are on and the gun will go off when it is dead center." Garbage!

The shooter must know his gun and his pull

If a pistol weighed 40 pounds and the trigger broke at only three, we could punish the trigger in quick time and get away with it. But, unfortunately, this isn't true. The handgun, even the heavy ones do not go more than 3 pounds and a trigger let-off of this weight is common. Because of these irrefutable facts the pressure has to be applied with a great deal of caution.

It is best to grip the gun with both hands. In target match shooting the rules require that only one hand be placed on the pistol but in practice the two-fisted hold is perfectly cricket. I believe in it. You can simply hold a lot steadier, overcome recoil faster and suffer less punishment with the two hands on the grip. I'd recommend you start this way.

The two-handed grip is best

Even tho' both fists are wrapped around the stock, the control hand is the right. It is this index finger which works against the trigger, while it may be OK to hold the pistol with both hands only the one finger sets off the charge. Lay it against the iron midway of the very end of the digit and the first joint. All the nerves come to an end here and this is the most sensitive part of the finger. To put only the tip against the trigger means that both of the joints must be bent quite abruptly. This makes possible the placement of the finger at right angles to the trigger — and in exact prolongation with the axis of the bore. These may seem like inconsequential details but they all help to shoot better.

The second hand, normally, the left, is wrapped around and over the right. The most of the pressure on the gun stock is exerted by the right hand; for all that the grasp of the left is plenty hard. A pistol, regardless of caliber, is never held lightly nor loosely. And the bigger the caliber the harder the pressure!

The pistol is fully extended to arm's length. Both arms that is. And to do this the marksman fully faces the mark. Not at any angle at all, but full-face. This then makes comfortable the full extension of both arms. The elbows are locked, the muscles at the shoulders which support the arms are locked and the body is supported and steadied by a separation of the feet of not less than 20 inches. Some shorties may not straddle out this much and some of the Jordans will separate the heel by a full yard. Every man is a law unto himself. There should be no tendency to lean backward at the hips to hold the gun in firing position and there seems little inducement to lean into the piece in anticipation of the recoil.

The one-handed shooter, the target man who fires the national match course, turns about 45 degrees from the target, separates his feet about the same distance, fully extends his hand, locking the elbow, and with head and body erect looks over the sights. Some one-handed shooters actually turn 90 degrees from the target and in this stance take up more of the recoil from the heavy kicking handguns. It has something to commend it. The only objection, as I have found it, is that the aiming eye must accept all the burden. The left plays a very secondary role since it is sort of around the corner as it were.

It is best when making a beginning to fire two-handed. The shooter progresses more rapidly and once he has attained a certain modicum of skill may experiment with the one-handed firing if he is interested. It most certainly is considerably more difficult and should be attempted only after a lot of shooting with both fists.

The new shooting game called "Practical Pistol Shooting," a training in which the gunner makes a fast draw and triggers off a series of shots in extremely short time periods at silhouette targets set up at comparatively short range, has seen the development of a slightly different shooting stance.

Many of the practical pistol shooters slightly advance the right foot toward the target, bend both knees slightly, fully straighten the left arm but permit a bend in the right at the elbow. This position is OK for fast shooting and altho' it would not do for deliberate slow fire it has been found quite satisfactory for the fast rapid fire. Some gunners push the gun forward with the right hand and pull backward with left. Others reverse this procedure. They believe it not only permits a steadier grasp but also tends to counteract the recoil.

As the pistol is pushed out from the body and as the arms straighten, the aiming eye picks up the sights. The front post is 1/8" in width from top to bottom and the rear notch is a few thousandths larger so that the post fits the rectangular opening with a bit of light to spare on either side of it. A great deal of care wants to be exercised to be doubly sure that ribbon of light is the same on either side. Just as meticulously the shooter wants to be careful the top of the front sight only comes even with the top of the back sight. Not even $\frac{1}{1000}$" below the top nor even half that much above. But precisely!

Too much accent cannot be placed on alignment of the sights

Too much accent cannot be placed on the alignment of the sights. It must be done perfectly. Our best pistol marksmen, shooters like Hershel Anderson and Bill Blankenship, do not focus the shooting eye on the target at all. They focus on the sights on the pistol and see the mark as a secondary sort of thing. This is because the alignment of the front and rear sights is so absolutely important.

As the front sight settles into the back notch, the marksman catches his breath. He does not suck air like a beached trout but simply locks his breath in his throat. If he breathes while he is aiming and squeezing the gun will bobble up and down and a decent let-off is impossible. Hold the breath but if you are so tardy with the shot that holding in becomes strained or painful then the pistol wants to be brought back to the raised pistol position, the air expelled, a rest taken and the whole sequence commenced anew.

Bullseye shooters frequently aim one place and expect to hit another. This is readily accomplished with an adjustable rear sight. The sights are pointed at the 6 o'clock point on the black but the bullet hits dead center. The advantage of this is that the front sight is iron and is usually blackened with a lamp to make it nonreflective and in this Stygian state shows up a lot more clearly against the white paper.

I do not like this system, it is better to sight the pistol to hit the middle of the mark. It does not matter whether the target is in the shape of a bullseye, the silhouette of man or animal, is a knothole, a floating chip in the creek, or a tin can, it is far more practical to zero the gun to hit where it is pointed.

At any rate, and before the first practice the handgun must be sighted in. This should be done at not more than 15 yards if the gunner is a rank beginner. Better that the sights be adjusted by an old hand but if no experienced shooter is available then the tyro should test the piece over a bench and essay the job himself. No pistol as it comes across the counter can be depended upon to be in zero. This is a chore for the new owner and it is extremely important. If he feels that he is not competent to bring the arm to a decent zero then he had better cast about for someone to help him.

When you read his work, you find yourself developing an affinity for William Reichenbach. Quaint phrases and outright quirkiness aside, he writes in an engaging and entertaining fashion. Better still, for the purposes of the present book, he makes good sense. Here, in a piece that comes from his little book Sixguns and Bullseyes *(1936), he takes a practical look at how handguns should*

William Reichenbach on how handguns should be held

be held. Thoughts on the matter have changed appreciably in recent decades, particularly in regard to using a two-handed grip as opposed to only one hand, but what Reichenbach has to say about comfort, feel, and fit is as applicable as ever.

HOLD

A baby, as we know, has little trouble finding the place where the milk grows. To find the proper hold for a Revolver is equally easy. Nobody but a perfect moron will pick the barrel-end as being just as convenient as the other extremity. But right there is where most people stop thinking and that's why we have so many people that can't shoot. There are 14 different ways of holding a soup-spoon, 6 ways of gripping a tomahawk and 431 ways of getting the goat of your mother-in-law, but there is only *one way* to hold the stock of a Revolver.

There is only *one* way to hold the stock of a revolver

"Why be so fussy?" will you say. My dear fellow, telling somebody what the correct hold is, is like an initiation into a Hindu-temple. I always get jittery when I undertake it and I shall go into my grave long before it is time. I have had more than one intelligent pupil who, getting along in jig-time, will suddenly neglect his hold. They all have a way of compressing their lips and putting the glint of stubbornness in their iris. Here I am, trying to convince the thickhead that his progress will stop at "80" or thereabouts. (Mind you, I am doing it for nothing.) And he had promised so faithfully not to branch out on his own until he got to his goal.

Well, in this Manual the pupil can't talk back! So listen brother: There is only *one* correct hold! Get it? Thank you!

First off, we must realize that holding the stock of a Revolver should entail no physical strain — the gun should feel natural. We have some apostles who jeer about "ladylike grip" and so on. Those birds, probably, never have shown anything in the way of fine shooting. Just don't pay any attention! You can please only one master and listening to a number of "know-it-alls" will only set you back. Alright, we place the stock between the middle finger and the ball of the thumb. Then we drape the other fingers lightly wherever they feel comfortable. Got that? Now place your thumb on the latch — and presto!

Mind you, just drape the fingers around the stock, and do *not* touch the stock with your fingertips at all.

The lower part of the trigger finger touches the frame and should steady it. The little finger, also with its lower portion, does the same further down the stock.

The action of the first two digits of the triggerfinger is being dealt with under the chapter entitled Squeeze.

No pressure in any part of your hand, mind you! That seems to be the whole secret of HOLD.

However, it may not be amiss to amplify this statement. There is a reason for everything, as you will see presently.

Suppose, we practice the thing a little —

Just a minute! Don't pick up the Revolver like that — Take your hand off the gun! Are you a right-hander? Alright, pick the gun up with your *left* hand and *fit* it to your right. The idea is to give your shooting hand every possible help. You need it!

A handgun is not a blackjack or a club that must be gripped tensely. Violence or noticeable pressures are oriented in the cylinder and barrel, not in your hand.

Let's analyze the situation! Not only for the sake of correct learning, but also as an aid in acquiring consistency. Your middle-finger has the function to support the weight of the gun. It is placed where the trigger-guard meets the grip.

The middle-finger has the function to support the weight of the gun

You recall that the other fingers were placed below, first the ring-and then the little finger. Only if you were very stubborn would you wish to change this order.

Alright! Now, these fingers touching the *front* of the grip, would tend to make the gun tilt downward. We don't want that! Here is where nature comes to our assistance. As you will observe, the ball of the thumb is still unemployed. How about it? Right! Place that against the back strap (The rear-edge of the grip) and — there we are. No more tilting, what?

But, we can't have the thumb floating around idly. Lay it on the latch.

Contrary to the beginner's usual conception, the gun must be held lightly! Just firmly enough to take care of a little bit of recoil. This light hold is beneficial in many ways. It tires you less. The gun remains steadier. Your motions and reactions are less acute — If you can bring yourself to regard the Revolver as a delicate instrument, you have gained much.

How does it feel?

We agree that the weapon is supported by the middle-finger; in fact, it literally hangs on it. Close to the second joint and on the side of the middle-finger (i.e. the side nearer the thumb) is the point of support. On the revolver, the corresponding point is directly in the rear of the trigger guard. This point serves also as a fulcrum. The pressure exerted by the middle, ring and little finger towards the rear is opposed by the ball of the thumb. The *vertical* movement of the muzzle, caused by the working of the mechanism and recoil, is checked by the thumb resting on the cylinder latch and by the ball of the thumb. The *horizontal* movement of the muzzle is governed by the palm and the sides of the trigger-and little fingers, as mentioned before and again the thumb, by its strategic position on the cylinder latch, comes into passive function.

By now you will readily appreciate the importance of what I said previously. *Do not touch* the revolver grip *with your finger tips*! The slight pressure they exert against the left side of the stock, the amount of which you cannot control,

Do not touch the revolver grip with your finger tips!

will destroy the delicate state of balanced forces (opposing pressures) which you are seeking to establish and maintain until after the weapon is discharged.

Now, try to memorize the procedure and practice holding the gun in the *same* way *every* time. Get into the habit!

Get into the habit

I might as well whisper a secret in your ear. It is all-important that, once you have found the correct hold, you must take and maintain it in exactly the same manner, with every shot — today — tomorrow — next week — all your life. Don't shift around! You should have invisible callouses in certain places in your hand and the stock should have invisible grooves and bumps, through your method of taking the same hold all the time. I said "invisible." You don't apply any pressures and therefore should not get callouses and wear grooves into the stock. I just used a sort of metaphor.

Another, and probably better, way of expressing what I mean would be to imagine the stock covered with a delicate film which, upon first correct contact with your hand, would show the impression of all the little skin wrinkles and folds of your hand. This impression, we go on imagining, must not be disturbed and, each time we resume our hold, all these skin wrinkles and folds should match the first imprint.

Start slowly and pedantically — Do it right! Practice it! And by and by, the gun will slip into the same place automatically — and that's what we want!

VIII
POSITIONS FOR
HANDGUN SHOOTING

Stance or foot placement plays a prominent role in most pistol shots. Although there may be some occasions, primarily connected with hunting, when the shooter lies prone or uses some type of support to enhance steadiness, we primarily think of handgun shooting in terms of standing shots. For a long time, an angled stance with the shooting hand extended was considered de rigueur, but the obvious advantages of two hands when it comes to steadiness, and the development of the Weaver Stance, changed that. Here we get a sampling of more traditional approaches on the subject, offered by two great gun writers, along with current thinking as reflected in the U.S. Army's training procedures.

Two approaches to handgun shooting positions

●

William Reichenbach had a special way of tendering advice, doing so in a pithy, humor-laced fashion that is virtually irresistible. In this short treatment of stance, taken from Sixguns and Bullseyes *(1936), he explains the long-accepted way of doing things when shooting with one hand.*

William Reichenbach discusses stance

STANCE

Ah me, you will sigh, what do we want with "stance?" We don't aim to shoot with our feet. Do you know that one of our foremost revolver-experts who read my exposition on stance in the first "Elusive Ten," wrote me that he thought it important enough to apply it in practice? Well Sir, we deal with this thing called "stance" because it is imperative to our success, not because we want to fill valuable printing space.

Did you ever observe a man slightly under the weather giving a speech to the world at large? We are not concerned here with what he may have been blubbering, but didn't you see that his body was swaying back and forth? — There we have it! *His body swayed*! Now, if the man had only had three legs, he would have presented a steadier picture, regardless of how much friend alcohol were urging him to sway in the breeze. We, of course, are more dignified. We don't hold speeches — not at street corners. We are busy drinking in knowledge, not alcohol, knowledge about "Swaying."

We can begin by making a little experiment. Alright! Stand in the middle of the room and close your eyes. After a short while you will have the feeling as if you were swaying — you *are* swaying! You are *falling*! You feel that, if nature had only provided you with another leg, things would be much steadier. Right? That's the trouble with having only two legs. A horse can *sleep* on its feet. We humans can't even stand steadily when fully awake. This is not a philippica against nature's shortsightedness; it is an endeavor to impress upon you the fact of "body sway." The best shooter, be he as steady with his arm as possible, will sway. His gunmuzzle is carried across the bullseye, in unison with the sway of his body. He has acknowledged that and he has taken steps to minimize the evil by assuming a correct stance.

Suppose, you were to acknowledge this fact now, instead of later? It would save a lot of time.

Alright then: The body sways in the direction of your chest. Just stand with your feet about 14" apart, the toes facing the target. Raise your hand and point with a finger at the bull. You will see that the finger moves mostly up and down.

Now point your toes both to the left and have your right shoulder face the target. Your finger will now travel across the bull from left to right and vice versa.

This kind of sway would interfere with your shooting, what?

Your shot-groups would be distorted. Swaying in the direction of the line of fire, your groups would tend to spread unduly in a vertical line, and horizontally, of course, if your torso were swaying across the line of fire.

Obviously since we cannot eliminate swaying altogether, we must try to minimize it. If we were to take a position somewhere between the two extremes just mentioned, it would be evident that our finger could not travel as much in one direction as before. You would find, in fact, that your finger — or, if you were holding a gun, the gun-muzzle — moves within a very restricted area, vertically and horizontally, but not enough to do much damage.

Following up our reasoning logically, we will now consciously apply the principle of correct stance:

The principle of correct stance

1. Stand with feet close together, facing in a direction of about 45 degrees to the left of the line of fire.
2. Move left foot straight to the left, a distance of 10 to 14", more or less, to find a comfortable position.
3. Now raise the heel of your right foot, turn on the ball of your foot to the left, until you reach a position of comfort.

As agreed before, even now the body will sway, namely in the direction which your chest is facing. But since — for right-handers — your target is over to the right your gunarm has to be swung in the direction of the target, also to the right, in a line between your chest and your shoulder. In other words, we introduce a sort of half twist in your torso and that is why the muzzle travel is so greatly shortened.

We can further reduce the disturbance by placing our body-weight correctly on both feet. We "toe-in," until we can feel pressure on the outer margin of each foot. We also distribute the weight equally on both feet and on each foot evenly between the ball and the outer edge and the heel. In short: We were born with full soles and we should use as much of the sole surface as possible. This should be a boon to people with flat feet, what?

I hope, I don't have to implore you not to dismiss the matter of stance as trivial. "Stance" is one of the seven fundamentals. Get into the spirit and practice "stancing." See that you spread your legs so that you feel comfortable. The spread is individual — There is no hard and fast rule about the matter of inches. The stance must be comfortable and theoretically correct. You see, the thing you want to avoid is: having any tension in any part of your anatomy and that includes your shoulders, arms, body, legs and feet.

Your left hand which you find to be hanging rather helplessly should not be cause for giving it any thought. It is best if you just put it in you pocket and forget it while your pistol is up.

Jeff Cooper is one of the leading handgun authorities of the twentieth century, and in this selection he provides a clear, succinct overview of the various positions for handgun shooters, along with some helpful hints on how to make them most effective when it comes to marksmanship. The piece originally appeared in Jack O'Connor's Complete Book of Shooting *(1965).*

Do not dismiss the matter of stance as trivial

Jeff Cooper's tips on position

GRIP, STANCE, AND POSITION

SHOOTING POSITIONS

**The
Weaver
Stance**

The Weaver Stance — If only one method of shooting is to be learned, it should be the Weaver Stance, invented by Jack Weaver, of Lancaster, California. It is basically a two-handed standing position, but not the fully erect, straight-armed position of the target range. The big difference is that the Weaver Stance is fast, while the other is deliberate. Jack had to defeat his share of quick-draw artists to prove it, but prove it he did. Tests have now shown that a master can keep all his shots on the international target at 25 meters, starting with the weapon holstered and safe, and including reaction time, *in one second per shot*. At three full seconds, which is the regular time allotted to Olympic competitors starting with the pistol ready in the hand, he can keep all his shots in the nine ring. The Weaver Stance may be used with deliberation, but it is essentially a position for fast shooting.

To assume the Weaver Stance, face square to the target, with the left foot leading just a little. The right arm is nearly straight, the left arm bent a little more as the left shoulder leads, and the head is sometimes bent slightly into the line of sight depending on the shooter's build. On shifting targets, the body is pivoted from the waist without disturbing the fixed relationship of arms and shoulders. This position is accurate, fast, and extremely versatile. It is the best position to use in about 80 percent of the situations in which a pistol is necessary.

After the Weaver Stance come two positions which call for about equal attention, the braced kneeling and the speed rock. They fulfill opposite needs, for kneeling provides 100-yard stability while the rock is a means of stopping a lethal adversary at arm's length.

Braced Kneeling Position — To assume the kneeling position, first place your feet so that your heels arc in line with the target. This may be done as the pistol is drawn. Then drop so that your right knee touches the ground and sit upon your right heel. In this position your left shoulder is more advanced than in the Weaver Stance, so your left arm is more sharply bent as it supports your right hand. The bent elbow then rests easily upon the left knee, left elbow, and left hand all in the same vertical plane. The position is rock-solid and permits a rifle-like shot from an unready condition in about three seconds. Successive shots of course may be delivered with equal accuracy and greater speed. This position is of more use to the beginner than to the expert, for given equal time, the expert can shoot like a machine rest from the Weaver Stance. However, I recommend it highly for recruit training as it builds confidence in the beginner.

The braced kneeling position is of more use to the beginner

Speed Rock Position — This is the gunslinger's position, so called because it is the fastest way to get off a shot and because most practitioners rock

312 THE MARKSMANSHIP PRIMER

the body slightly backward by bending the knees in order to start the barrel up toward level even before the weapon clears leather. In the rock — as used by a man (not a blank-shooter) who must hit a target — the grip is naturally one-handed, but the wrist and forearm are solidly locked. The pistol is pointed at belt level and fired as it lines up. This is a technique that calls for much practice and one that, to my knowledge, is never officially taught. Its speed advantage is perhaps a half second over the Weaver Stance, and its accuracy potential is limited to large targets at 20 feet or less, but it has saved lives. For the policeman who makes a traffic stop and is greeted by unexpected gunfire at 10 feet it is a most comforting skill to acquire.

The speed rock position is accurate only up to about 20 feet

F.B.I. Crouch — Related to the rock, but less useful, are the F.B.I. crouch and the so-called "lock-on." In these the pistol is drawn and pointed with some deliberation, but not from higher than diaphragm level. Good shooting may be done this way, but not as accurately as from the Weaver Stance and not much, if at all, faster. It is sometimes used in competition to split a difference against a specific antagonist whose abilities are known. It is also the only way that so-called hip shooting can be done with an improperly designed holster, as the speed rock works only from a speed holster. However, in practically all cases, if you aren't wearing a speed holster you had best settle for the Weaver Stance.

The so-called "lock-on"

Prone Position — There are many other shooting positions for the pistol which are interesting to experiment with, even though they may not be of much real use. For sighting-in or for an occasional ridge-top shot while hunting, the prone position is convenient. I have also used it in freestyle competition when the time allowance was ample. Prone is taken simply by lying full length on the ground and extending the basic two-hand grip straight forward. The pistol is supported firmly by the joined fingers of the left hand, with the little finger resting on the ground.

Care should be taken that no part of the weapon touches anything but the hands, and that the muscles of the right hand keep the same tension as when standing, otherwise the point of impact may be changed.

When using a bench rest the technique is the same as in prone except for that part of the body below the shoulders.

Sitting Position — The sitting position is not as useful to the pistolero as it is to the rifleman, since the accuracy differential between sitting and kneeling is pronounced with a rifle and negligible with a pistol, and the kneeling position is quickly and easily assumed while the sitting position is awkward to get into. Nevertheless, the sitting position is taught by the F.B.I, and has some usefulness in the field, especially when shooting from a forward slope across a canyon. To take it, sit down facing the target and assume the basic two-hand

The sitting position has some usefulness in the field

grip, with both arms straight. The torso is forced well forward so that, on level ground, the elbows are forward of the knees, which support the upper arms lying between them. This position is easily varied to suit different angles of elevation, from about 30 degrees downward to 45 degrees upward, which gives it its main usefulness. For firing horizontally from level ground it is not very practical; not as accurate as prone and hardly faster, and not as fast as kneeling and hardly more accurate.

If a backrest is available, such as the trunk of a tree, the braced sitting position may be taken, which is fully as accurate as prone or a bench rest. In this one the torso leans well back, somewhat as in a modern racing car, and the pistol hands are pressed between the knees, the feet being placed somewhat outboard for extra stability. From this you can shoot as well as the pistol can, but obviously conditions must be just right. It should be pointed out that a revolver fired from this position may scorch the trousers severely, as its flash gap is not clear of the shooter's legs.

Offhand is the official target shooter's position

Offhand Position — Offhand is the official target-shooter's position. Highly trained specialists can shoot brilliantly from it, but it is likely to discourage the ordinary man, since it is the least accurate sighted method of shooting a pistol. A conventional offhand position is taken by facing 30 to 45 degrees to the left of the direction of fire (depending upon the individual build), with the feet about a half pace apart, and extending the unsupported arm straight at the target. This traditional stance serves no useful purpose that I can see — though I used it unquestioningly for twenty years — and should be confined to traditional target shots and people with one arm.

A variation of offhand — the one-hand point — does have value in rough and tumble situations where one hand is necessary to hold on. Short-range unsighted fire is delivered in this manner when riding a horse, riding postilion on a motor-cycle, or hanging onto a bouncing jeep or a speedboat. The left hand holds the controls or a support, the body is placed as necessary, and the right arm is extended not quite fully, since a completely extended arm lacks directional strength. The pistol is held about chin high, and the eyes focus on the target. The weapon appears as a vertical black bar just under the target, and the sights are not used. This is a wild way to use a pistol, but it works. Ray Chapman recently shot an X-possible on combat targets from the rear seat of a speeding motorcycle over rough ground using this method.

Barricade Position — Another position taught by the F.B.I. is the barricade position. To take it, shooter stands erect behind the barricade and places his inside hand flat on the edge a bit above shoulder height, allowing the web and thumb to extend outward. The pistol is held in the outside hand, which is placed in the web of the hand on the barricade. All of the body except the hands and half of the head remain behind cover. F.B.I. technique calls for the use of the right hand when

The one-hand point

shooting around the right side of things, and the left hand around the left.

However, with a little adjustment, the master hand can be used in either case with only a minute increase in exposure, and I suggest this for shooters who have extreme difficulty with the weak hand, rules or no rules.

The U.S. Army's Pistol Combat Training Techniques

From a contemporary perspective, one would assume that the U.S. Army would offer recruits what it considers the optimum in field training. This piece comes from a manual entitled Combat Training with Pistols, M9 and M11 *(2003). Although the text is somewhat dry, the information is eminently practical. Of course, it should be noted that the manual was written specifically with combat situations in mind, and proven combat shooting techniques may not always produce the most effective marksmanship in other circumstances.*

PISTOL MARKSMANSHIP TRAINING

The main use of the pistol is to engage an enemy at close range with quick, accurate fire. Accurate shooting results from knowing and correctly applying the elements of marksmanship. The elements of combat pistol marksmanship are:

- Grip.
- Aiming.
- Breath control.
- Trigger squeeze.

- Target engagement.
- Positions.

GRIP

A proper grip is one of the most important fundamentals of quick fire. The weapon must become
an extension of the hand and arm; it should replace the finger in pointing at an object. The firer
must apply a firm, uniform grip to the weapon.

One-Hand Grip — Hold the weapon in the nonfiring hand; form a V with the thumb and forefinger of the strong hand (firing hand). Place the
weapon in the V with the front and rear sights in
line with the firing arm. Wrap the lower three fingers around the pistol grip, putting equal pressure
with all three fingers to the rear. Allow the thumb
of the firing hand to rest alongside the weapon
without pressure. Grip the weapon tightly until
the hand begins to tremble; relax until the trembling stops. At this point, the necessary pressure
for a proper grip has been applied. Place the
trigger finger on the trigger between the tip and
second joint so that it can be squeezed to the rear.
The trigger finger must work independently of
the remaining fingers. (Note: If any of the three
fingers on the grip are relaxed, the grip must be
reapplied.)

Two-Hand Grip — The two-hand grip allows the
firer to steady the firing hand and provide maximum support during firing. The nonfiring hand

**Proper grip
is one of the
most impor-
tant funda-
mentals of
quick fire**

becomes a support mechanism for the firing hand by wrapping the fingers of the nonfiring hand around the firing hand. Two-hand grips are recommended for all pistol firing.

Fist Grip — Grip the weapon as with the one-hand grip. Firmly close the fingers of the nonfiring hand over the fingers of the firing hand, ensuring that the index finger from the nonfiring hand is between the middle finger of the firing hand and the trigger guard. Place the nonfiring thumb alongside the firing thumb.

Palm-Supported Grip — This grip is commonly called the cup and saucer grip. Grip the firing hand as with the one-hand grip. Place the nonfiring hand under the firing hand, wrapping the nonfiring fingers around the back of the firing hand. Place the nonfiring thumb over the middle finger of the firing hand.

Weaver Grip — Apply this grip the same as the fist grip. The only exception is that the nonfiring thumb is wrapped over the firing thumb.

Isometric Tension — The firer raises his arms to a firing position and applies isometric tension. This is commonly known as the push-pull method for maintaining weapon stability. Isometric tension is when the firer applies forward pressure with the firing hand and pulls rearward with the nonfiring hand with equal pressure. This creates an isometric force but never so much to cause the firer to tremble. This steadies the weapon and reduces barrel rise from recoil. The supporting arm is bent with the elbow pulled downward. The firing arm is fully extended with the elbow and wrist locked. The firer must experiment to find the right amount of isometric tension to apply. (Note: The firing hand should exert the same pressure as the nonfiring hand. If it does not, a missed target could result.)

Natural Point of Aim — The firer should check his grip for use of his natural point of aim. He grips the weapon and sights properly on a distant target. While maintaining his grip and stance, he closes his eyes for three to five seconds. He then opens his eyes and checks for proper sight picture. If the point of aim is disturbed, the firer adjusts his stance to compensate. If the sight alignment is disturbed, the firer adjusts his grip to compensate by removing the weapon from his hand and reapplying the grip. The firer repeats this process until the sight alignment and sight placement remain almost the same when he opens his eyes. With sufficient practice, this enables the firer to determine and use his natural point of aim, which is the most relaxed position for holding and firing the weapon.

The firer should determine his natural point of aim

AIMING

Aiming is sight alignment and sight placement.

Sight alignment is the centering of the front blade in the rear sight notch. The top of the front sight is level with the top of the rear sight and is in correct alignment with the eye. For correct sight alignment, the firer must center the front sight in the rear sight. He raises or lowers the top of the front sight so it is level with the top of the rear sight. Sight alignment is essential for accuracy because of the short sight radius of the pistol. For example, if a $\frac{1}{10}$-inch error is made in aligning the front sight in the rear sight, the firer's bullet will miss the point of aim by about 15 inches at a range of 25 meters. The $\frac{1}{10}$-inch error in sight alignment magnifies as the range increases — at 25 meters, it is magnified 150 times.

Sight placement is the positioning of the weapon's sights in relation to the target as seen by the firer when he aims the weapon. A correct sight picture consists of correct sight alignment with the front sight placed center mass of the target. The eye can focus on only one object at a time at different distances. Therefore, the last focus of the eye is always on the front sight. When the front sight is seen clearly, the rear sight and target will appear hazy. The firer can maintain correct sight alignment only through focusing on the front sight. His bullet will hit the target even if the sight picture is partly off center but still remains on the target. Therefore, sight alignment is more important than sight placement. Since it is impossible to hold the weapon completely still, the firer must apply trigger squeeze and maintain correct sight alignment while the weapon is moving in and around the center of the target. This natural movement of

The last focus of the eye is always on the front sight

the weapon is referred to as wobble area. The firer must strive to control the limits of the wobble area through proper grip, breath control, trigger squeeze, and positioning.

Focusing on the front sight while applying proper trigger squeeze will help the firer resist the urge to jerk the trigger and anticipate the moment the weapon will fire. Mastery of trigger squeeze and sight alignment requires practice. Trainers should use concurrent training stations or have fire ranges to enhance proficiency of marksmanship skills.

BREATH CONTROL

To attain accuracy, the firer must learn to hold his breath properly at any time during the breathing cycle. This must be done while aiming and squeezing the trigger. While the procedure is simple, it requires explanation, demonstration, and supervised practice. To hold his breath properly, the firer takes a breath, lets it out, then inhales normally, lets a little out until comfortable, holds, and then fires. It is difficult to maintain a steady position keeping the front sight at a precise aiming point while breathing. Therefore, the firer should be taught to inhale, then exhale normally, and hold his breath at the moment of the natural respiratory pause. (Breath control, firing at a single target.) The shot must then be fired before he feels any discomfort from not breathing. When multiple targets are presented, the firer must learn to hold his breath at any part of the breathing cycle. Breath control must be practiced during dry-fire exercises until it becomes a natural part of the firing process.

TRIGGER SQUEEZE

Improper trigger squeeze causes more misses

Improper trigger squeeze causes more misses than any other step of preparatory marksmanship. Poor shooting is caused by the aim being disturbed before the bullet leaves the barrel of the weapon. This is usually the result of the firer jerking the trigger or flinching. A slight off-center pressure of the trigger finger on the trigger can cause the weapon to move and disturb the firer's sight alignment. Flinching is an automatic human reflex caused by anticipating the recoil of the weapon. Jerking is an effort to fire the weapon at the precise time the sights align with the target.

Trigger squeeze is the independent movement of the trigger finger in applying increasing pressure on the trigger straight to the rear, without disturbing the sight alignment until the weapon fires. The trigger slack, or free play, is taken up first, and the squeeze is continued steadily until the hammer falls. If the trigger is squeezed properly, the firer will not know exactly when the hammer will fall; thus, he will not tend to flinch or heel, resulting in a bad shot. Novice firers must be trained to overcome the urge to anticipate recoil. Proper application of the fundamentals will lower this tendency.

To apply correct trigger squeeze, the trigger finger should contact the trigger between the tip of the finger and the second joint (without touching the weapon anywhere else). Where contact is made depends on the length of the firer's trigger finger. If pressure from the trigger finger is applied to the right side of the trigger or weapon, the strike of the bullet will be to the left. This is due to the normal hinge action of the fingers. When the fingers on the right hand are closed, as in gripping, they hinge or pivot to the left, thereby applying pressure to the left (with left-handed firers, this action is to the right). The firer must not apply pressure left or right but should increase finger pressure straight to the rear. Only the trigger finger should perform this action. Dry-fire training improves a firer's ability to move the trigger finger straight to the rear without cramping or increasing pressure on the hand grip.

Dry-fire training improves trigger squeeze

Follow-through is the continued effort of the firer to maintain sight alignment before, during, and after the round has fired. The firer must continue the rearward movement of the finger even after the round has been fired. Releasing the trigger too soon after the round has been fired results in an uncontrolled shot, causing a missed target.

The firer who is a good shot holds the sights of the weapon as nearly on the target center as possible and continues to squeeze the trigger with increasing pressure until the weapon fires.

The soldier who is a bad shot tries to "catch his target" as his sight alignment moves past the target and fires the weapon at that instant. This is called ambushing, which causes trigger jerk.

TARGET ENGAGEMENT

To engage a single target, the firer applies the method discussed in paragraph 2-4. When engaging multiple targets in combat, he engages the closest and most dangerous multiple target first and fires at it with two rounds. This is called controlled pairs. The firer then traverses and acquires the next target, aligns the sights in the center of mass, focuses on the front sight, applies trigger squeeze, and fires. He ensures his firing arm elbow and wrist are locked during all engagements. If he has missed the first target and has fired upon the second target, he shifts back to the first and engages it. Some problems in target engagement are as follows:

Controlled pairs

Recoil Anticipation — When a soldier first learns to shoot, he may begin to anticipate recoil. This reaction may cause him to tighten his muscles during or just before the hammer falls. He may fight the recoil by pushing the weapon downward in anticipating or reacting to its firing. In either case, the rounds will not hit the point of aim.

Trigger Jerk — Trigger jerk occurs when the soldier sees that he has acquired a good sight picture at center mass and "snaps" off a round before the good sight picture is lost. This may become a problem, especially when the soldier is learning to use a flash sight picture.

Heeling — Heeling is caused by a firer tightening the large muscle in the heel of the hand to keep from jerking the trigger. A firer who has had problems with jerking the trigger tries to correct the fault by tightening the bottom of the hand, which results in a heeled shot. Heeling causes the strike of the bullet to hit high on the firing hand side of the target. The firer can correct shooting errors by knowing and applying correct trigger squeeze.

POSITIONS

The qualification course is fired from a standing, kneeling, or crouch position. During qualification and combat firing, soldiers must practice all of the firing positions described below so they become natural movements. Though these positions seem natural, practice sessions must be conducted to ensure the habitual attainment of correct firing positions. Practice in assuming correct firing positions ensures that soldiers can quickly assume these positions without a conscious effort. Pistol marksmanship requires a soldier to rapidly apply all the fundamentals at dangerously close targets while under stress. Assuming a proper position to allow for a steady aim is critical to survival.

Pistol-Ready Position — In the pistol-ready position, hold the weapon in the one-hand grip. Hold the upper arm close to the body and the forearm at about a 45-degree angle. Point the weapon toward target center as you move forward.

Standing Position without Support — Face the target. Place feet a comfortable distance apart, about shoulder width. Extend the firing arm and attain a two-hand grip. The wrist and elbow of the firing arm are locked and pointed toward target center. Keep the body straight with the shoulders slightly forward of the buttocks.

Kneeling Position — In the kneeling position, ground only your firing-side knee as the main support. Vertically place your firing-side foot, used as the main support, under your buttocks. Rest your body weight on the heel and toes. Rest your non-firing arm just above the elbow on the knee not used as the main body support. Use the two-handed grip for firing. Extend the firing arm, and lock the firing-arm elbow and wrist to ensure solid arm control.

Crouch Position — Use the crouch position when surprise targets are engaged at close range. Place the body in a forward crouch (boxer's stance) with the knees bent slightly and trunk bent forward from the hips to give faster recovery from recoil. Place the feet naturally in a position that allows another step toward the target. Extend the weapon straight toward the target, and lock the wrist and elbow of the firing arm. It is important to consistently train with this position, since the body will automatically crouch under conditions of stress such as combat. It is also a faster position from which to change direction of fire.

Prone Position — Lie flat on the ground, facing the target. Extend your arms in front with the firing arm locked. (Your arms may have to be slightly unlocked for firing at high targets.) Rest the butt of the weapon on the ground for single, well-aimed shots. Wrap the fingers of the nonfiring hand around the fingers of the firing hand. Face forward. Keep your head down between your arms and behind the weapon as much as possible.

Standing Position with Support — Use available cover for support — for example, a tree or wall to stand behind. Stand behind a barricade with the firing side on line with the edge of the barricade. Place the knuckles of the nonfiring fist at eye level against the edge of the barricade. Lock the elbow and wrist of the firing arm. Move the foot on the nonfiring side forward until the toe of the boot touches the bottom of the barricade.

Kneeling Supported Position — Use available cover for support — for example, use a low wall, rocks, or vehicle. Place your firing-side knee on the ground. Bend the other knee and place the foot (nonfiring side) flat on the ground, pointing toward the target. Extend arms alongside and brace them against available cover. Lock the wrist and elbow of your firing arm. Place the nonfiring hand around the fist to support the firing arm. Rest the nonfiring arm just above the elbow on the nonfiring-side knee.

IX
STRIVING
FOR ACCURACY

A variety of considerations enter into the accuracy equation. These include problems with stance or trigger squeeze, the heretofore unrecognized matter of which eye is dominant, improper technique, lack of practice, and use of a handgun unsuited to the shooter. Yet every shooter wishes to improve his shooting; that is why we constantly strive to improve our marksmanship. Here we have glimpses of a number of factors the serious shooter needs to contemplate as he works on his shooting form.

●

Sound journalist that he unquestionably was, Jack O'Connor knew to turn to others more expert than he when the occasion demanded such an approach. That is precisely what he does here: he takes wisdom from first-rate handgunners he knew and distills it into readable, reliable coverage. The material comes from his Sportsman's Arms and Ammunition Manual *(1952).*

Jack O'Connor discusses expert pistol shooting

EXPERT HANDGUN SHOOTING

*The Experts Know How to Handle Handguns
— Here are all the Tricks of Their Trade*

Few will dispute the fact that the handgun is the most difficult of all weapons to shoot well; also that, once sufficient skill is developed, using a handgun is one of the highest forms of shooting pleasure.

Handgun shooting is just like offhand rifle shooting, although more so. Every rifle-shooting fault is enormously magnified with the handgun. The prone rifle shot can do a little flinching and cover it up pretty well because of his tight sling, heavy firearm, and steady position. If he tries to shoot offhand, wild shots make his flinch apparent. Nevertheless the rifle is both heavy and long-barreled, and what a nice flinch can do to a rifle shot is nothing compared with what it can do to a handgun shot.

Every rifle-shooting fault is magnified with the handgun

Usually I am not too enthusiastic about the theory of training in one subject to become proficient in another. If a man wants to learn Spanish he should study Spanish, not Latin. And if he wants to think well and clearly on social and political subjects, he should study psychology and logic to find out how his mind works, and then do some plain and fancy contemplating on social and political subjects, instead of sharpening his wits through the study of dead languages and mathematics, as old-fashioned teachers used to advise.

However, supplementary shooting of the handgun is one of the finest of all ways to keep a rifleman on the beam, to perfect his trigger control, to steady his hold, to sharpen his sighting. The unsteady one-hand hold, the short sight radius, the light weight of the handgun — all make for mistakes that prove fatal, though a rifleman could make the same mistake and score fairly well. As a consequence a good handgun shot is almost always a *very* good rifle shot, whereas the reverse is a long way from being true.

For years a friend of mine did a lot of handgun shooting. He almost never shot a rifle, however, because he was not a hunter. Then some friends talked him into buying a .30/06. Much to their astonishment this "beginner" started immediately to knock their ears down in offhand matches. Why? He had already mastered steady holding and trigger control with a vastly more difficult weapon.

I am not going into the selection of a handgun here, except to say that the smart thing to do is to start with a .22 because the ammunition is inexpensive and its light report and relatively gentle recoil are not likely to bother the novice. The smart thing also is to get as good a weapon as one can afford. I have always liked the feel and heft of the revolver, but most .22 target sharks use automatics and there is no doubt that the short-barreled, light automatics like the little Colt Woods-

A good handgun shot is almost always a *very* good rifle shot

Start with a .22

man with the 4½-in. barrel are sweet to pack around for plinking and general small-game shooting.

Form in any sport is acquired only by thought and practice. Give a man a tennis racket or a golf club for the first time and he will pick it up all wrong. His stance will be terrible. For the most part there is nothing "natural" about good form.

There is nothing "natural" about good form

Likewise, the man who first picks up a handgun will do everything wrong. He will grasp it as if it were a dagger that he was about to sink in someone's back. He will hold it with a bent arm. He will waver and wobble the trigger.

All of which reminds me of a story. Back in my boyhood, a couple of Western ranchers had a falling out over a stolen calf and decided to go a-gunning for each other. They eventually met in a saloon. One walked in the front door just as the other, who had been powdering his nose, emerged from a rear door. They emptied their guns — and did no damage except to the bar mirror and the walls. Before they could reload, friends overpowered them. The law came in. They were fined, warned by the judge to keep the peace, and then turned loose.

They next met on the open range, and this time they started popping away at each other at about 80 yd. Again neither got a hit.

Then it struck one of them as being funny. "Joe," he called, "got an ax?"

"Not with me, you damned fool!" Joe replied.

"You go home and get yours and I'll get mine. We ain't a-doin' no good with these here six-shooters!"

Then they both began to laugh, and for years they told that story on each other. It turned out that somebody else had stolen the calf after all.

In getting the correct hold for a handgun, the first thing to remember is that it should be held at arm's length. A general tendency of beginners is to hold with a bent arm, but this is wrong. Try to think of the gun being held so that there is a straight line from the shoulder right through the sights to the target.

The handgun should be held at arm's length

Furthermore, the gun should be held from the shoulder with no conscious tightening of the muscles of the arm. An attempt to get steadiness through stiffened arm muscles will produce an exactly opposite effect; arm and gun will vibrate every which way. Held from the shoulder, with the arm virtually limp, gun and arm will act as if one piece, and movement will tend to be up to control.

Left to himself, the beginner probably will *grasp* the gun rather than *hold* it. He'll clamp down on the grip as if it were the last dollar he had in the world. Instead, the handgun should be held firmly but lightly. The frame just back of the trigger guard should rest on the middle finger. (Think of it as being balanced there.) The thumb should extend high along the frame for steadiness, and also because the thumb in that position promotes *holding* rather than *grasping*, to use that term again.

Many
beginners
put too
much index
finger
through the
trigger
guard

Many beginners (and also some darned good handgun shots) put too much index finger through the guard, so that the pad of flesh between the first and second joints contacts the trigger. This is O.K. for rifle shooting, where the feeling should be that one is simply gently tightening up with the whole hand. In handgun shooting, however, the sensitive ball of the fingertip should be employed to touch her off. If the index finger is too far through the guard, it often contacts the guard as well as the trigger, and part of the pressure is actually being put upon the guard. The trigger finger must remain free to complete the squeeze at the right time.

If your sole acquaintance with a handgun comes from having played cowboy and Indians with a cap pistol in your youth, this method of holding the handgun may seem awkward at first. However, that's equally true of a golf club or a tennis racket, and using the correct grip will soon seem as natural as rolling the eyes and uttering a gentle sigh when a lovely maiden comes floating by.

Most good
handgun
shots stand
with their
feet at a
45-degree
angle

Most good handgun shots stand with their feet at about a 45-degree angle to the line of the arm. However, I have seen some very sharp characters face the target. Others continue the straight line of muzzle to shoulder through the other shoulder; in other words, they face away from the target at a right angle. But since the first method is the easiest and most natural, the beginner should form the habit of using it. Thrust the left hand in your pocket or rest it on your hip, so there is no temptation to wave it around and destroy balance.

Anyone taking up the handgun is appalled by the fact that the front sight wobbles and wibbles so. He hears talk about the champions' rock-steady holding, and feels like a very inferior fellow indeed.

Between us girls, I think that the "rock steady" handgun hold is purely relative — that actually there ain't no such thing. Holds range from very wobbly to fairly steady. Even a rifle resting with fore-end and butt on sandbags on a bench rest isn't "rock steady." The more a man practices, the more he develops the important muscles in hand, forearm, and shoulder, the steadier he can hold. He will never, however, become a machine rest. If he did, all the fun would be gone.

Stage fright, weak and untrained muscles, too much smoking, and not enough sleep will make the extended arm with the handgun wobble; but even at that the wild and unpredictable shots are caused, not by wobble but by flinching.

So if you're a beginner, don't worry too much about wobble. If the trigger is squeezed off smoothly and the sights remain more or less in line, the shot won't be too sour. Let me repeat: It is *flinching* — not wobble — that causes those wide shots. One way to convince yourself of that is

Don't worry about wobble

to shoot with a deliberate and exaggerated wobble; if you manage to keep the sights lined up, you'll find that you still do fairly well.

Now let us suppose that, instead of feeling strange, as it did at first, the orthodox grip has come to seem natural. You've learned to hold the handgun firmly yet not hard, because holding *hard* only accentuates the tendency to wobble. You're ready to try some dry firing — holding the handgun sights on a mark and squeezing off the shot with no disturbance of aim. (Dry firing, by the way, isn't going to hurt your handgun and every good shot does worlds of it.) If you can put up a 25-yd. pistol target in the backyard, well and good. Failing a backyard, paste a small bull on the window and go to it.

Shooting the handgun is a grand hobby

Shooting the handgun is a grand hobby, and one that is neither expensive nor troublesome to follow. The small-bore rifleman has to be loaded up with a long and heavy rifle, a heavy scope sight of high power, a spotting scope and stand, and what not. The pistol shot can put all his gear in a container no bigger than a brief case. One of the best small-bore shots I know has switched almost entirely to the handgun because he grew weary, he says, of taking care of so much rifle equipment.

A good man with a handgun can get a lot of game, if he has to, and a .22 pistol or revolver is an excellent supplementary weapon to take along on a big-game hunt. On a 30-day trip into the Rockies one time my companion carried a Colt Woodsman and used it very effectively. Almost every day we'd run into grouse of some sort on the trail and my pal had no trouble giving the whole camp an occasional feast of wild chicken. To the wilderness dweller a .22 handgun is almost a necessity for supplementing the diet with grouse and rabbit and, perhaps, porcupine.

I know some very good handgun shots who hunt varmints with their favorite weapons and who would rather knock over one jack rabbit with a .22 hollow point or a .38 Special at 75 yd. than a dozen with a rifle. One amazing character I know has killed *two* mountain lions with a handgun. Wait a minute and I'll make it worse. They had NOT been treed by dogs. In both cases he saw them when they were crossing mountain roads. He got one with a Colt Woodsman and the other with a little automatic for the .25 A.C.P.

To me, the most interesting thing about the handgun is the training it gives and the lessons it teaches the rifleman. Do you tighten up too much? Do you jerk the trigger? Do you have poor breathing habits? If you want to find out (and have a lot of fun doing it), try the handgun!

This selection comes from the Army Marksmanship Unit Pistol Training Guide *(1980). Poor trigger control, especially jerking or snatching the trigger (rather than pulling with a smooth, even motion, normally referred to as "squeezing"), can be a problem when shooting any type of firearm. However, shortcomings in this arena are magnified when working with handguns.*

Trigger control as taught by the U.S. Army

This straightforward text describes proven ways to optimize control of the trigger when firing a handgun.

TRIGGER CONTROL

GENERAL

Correct trigger control must be employed in conjunction with all other fundamentals of shooting. The physical act of applying pressure on the trigger to deliver an accurate shot may vary from individual to individual. Proper trigger control for each individual gradually assumes uniformity when the techniques of proper application are mastered. Many shooters, for example, maintain a degree of trigger control with a relatively light grip, while another shooter may use a very tight grip. Some shooters prefer to apply consistent trigger pressure at a rapid rate, while maintaining correct sight alignment. For another shooter, a slower, deliberate application may achieve the same results. An ever increasing number of shooters use the positive approach to trigger control, that is, once it is initiated, it becomes an uninterrupted, constantly increasing pressure until the weapon fires.

Many shooters use the positive approach to trigger control

Trigger control is of very great importance in producing an accurate shot. When the shooter exerts pressure on the trigger, he must do so in a manner that does not alter the sight alignment, or position of the pistol. Consequently, the shooter must be able to exert smooth, even pressure to the trigger. Furthermore, the trigger must be pressed in conjunction with maximum concentration, peak visual perception of sight alignment and minimum arc of movement.

In order to produce an accurate shot, the shooter must carry out many diverse, but related, actions. Fulfilling this action is compounded by the fact that the pistol is in some degree of motion throughout the period of sighting and aiming. The movement varies according to the stability of the shooter's stance. Consequently, the sight alignment deviates from the aiming area. Often it will move through the aiming area, pausing only for a short period of time in perfect alignment with the target. It is impossible to determine when, and for how long the properly aligned sights will stay in the center of the aiming area. This difficulty is aggravated further by the fact that the shooter is trying to execute coordinated actions when reflex action seeks to contradict them. Such a situation requires the development of conditioned reflexes, and improvement of coordination.

For an accurate shot, the shooter must carry out many diverse actions

The coordinated action of correct aiming, timely pressure on the trigger and the correct delivery of the shot is difficult and can be accomplished only by overcoming former uncoordinated reflexes or by acquiring new ones. Only through constant training and attention to accepted techniques can these new reflexes be acquired.

FACTORS PROVIDING FOR THE CORRECT CONTROL OF THE TRIGGER

The pressure put on the trigger must come from independent movement of the trigger finger only. The gripping fingers and the thumb do not move or tighten. Keep the grip pressure constant. Align the sight, settle into your normal aiming area and exert positive, uninterrupted, increasing pressure, straight to the rear, until the hammer falls. You must not look for a perfect sight picture combination of rear sight-front sight-bull's eye. Instead, **Focus the eye on the front sight** focus your eye on the front sight, keeping it perfectly aligned in the rear sight notch. The blur of the out-of-focus target may move about slightly, but this movement is relatively unimportant. Any time the weapon is fired with good sight alignment within the normal arc of movement and it is a surprise shot, the shot will be a good one, and will hit the target within your ability to hold.

Trigger control has a series of actions that take place if a smooth release of the firing mechanism is accomplished.

Slack and Initial Pressure — Any free movement of the trigger, known as slack, has to be taken up prior to a light initial pressure. This action assures that the tolerances in the firing mechanism linkage are taken up and are in firm contact before positive trigger pressure is applied.

Initial pressure is an automatic, lightly applied pressure, approximately one-fourth or less of the total required to fire the weapon. This careful action is an aid in the positive pressure that will release the hammer quickly and smoothly.

In order to fire a controlled shot the shooter must learn to increase the pressure on the trigger positively, smoothly, gradually, and evenly. This does not mean, however, that the trigger must be pressed slowly. It must be pressed smoothly, without interruption, but the release of the trigger must take no more than 2 to 5 seconds. Numerous accurate rapid fire strings of five shots in ten seconds are fired in a cycle that allows only one second or less to employ the principals of correct trigger control.

Release of the trigger must take no more than 2 to 5 seconds

Smooth trigger action makes special demands on the trigger finger when pressing upon the trigger; its correct functioning determines to a great extent the quality of the shot. The most carefully attained sight alignment will be spoiled by the slightest error in the movement of the trigger finger.

Function of Proper Grip — In order for the index finger to be able to perform its function without spoiling the aim, it is first necessary to have the hand grasp the pistol correctly and create the proper support; permitting the trigger finger to overcome the trigger tension. The pistol grips must be grasped tightly but without any tremor. It is also necessary that the index finger clears the side of the stock. The movement of the index finger must be independent as it presses on the trigger, and also not cause any lateral change to the sight alignment.

Proper Placement of the Trigger Finger — It is necessary to apply pressure on the trigger with either the first bone section of the index finger, or with the first joint. The trigger must be pressed straight to the rear. If the finger presses the trigger to the side, undesirable things will happen. The weight of trigger pull will increase; because of additional friction on certain parts of the trigger mechanism an otherwise flawless trigger action will take on the characteristics of a poor trigger when side pressure is exerted on the trigger. Another consideration is the effect that side pressure has on sight alignment. Only slight pressure to the side is required to bring about an error in sight alignment. The prime cause of exerting pressure to the side is improper placement of the trigger finger.

The effect of side pressure on sight alignment

Ideal trigger finger placement may be modified to a degree by the requirement that the grip provide a natural alignment of the front and rear sights. The shooter frequently must make a compromise to overcome the undesirable effects of not being able to utilize each factor to full advantage.

Coordination — It must be emphasised that match shooting is successful only when all the control factors are consistently in coordination.

Ability to control the trigger smoothly is not sufficient in itself to produce an accurate shot. The trigger must be activated in conjunction with correct sight alignment, minimum arc of movement, and maximum undisturbed concentration. This might be called cadence, rhythm or timing. Under any name, it comes only to those who practice frequently. Occasional ability is not the answer to championship shooting. A three-gun aggregate requires 270 successful results. Consistent, exacting performance is enhanced by an ability to compensate automatically for errors. It is necessary during firing to press the trigger under varying conditions of pistol movement in conjunction with correct sight alignment. In order to apply coordinated pressure on the trigger, the shooter must wait for definite times when all factors and conditions are favorable. Frequently, it will be impossible to exercise maximum control. However, the shooter must never attempt to fire until he has completely settled into a minimum arc of movement.

Occasional ability is not the answer to championship shooting

APPLICATION OF TRIGGER PRESSURE

Positive Uninterrupted Trigger Pressure-Surprise Shot Method — is primarily the act of completing the firing of the shot once starting the application of trigger pressure. The shooter is committed to an unchanging rate of pressure, no speed up, no slowdown or stopping. The trigger pressure is of an uninterrupted nature because it is not applied initially unless conditions are settled and near perfect. If the perfect conditions deteriorate, the shooter should not fire, but bench the weapon, relax, replan, and start again.

In instances when the pistol is stable and steady, and the periods of minimum arc of movement are of longer duration, it is immaterial whether the release of the trigger is completed a second sooner or a second later. Anytime that the shot is fired with minimum arc of movement and the sights are in alignment, it will be a good shot. Therefore, when the shooter has established stable minimum arc of movement and sight alignment, he must immediately begin to press on the trigger, smoothly but positively, and straight to the rear without stopping, until a shot is produced. This method of controlling the trigger action will give the shooter a surprise break of the shot before any muscular reflex can disturb sight alignment.

A method of trigger control that is *not* recommended

Interrupted Application of Trigger Pressure or the "Point" Shooting Method — This is a method of trigger control not recommended, although used by some shooters. Some shooters think they can pick the trigger release time even after years of experience.

The shooter will align the sights and exert initial pressure on the trigger. He will then make every effort to hold the weapon motionless. During extremely brief moments of motionlessness, pressure is applied on the trigger. If the sight alignment changes and is not perfect, or the arc of movement of the weapon increases, the pressure on the trigger is halted and trigger tension maintained. When sight alignment is again perfect and movement diminishes, pressure on the trigger is resumed until the shot breaks, or after the slack in the trigger is taken up, Initial pressure is applied and the shot released by a single swift movement of the trigger finger when there is a decrease in the minimum arc of movement. In this case the presence of perfect sight alignment is not considered essential in initiating trigger action. Abrupt action in applying trigger pressure will disturb the existing sight alignment and other fundamental control factors are subordinated to a minimum arc of movement. The application of all other fundamentals is required regardless of whether or not they are optimum.

While applying positive trigger pressure straight to the rear, if any thought enters the shooter's mind to speed up or slow down this trigger pressure, it will result in the concentration on sight alignment being broken down.

The decision to increase the trigger pressure may result in a reflex action commonly known as anticipation and usually results in heeling the shot (The bullet strikes the target at approximately one o'clock). The recoil becomes more imminent and the brain will send a signal for the arm and hand muscles to react prematurely a split second before the shot is fired; resulting in frequent bad shots and low scores.

The reflex action known as anticipation

ERRORS MADE IN TRIGGER CONTROL AND MEANS OF COMBATING THEM

The most serious error is jerking

The most serious and disrupting error made by the shooter is jerking — that is, the abrupt application of pressure on the trigger accompanied with muscular action of the hand and arm muscles.

If jerking was limited to abrupt pressure on the trigger, and the rapid displacement of the axis of the bore, it would cause only part of the results.

Jerking is usually accompanied by: the sharp straining of all the muscles in the arm and shoulder; the abrupt tightening of the hand on the grip; failure to press the trigger directly to the rear.

All of these factors, taken together, lead to a great shifting of the pistol to the aide and down and only a very poor shot can result.

Most frequently, jerking is observed in new shooters. Usually, because of a large arc of movement, favorable moments for producing a good shot are of very short duration.

The cause of trigger jerking

The cause of trigger-jerking, is the practice of "snatching a ten-pointer," as the expression goes. The shooter tries to fire at the moment when the centered front sight, as it moves back and forth, passes under the lower edge of the bull's eye, or comes to a stop, for a brief time, near the center of the aiming area. Since these moments are fleeting the inexperienced shooter strives to exert all the necessary pressure on the trigger at that time. This rapid and abrupt trigger pressure is accompanied not only by the work of the muscles in the index finger, but also by the sympathetic action of a number of other muscles. The involuntary action of these muscles produces the "jerk," and the inaccurate shot that results. The young shooter, in anticipation of the recoil of the pistol and its loud noise, strains his muscles by flinching, to counteract the anticipated recoil. This is also known as heeling the shot.

Heeling the shot

Practice has shown that a young shooter must be warned sufficiently early in his training about the dangers of jerking the trigger and effective steps taken to instruct him in the correct technique of accurate shooting.

Difficulty in detecting errors in trigger control is frequently because the pistol shifted during recoil and errors are not recognized. The shooter has a more difficult time in evaluating his actions than a coach, and often does not realize that he is jerking the trigger, blinking his eyes, or straining his arm and shoulder muscles.

The easiest way to correct jerking in the young shooter is by the coaching of an experienced coach. A coach can more readily detect errors and correct habits that will produce poor trigger control. Frequently a shooter does not consider it necessary to prove conclusively whether or not they are jerking on the trigger. It is necessary, though, to know that if he does not get rid of the detrimental habit of jerking on the trigger, he will never succeed in achieving good results.

Signs of jerking are an increase in the size of the area of the shot group or shots off to the side which are not called there; chiefly to the left and down (for right handers). To correct this condition, the shooter must make a change in his training exercises, but in no instance must he stop them.

Dry-fire practice will enable the nervous system to rest from the recoil of the shot. By this practice some of the reflexes which are detrimental to firing (tensing of the arm in order to counteract the recoil, the straining of the muscles in expectation of the shot, blinking from the noise of the shot), are not being developed. They will, in fact, begin to decrease and may completely disappear.

Secondly, the shooter may continue regular-training, but occasionally he may practice "dry". This way, he will not lose the stability of this position, as well as the useful reflexes which the shooter has developed during the process of previous firings.

By aiming carefully and noting attentively everything that happens to the pistol when he presses on the trigger, the shooter will discover his errors and eliminate them. Training by means of **Dry-fire** ball and dummy and dry firing is of great benefit. **practice is** It makes it possible to develop correctly and care- **of great** fully the technique of pressing the trigger, and con- **benefit** tributes to acquiring proper habits in controlling the trigger.

When beginning to use dry firing the shooter must first overcome the desire to "grab" for a shot when the centered front sight is under the bull's eye. Despite the arc of movement the shooter must teach himself only to press smoothly on the trigger and to use the uninterrupted positive control method of trigger action. When the smooth control of the trigger again becomes habitual and he no longer has to devote special attention to it, he can again shoot live cartridges. After starting again to shoot live cartridges, the first training exercises should involve firing at a square of blank white paper, rather than at a target with a black aiming area. Simultaneously, the shooter must devote special attention to analyzing his performance, counteract the desire to jerk on the trigger, and be conscious of reacting incorrectly to the firing of a shot.

Another error committed by a shooter when controlling the trigger is "holding too long," that is, the drawn out action of pressing the trigger.

The "holding too long" error

A consequence of holding too long is that the shooter does not have enough air to hold his breath, his eye becomes fatigued, and his visual acuity decreases. In addition, his stance loses part of its stability. Consequently, when he holds too long, the shooter presses on the trigger under unfavorable conditions.

Holding too long is a consequence of excessively slow and cautious pressure on the trigger. This is caused by the shooter's fear of producing a bad shot. Such indecisiveness and over-caution may be regarded as the opposite of jerking. Moreover, holding too long stems from the lack of coordination of movement which frequently occurs during those stages of training when the process of inhibition outweighs the process of stimulation. Simply stated, the shooter cannot force himself to exert positive pressure on the trigger at the proper time. One favorable moment after another goes past, and soon the chances for an accurate shot are gone. Naturally, the trigger control phase has been extended far beyond its effective duration. This situation frequently occurs after a period of dry-fire training exercises. The shooter loses the sense of the trigger's true weight when he fires for extended periods of time with a round in the chamber. When the trigger is released in a dry shot, the trigger seems to be rather light, but when the shooter switches to live rounds, the trigger weight seems to be considerably greater. He feels that he must exert greater effort to overcome this seemingly greater weight. Frequently, the shooter will blame his troubles on faulty adjustment of the trigger mechanism. Nothing is gained from such assumptions. More times than not, the shooter returns to normal trigger control since the root of the evil is lack of coordinated control and not trigger adjustment.

The shooter cannot force himself to exert positive pressure on the trigger at the proper time

The restoration of coordination of movement, and the return to the correct balance between stimulation and inhibition is brought about primarily through systematic practice, match training and dry-fire exercises. It is precisely this method of training which develops the necessary coordination of the shooter's actions. When the shooter's movements become automatic, the trigger finger will operate in an unstrained manner, and the shot will break at the proper moment. It is important that each training session begin with a few dry-fire exercises. It has been demonstrated that such exercises are necessary for the development of accurate shooting. Such exercises may also be repeated after record shooting to restore equilibrium in the nervous processes.

Frequently, a shooter, when firing for record, is unable to fire a shot. After several unsuccessful tries, a loss of confidence will arise. Rather than risk a wild shot the shooter should unload the pistol, time permitting, and dry-fire a few shots. After restoring coordination of movement and regaining his confidence, the shooter Is far better prepared, both physically and mentally, for the delivery of an accurate shot. Firing the shot during the first few seconds after settling into a good hold will guarantee confidence.

We have considered the fundamental errors that arise in trigger control. Let us now consider a problem that is also closely related to trigger control — trigger adjustment.

The firing of an accurate shot depends to a great extent on the quality of the trigger adjustment. An incorrectly adjusted trigger aggravates the errors committed by the shooter as he exerts pressure on the trigger. Incorrect adjustments in-

Trigger adjustment

clude: excessive trigger weight; excessive long creep (movement of trigger); too light trigger weight; variable trigger weight.

The shooter should not try to overcome these difficulties with modification in his trigger control but take the problem and pistol to the armorer (gunsmith) for solution.

The U.S. Army on sight alignment

Taken from the same source as the previous selection, this piece deals with the critical matter of alignment. Although stellar marksmanship certainly involves hand-eye coordination, the accurate shooter aims rather than points. Here are data on how to align one's eyes with the handgun's sight for maximum effectiveness.

SIGHT ALIGNMENT

Sight alignment is the most important contribution to firing an accurate shot.

In order for the bullet to hit the center of the target, the shooter must aim the pistol and give the barrel a definite direction relative to the target.

In theory, accurate aiming is achieved when the shooter places in exact alignment, the rear sight with the top and ideas of the front sight, and holds them in alignment in the aiming area.

A requisite for correct aiming is the ability to maintain the relationship between the front and rear sights.

When aiming, the front sight is positioned in

the middle of the rear sight notch with an equal light space on each side. The horizontal top surface of the front sight is on the same level as the top horizontal surface of the rear sight notch.

RELATIONSHIP OF SIGHTS

It is necessary to be acutely aware of the relationship of the rear sight to the clearly defined front sight. Normal vision is such that the rear sight of the pistol will be as nearly in focus as the front sight. Some shooters may be able to see only the notch of the rear sight in sharp focus; the outer extremities may become slightly blurred.

Angular Shift Error — If the shooter does not observe correct aiming (maintaining the top surface of the centered front sight on a level with the top of the rear sight and equal light space on each side of the front sight), there will be few accurate shots. Most often, he locates the front sight in a different position in the rear notch. This accounts for a greater dispersion of shots on the target, since the bullets will deviate in the direction in which the front sight is positioned in the notch. This aiming error is known as angular shift error.

Angular shift error

Parallel Shift Error — If the hold (arc of movement) is deviating in near parallel error from the center of the aiming area, the shooter should know that these deflections will not lower the score to the extent of angular shift error. Therefore, sight alignment is the most critical of the two. Thus, the accuracy of a shot depends mainly upon the shooter's ability to consistently maintain correct sight alignment. The main effort should be toward keeping your sights aligned. Holding the pistol perfectly still is desirable but it is not mandatory.

POINT OF FOCUS

Correct sight alignment must be thoroughly understood and practiced. It appears on the surface as a simple thing — this lining up of two objects, front and rear sights. The problem lies in the difficulty in maintaining these two sights in precise alignment while the shooter is maintaining a minimum arc of movement and pressing the trigger to cause the hammer to fall without disturbing sight alignment.

The solution is partly in focusing the eye on the front sight during the delivery of the shot.

It is imperative to maintain "front sight point of focus"

It is imperative to maintain "front sight point of focus" throughout the sighting and aiming of the pistol. The shooter must concentrate on maintaining the correct relationship between front and rear sight, and the point of focus must be on the front sight during the short period required to deliver the shot. If the focus is displaced forward, and the target is momentarily in clear focus, the ability of the shooter to achieve correct sight alignment is jeopardized for that moment. Frequently,

STRIVING FOR ACCURACY   355

this is the moment that the pistol fires. A controlled, accurate shot is impossible under these conditions.

When the eye is focused on the target the relatively small movement of the arm appears magnified. However, when the eye is correctly focused on the front sight this movement appears to have been reduced.

CONCENTRATION

If the sights are incorrectly aligned, the net result is an inaccurate shot. Carelessness in obtaining correct sight alignment can usually be traced to the shooter's failure to realize its importance. Many shooters will, in the initial phase of holding, line up the sights in a perfect manner. However, as the firing progresses and the shooter is concentrating on delivering the shot, he often loses correct sight alignment which he attained in the initial phase of his hold. Usually, when the shooter is unable to maintain a pin-point hold, his concentration on sight alignment wavers. An accurate shot is lost because the shooter is thinking of his arc of movement and not the perfection of sight alignment.

Another factor which contributes to the deterioration of sight alignment, is the feeling of anxiety which arises over the apparently stationary pressure on the trigger when attempting to fire. An im-

An inaccurate shot will result when sights are incorrectly aligned

pulse is generated to get more pressure on the trigger, so that the shot will be delivered. When the shooter thinks about increasing the trigger pressure, a degree of the intense concentration required to maintain correct sight alignment is lost. Even if trigger control and the hold are good, the net result will be a poor shot. Sight alignment must remain uppermost in the shooter's mind throughout the firing of the shot. Positive trigger pressure must be applied involuntarily. Consistently accurate shots are produced when the shooter maintains intense concentration on sight alignment during the application of trigger pressure, while experiencing a minimum arc of movement. Control of the shot is lessened in direct proportion to the loss of concentration on sight alignment.

For the average shooter, sustained concentration is probably limited to 3 to 6 seconds

The average, advanced shooter is probably limited in sustained concentration to a period of 3 to 6 seconds. This short space of time is the optimum period in which a controlled shot can be delivered. This concentration interval should be attained simultaneously with acquiring a minimum arc of movement, a point of focus, satisfactory sight alignment, and the involuntary starting of positive trigger pressure. If exact sight alignment is maintained, and the trigger pressure remains positive, the shot will break during the limited time the shooter is able to control his uninterrupted concentration. Result! A dead center hit on the target.

THE EYE

The principal difficulties which confront the shooter during aiming are determined to a great extent by the inherent characteristics of the eye and its work as an optical apparatus.

Recoil and the dread of recoil, even if subconscious, can be the bugbear of the handgun shooter. It may not figure prominently in the shooting of .22 pistols, but as the handgun's caliber moves up and the kick does likewise, the shooter faces an issue he must deal with. Charles Askins, Jr., addresses the matter in this selection taken from Colonel Askins on Pistols & Revolvers *(1980).*

Charles Askins, Jr. on recoil

KICKING HANDGUNS

If a man had 6 fingers on either hand he would be a better pistol shooter, maybe even seven digits would help the more. Too, if the wrist joint was not quite as flexible this would be a further assist. Recoil in the pistols is controlled by the fingers and the more of them the better. It might be for the really ambitious that a surgical graft of another finger or two would not be such a bad idea.

The uplift of the muzzle when the trigger is mashed is a most important item in the success of the shot for the gun commences recoil on the instant the propellant is sparked to fire. By the time the bullet quits the barrel the muzzle has raised and this is the final direction of the bullet. If the shooter's hand is weak and the grip ineffectual the muzzle upchuck will be considerable. What's even worse is that if it isn't constant from shot to shot the hits will be strung up and down on the target.

Target pistol shooters are compelled to bang off their rounds using only the one hand on the grip. This is in accordance with the rules. The new school of thought, exemplified by the silhouette marksmen, the hunting fraternity, and even the cops is that both hands should be gripped about the gun stock. It is the only smart way to go. To control the kick which has such an influential bearing on the goodness of the hit the more hands on the stock the better!

The two-hand grip is the way to go

The grip is second in importance only to the trigger let-off, the pistol is somewhat like the scattergun, it is never still and while we may get so good we can hold it almost rock steady we never entirely succeed. For this reason the pistol is a close relative of the shotgun, both are fired while in movement.

The trigger squeeze must be coordinated with that movement. The tighter, quieter and harder the grip the less wobble and the easier the squeeze. Any shooter almost regardless of who he may be can hold a gun steadier with two hands rather than with one.

And by the same token [any shooter] can control the recoil more effectively with the 2-fisted hold rather than the one. We have grown, these past two decades into a fraternity of big bore men. The twenty-two and the .38 used to be the popular shooting irons; with the old .45 Auto running a distinctly poor third. This isn't so today. The magnums are now edging forward most especially with the hunting clan. The .45 ACP from a distant 3rd choice is now clearly the gun preferred by the combat shooters. The cops stick to the thirty-eight not so much from choice but through the obstinancy of their city fathers.

The recoil of the magnums has a formidable bearing on accuracy, the more the kick the faster and the higher the barrel climbs and the more probability of a wide hit. To control this jump at least in some measure is the name of the game. One of the big factors in the successful manhandling of the big bores is the grasp on the stock.

Regrettably the stock makers have not really given much serious thought to the design of a grip for the 2-hand hold.

The stocks on all the big handguns are obsolescent because they are all designed for only the one hand. This will be corrected in time but right now we have to live with it, a complication that has got to be resolved is that the gunner wants a grip small enough to make a one-hand draw but afterward will then catch the grip with the left hand overlapping the right.

While the stock may be big enough to nicely contain the one hand there simply isn't room enough for the other. It overlaps the principal hand, usually the right, and while it is decidedly

Recoil has a formidable bearing on accuracy

important it is very much the accessory hand. Just how this is going to be improved is a problem for the stock designers. We'll hope they are working on it.

Recoil is controlled so far as possible by a tremendously hard grip. A force exerted by both hands. A grip so strong that during the first few months of practice the hands will tremble because of the inordinately hard grasp. With time and more firing the force put on the stock can be maintained and there will be no tremble. Unfortunately we do not have a grip indicator with a handy dial gauge to show the pressure to be 50 psi or whatever is proper. If we only had a neat little meter which showed when the grip-pressure got up to the proper limits the grasp could then be kept uniform. After that we'd all shoot better.

The wrist can be a weak link in the equation

Another weak link in the equation is the wrist, it is a swivel and bends and gives under the force of the up-turning muzzle. If, somehow, there was a lock on that swivel what a boon it would be!

Since we can't snap that latch the gunner wants to stiffen the wrist against the kick all he possibly can. With the Big Berthas he must also lock the elbows. This is easily done but a conscientious effort has to be made at least in the beginning for the recoil with calibers such as the .41 and the .44 magnums will break the elbow joint unless the gunner is prepared to resist it.

There are two movements when the pistol is fired. One direction is upward and the other and secondary motion is angular and is away from the supporting hand. The palm of the hand provides the principal resistance to the kick while the fingers are secondary in their support. If the hand was better designed to hold the pistol there would be 10 fingers, 5 on a side and these when wrapped around the butt would dampen not only the up-chuck but also the tendency of the gun to kick to the left.

The fingers are not as strong as the palm and so these give way under the recoil. The muzzle not only rises but it kicks off in the direction of the fingers. That is to the left which sees a hit not only high but to the 9-10 o'clock point on the target. The addition of the left hand, wrapped as it is over the fingers of the right dampen this flip on the muzzle leftward.

That is one of the major advantages of firing any handgun with the 2-fisted grip. Some fine day when the shooting fathers become a little less hidebound there is no doubt in my mind that the rule will be revised to permit strictly bullseye shooters to compete with both hands on the gun. Scores will improve when this becomes reality.

Recoil is determined by the size and the weight of the bullet, by the weight of the powder charge and the poundage of the firearm. It follows that if a big ball of sizeable heft and backed by a strapping quantity of propellant is fired in a light frame gun there is going to be a lot of punishment! These are immutable laws and the guns and ammo de-

Recoil is determined by the size and weight of the bullet

signers are fully aware of them. It is for these reasons that handguns for the magnum calibers are designed around heavy frames. This is ordnance that weighs upwards of 44 ounces and some go as much as 60 ounces.

Since the recoil begins on the instant the powder commences to burn it is contended that one solution is to make the barrel shorter so that the ball and powder combo is more quickly free of the bore. The further contention being that the muzzle will not rise so high since it is free of the ball the more quickly. These theories are in fact partly true; the only fly in the ointment is that the shorter the barrel the lighter the gun and the greater the impact of the gases on the atmosphere at the muzzle.

This impact is one of the most violent phenomena in the whole recoil equation and must be given much weight in any consideration of the problem.

Hatcher on recoil velocity   Hatcher has this to say about recoil: "For example if we have a .38 Spl gun weighing two pounds and it fires a bullet which weighs 158 grains with a velocity of 860 fps, we would expect the gun to have a recoil velocity of 860 divided by the weight of the gun and multiplied by the weight of the bullet in pounds. As there are 7,000 grains in a pound, the bullet weighs $158/7000$ths of a pound, hence the recoil velocity would be $860 \div 2 \times 158 \div 7000$ which works out to 9.7 foot seconds.

"This is the velocity of recoil; but we are more

interested in the energy of recoil than we are in the velocity. The weight of the gun, combined with the velocity is what makes it hard to hold. Velocity in itself does not mean much without weight. Thus a tennis ball coming very fast is easy to stop; it has velocity but not much weight. A baseball has more weight and at the same velocity would obviously be much harder to stop.

"The energy if the recoil of a gun is equal to one half the mass of the gun times the square of the recoil velocity, or 54 ½ MV^2. The mass of the gun is the weight divided by the acceleration of gravity, or 2 pounds divided by 32.2; and the velocity squared is 9.7 multiplied by 9.7, or 94.09. Hence the recoil energy would be ½ of 2 ÷ 32.2 = 94.09, or 2.9 foot pounds.

The development of such improvements as the Mag-Na-Port, a design which incorporates ports or orifices in the top side of the barrel just back of the muzzle and which then jets the gases skyward before these same gases pass the muzzle is a monumental step in the right direction.

While the Mag-Na-Port is best adapted to revolvers it can be accomplished in the big automatics altho I am uncertain just how successfully since the ports in the barrel must necessarily be in perfect alignment with like ports in the slide.

Unfortunately, the large frame revolver, the common choice for the make up of the big magnum calibers, is sorry indeed for the control of heavy recoil. It is immutable that the deeper the frame on the revolver the harder it will kick. The

The large frame revolver is sorry indeed for the control of heavy recoil

frame was designed during the last century and no improvements have been made since. The barrel stands some inches above the grip and because of this height the kick develops a turning motion which accentuates the punishment.

The big auto pistols are much better designed for heavy recoil

The big auto pistols are much better designed for heavy recoil because the barrel does not stand nearly so high above its support. This, beyond question, is one of the reasons the .45 ACP has crested in popularity among the combat shooters.

Ask the average handgunner and he will be certain the peewee .22 caliber has utterly no up-chuck at the business end. This is an illusion, it does develop recoil and while it is of little conse-quence to the garden-run user there are certain marksmen who give it full measure of serious con-cern. These are the fellows who shoot the Olympic rapid fire game.

This match firing requires a shot on each of 5 silhouettes in a time interval of 4 seconds. The shooter must commence with the pistol pointed to-ward the ground and upon the appearance of the targets which all swing into view simultaneously, has to aim and squeeze the trigger meanwhile swinging along to the next silhouette. It should be explained that so keen is the competition that it is not just a game of plugging each man-shaped tar-get but an oblong 10-ring in the chest has to be punctured to insure a reasonable chance of being among the winners. Recoil, faint tho' it may be, is a factor. The Olympic aspirants all fire very spe-

cial .22 Short cartridge, a round that is more accurate than the run of the mill but a selection, I
suspect, more notable for its lightness of recoil.

Such accessories as the Bo-Mar heavy rib, an
attachment for all big auto pistols and some few
revolvers has integral sights both fore and aft but
more especially is designed to add weight the entire length of the rib. Its prime purpose is to hold
down muzzle flip.

The Clark heavy slide for the Model 1911 pistol accomplishes the same ends from a slightly different direction. Clark chops two slides in two and
then welds the longer pieces together again. The
finished slide is a full one-inch longer than standard. Besides the elongated slide there is a special
barrel from Douglas to fit the elongated piece.
While this precision job adds to the sighting radius, which God knows is appreciated on the .45
Auto, more particularly it does muchly appreciated things to the recoil.

Interestingly one of the very most accurate
shooting arms in the handgun firmament is the
Feinwerkbau air pistol. It is a .17 caliber and is
shot at 10 meters. This pistol will shoot tighter
groups than all save an exceedingly small number
of the best Continental-tuned free pistols. Even
tho the Feinwerkbau does not burn powder it too
develops recoil.

There is a spring and a plunger with a piston
attached and upon the release of the trigger this
piston is driven forward compressing the air

needed to give the .177 cal pellet some 450 fps velocity. The very movement of the piston is so disturbing it may be likened to the conventional kick of the powder-burning firearm.

To overcome this vibration the designers have struck on a novel system which on the release of the trigger also loosens the entire action of the gun which floats on horizontal rails for a fractional part of an inch. The weight of the barreled action magically compensates for the vibration of the rapidly moving piston and spring and thoroughly dampens these parts. The extraordinary design feature accounts in no small part for the phenomenal accuracy of this remarkable pistol.

Before the larger powder-burning handguns, and most especially the magnums are to be made truely accurate a similar development must come along. Recoilless artillery fires both frontward and backward. There is a moderate escape of gas rearward which reduces the recoil to negligible proportions. Fantastic tho' it may seem the big magnum handguns need much the same application.

Charles Askins, Jr. on hunting sights

This selection, also from Colonel Askins on Pistols & Revolvers *(1980), is included here because of the manner in which hunting sights can improve the sportsman's accuracy. Clearly, this piece has equal applicability to the next chapter of this primer, which focuses on hunting with handguns. Drawing on his vast wealth of experience, Charles Askins, Jr., weighs in on hunting*

sights and gives the handgunner obvious reason
to consider them and their performance carefully.

HUNTING SIGHTS

Probably the poorest sights on a hunting pistol are those of plain black iron. It does not much matter the color of the animal nor the background, his surroundings, the time of day, nor the position of the sun, those coal-black sights will show up poorly. I am a believer in a front post that is as star-spangled as the old fashioned barber pole. And if the rear notch is set in a bilious green, Navy brindle, or Polar bear white that is OK too.

The poorest sights are those of plain black iron

For strictly target panning the straight iron patridge out at the business end and a rear sight just as unprepossessing in appearance is alright but for game-taking this ain't so hot.

The facts are, in truth, a gold faced front post and a white inset rear may be easier to see and quicker to pick up but for gilt-edged accuracy this combo leaves quite a lot to be desired on the score of good precision. The contrasting colors don't do anything for visual acuity and this accounts for somewhat poorer performance but my contention has always been that the shooter can give up something here in favor of faster sight alignment.

There are two or three factors in the handgunning equation that are important. I have always contended the most important is the trigger mash but the sight picture is only a half-step behind.

No one can shoot any better than he can aim and when the shot gets beyond fifty yards the sight becomes quite critical. If it wasn't for the fact that the post in front and the notch behind were so close together it would not be such a problem but that proximity of one to the other makes alignment super critical!

The best target marksmen do not focus on the target but on the front post

The best of our target marksmen do not focus the aiming eye on the target at all but concentrate on the front post.

This, in effect, causes the bullseye to blur somewhat but it brings the sights into sharpest focus. This, they have found, accounts for closer hits and is conducive to better accuracy and performance.

This is alright for the bullseye panner but it is not recommended for the game shot. He has to keep his eye on the critter and simply move his sights into the line between shooter's eye and the living target. If there is something lost in the process so be it. The idea that the game is going to be a blur while the sights are in sharpest outline won't work when you are stalking whitetails!

Because ordinary pistol sights are a pair it is argued by some of the strategists that the best solution is a low-power scope sight. This dingus eliminates half the equation and in theory, at least, improves the prospects of a close hit. Too, the problem of fuzziness in either the rear notch or around the front post is negated. The crosshairs, if the scope is in adjustment, don't develop those funny aberrations that are all too common with the conventional sights.

Thompson/Center, the makers of the excellent line of Contender single-shot hunting handguns, has a new one that is yet to be proofed in the game fields. It is an optical sight which has no magnification, projects an illuminated crosshair into infinity, has windage and elevation adjustments, weighs 5 oz, is only 2¾" in length, and readily attaches to the Contender handgun. This accessory like the low-powered short-tube conventional scope, eliminates one of the two iron sights.

I am something less than enthusiastic about a glass sight on the belt gun. It violates, in my conception, the true utilization of the one-hand shooting iron. A handgun is meant to be short, handy, fast, and highly portable. When we hang an optical sight, however small, however compact, on the pistol it loses a lot of its utility. I want my hunting arm to be readily carried either at the hip or in a half-breed rig and the only way this can be comfortably done is to stick with the original sights. Maybe sights colored up like a Navajo at the annual corn dance but standard so far as size and shape are concerned are the answer.

Sights have been wonderfully improved these past three decades, handguns except target models which were few, all had a rear notch machined into the top strap with a front that was usually a half-moon in configuration. Only a smallish hand-

I am less than enthusiastic about a glass sight on a belt gun

ful of pocket models are so unhappily blessed
today. A pistol because it is so short, with its ab-
breviated barrel and its sights all too close together
needs the finest most precise kind of sights. And
by this I mean sights that are not only adjustable
but finely movable at that. The idea that all you
need is a groove in the top of the frame and a
semicircular blade in front is utterly wrong!

There was once a well established prejudice
against any kind of an adjustable sight on a handgun. "These movable sights are too flimsy," was
the consensus of opinion and it was most especially strong among that clan which took to the
woods. The cops were just as adamant, they were
double-damn certain that any kind of a movable
sight was sure to be so weak it would not hold up
on a service gun. This prejudice has now all but
disappeared.

During those days when the only handguns
that had adjustable sights were target models, Colt
had a novel system whereby the rear sight was
movable only laterally, and this permitted it to be
gotten in zero from side to side; the front sight
was adjustable for elevation. These were the crud-
est sights imaginable. Both had to be gotten in
zero and then left strictly alone. The bucko who
was so sanguine as to try to move his sights from
distance to distance, as from 25 yards to 50, was
soon hopelessly lost. Smith & Wesson had a fixed
front sight and a rear that was adjustable for both
deflection and elevation. The side-wise movement

was accomplished by backing off on the left-hand screw and tightening on the right. This, believe it or not, was pretty definitive. The only point was that once you had the pistol in adjustment you left it alone!

The elevation was done with a single flimsy screw and once the zero had been found a second screw was supposed to lock the first in place. Sometimes it held but more often it worked loose under the impetus of the recoil and then the gunner was all at sea.

There was a manufacturer in San Francisco, named D. W. King who had a sight company called the King Gunsight, and he was very definitely ahead of his time. He developed a rear sight that was movable for both elevation and deflection and the adjustments were simple and uncomplicated and what was maybe even more important the lock on both would hold against the kick of the gun! Attached as an integral part of the rear sight was a raised ventilated rib. This was new and startling and handgun hunters did not know whether they wanted such a dingus or not. At the front end of this rib was front sight which was quite innovative too. It consisted of a one-eighth-inch red plastic post. King used to call his post "red ivory" but this was just advertising hocum, it was common plastic but it held its color very well. The notch behind was outlined in an inset white and between the two visibility was excellent. Just behind the red post and inset in the rib was a mirror made of chromium steel. This was supposed to pick up the light and reflect it on the post. This was another gimmick but it looked good and everyone who used the King sights and accompanying rib were happy with it.

Front sights on the hunting gun are placed from ½ inch to as much as a full inch above the axis of the bore, this because of the recoil which commences once the powder is sparked to flame. Actually these high standing sights are part blessing and part nuisance. They are quick and easy to find when a fast shot is needed but they are also terribly easy to cant. A canted shot is one that is fired when the sights are not truly perpendicular. A front sight canted to the left will pour the hit out in that direction. To my notion the advantages of the extra high front post outweigh its drawbacks. The old .45 Auto has a front sight, on the issue model, that is altogether too low and hard to see. When some enterprising pistolsmith adds a set of his high sights it is a decided improvement.

Sight design, the outline that is, has been muchly bettered here of late. Instead of the old half-moon configuration or something near it, we now have a ramp base with a post that slants away from the eye quite pleasingly. For the woods gun this can scarcely be improved. The base with its ramp effect, along with the post itself gets a front sight above the barrel far enough and high enough so it can be seen quickly and easily.

It used to be that bead sights were common on

the one-hand gun. If it was just plain vanilla the bead was made of black iron; if on the other hand, it was all jazzed up it would be of gold, or ivory or maybe canary yellow. The rear notch, U-bottomed to conform to the bead might be outlined in white. This was thought to be the *one plus ultra* of refinement and while maybe you never see a combo like that these days the truth is that out to 25 yards the big gold bead in front and the white outlined rear notch worked very well. It distinctly was not a target proposition and for shots on game beyond off-the-muzzle yardages it was pretty ineffectual but for all that it had its uses. Rear sights must stand up above the frame and be highly visible. The sight must be so prominent that it instantly catches and holds the eye once the pistol is lifted into the line between the man and his target. I like the Dan Wesson which has a sight that is $^{12}/_{32}$" in height; and the Ruger Blackhawk which stands $^{10}/_{32}$" in height. Along with this good size the rear face of the sight must be grooved, stippled or checkered to dampen sun glare.

A great failure of many manufacturers is to provide us with a rear notch that is too shallow. This is a fault of S&W sights and it has been that way for a very long time. Too, Smith sights usually have a notch that is too narrow so that the front post fits too snugly.

This lends itself to shots that plop to the left or right because the gunner cannot align the post with the good precision that is needed. A hunting

Rear sights must stand up above the frame and be highly visible

rear worth its salt should be not less than .09"
in depth and if it runs a full $\frac{1}{10}$-inch so much the
better.

Just as importantly, maybe even more critical,
is the fit of the front post in the rear notch. Far, far
too many sights as they come from the factory are
altogether too snug one with the other. There
should be a good ribbon of light on either side of
the front sight as it is held in alignment within the
rear notch. I'd reckon if these ribbons could be
measured that each would be not less than $\frac{1}{64}$-
inch. It is a fact that it is scarcely possible to have
too much light around the front post. The eye automatically centers the front sight in the rear anyway and because so often hunting conditions are
poor indeed on the score of good light the more
space between the sights the better.

The width of the front sight is the most critical part of the equation

The width of the front sight is a most critical
part of the equation. It used to be that all front
sights, almost regardless of the type of handgun,
had blades of $\frac{1}{10}$-inch. This was a standard and
even today, and especially on foreign imports you
will find front sights that are still this dimension.
This is poor indeed!

The first shooters to abandon the all-too-nar-
row front post were the target gunners. These
marksmen went to a $\frac{1}{8}$-inch sight and they have
clung to it ever since. Today, all our hunting revolvers and auto pistols have sights of this width.
It is very near the perfect choice.

One time I had a series of front sights made up
and these ran $\frac{1}{10}$", $\frac{1}{8}$", $\frac{1}{6}$", $\frac{1}{5}$" and one-quarter

inch in widths. I attached these sights, one after the other, to a Colt python with 6-inch barrel. The ammo was limited to Federal wadcutters .38 Spl. I shot 10 scores at 50 yards with each front sight. I commenced with the $\frac{1}{10}$" width and as the front posts grew broader I simply filed out the rear notch to compensate for the wider front.

The one-tenth-inch post shot the highest scores and made the best groups. I believe this indicated the popularity of this sight for lo these many years. The $\frac{1}{8}$" was next best. It shot scores almost on a par with the one-tenth but what was more revealing, I think, was that it was done with less eye strain and less hard work.

The $\frac{1}{6}$" front post was not so hot at 50 yards, it simply covered too much of the bullseye and scores and groups were enlarged. Where this sight really showed its worth was at 25 yards rapid fire. It was quick and easy to pick up, was plenty accurate enough for the 10-second stanza during which the shooter has to bang our 5 rounds, and generally indicated its real worth at the closer range.

The $\frac{1}{5}$", and $\frac{1}{4}$" blades were utterly no good at the long range. However at 25 yards both turned in very credible jobs.

If there were any lessons to be gotten from this test it was to pin down why the $\frac{1}{10}$" front post has had its adherents; and why the $\frac{1}{8}$" is the happy choice of virtually all today's handgunners. The latter is by long odds the better choice.

The pistol sights both front and rear, are in-

The $\frac{1}{8}$"-wide front sight is the choice of all of today's handgunners

tended to be viewed at a distance of 24 inches. This is the average length of arm of the shooting man and his gun when extended in firing position and presents the sights in a certain perspective.

When the gunner bends the shooting arm at the elbow, or rests both elbows on his knees as when firing two-fisted and in the sitting position; or when he tries to fire prone, the sights are immediately thrown out of the accustomed perspective. When this occurs accuracy suffers, the front sight commences to loom up too large, the back notch appears out of proportion, and alignment is poor. Unless the pistol and its sights can be kept extended at the usual 24-inch distance from the aiming eye trouble will ensue.

There is another side of this coin. With a lot of hunting guns sporting barrels of 8 ½" to 10 inches, the front sight gets to be like 30 to 34 inches from the aiming eye. If that post is only ⅛" in width it can look awfully skimpy and sometimes not too well defined. On all my handguns that I intend for serious hunting usage, I replace the standard post with another that measures ⁹⁄₆₄-inch. On a brand new .45 Colt Contender with 10-inch bbl, I have swapped the regular front post for an even wider post. It goes ⁵⁄₃₂-inch, and this looks good at the end of that ten-inch barrel, I'll tell you.

The only two worth-while shooting positions in the game fields

In my opinion there are only two worthwhile shooting positions in the game fields; one is off-hand with a two-fisted hold; and the other is sitting with the one-hand grip, the arm rested over the right knee and the left hand behind the body and bracing it for greater steadiness. The business of taking up the sitting posture like a rifleman with the elbows on the knees and the gun gripped in two hands is for the birds. It places the sights too close to the eye and because both elbows are bent, is not steady at all. The prone position is ridiculous. The body is close to the ground, the head is thrown back so abruptly and the sights are too close to the aiming eye that it is futile.

Because of the inherent inaccuracy of the handgun at any very great distances plus the crudeness of the sights, shots at game want to be limited to close range. I recollect a fellow who should have known better who bragged about killing a pronghorn at 217 yards. The pistol was the AutoMag which for some reason was at that time rated as being just slightly more lethal than a nuclear weapon but in truth is far outdistanced at any such ridiculous yardages. The bullet in going 217 yards will fall 70 inches which means that either the gunner held over the back of the game and thus could not see it, or he simply jerked the trigger so hard the muzzle was pointed high when the gun fired. At any rate it was a contemptible thing to do and should never had been told in public.

A hunting handgun ought to be sighted in at 50 yards to hit point of aim. If chances are offered at 100 yards these should be passed up, this business of trying for a trophy at such yardages places the

A hunting handgun ought to be sighted in at 50 yards

shooter in a very questionable bracket. He is one of these jazbos who will freely risk a wounded and lost animal simply for the sake of trying the impossible. It is a reflection of good sportsmanship, stalking skill and woodsmanship to fetch the animal into the sights at 50 yards rather than to hazard the shot at distances beyond. There are a lot of jokers who will recite, chapter and verse, how with the .30 Herrett, or the .30-30 in the Contender, or the .44 Mag loaded with 26 grains of Bullseye have knocked off moose, caribou, elk and mule deer at distances so lengthy it took a long horseback ride just to get to the dead critter.

For those who have these tales to spin I can tell you 10-for-1 about the questionable sportsmen who tried the doubtful shot, crippled the game, and the trailing a failure left a fine animal to die miserably. The handgun is a hunting arm when it is used well within its limitations. And it does have decided capabilities in the game fields, keep the shots close and both gun and man will come off looking much better.

X
HUNTING WITH THE HANDGUN

Modern hunters enjoy a challenge. The days when putting meat on the table for the evening meal was the focal point of hunters belong to a world we have lost, and as a result, today's sportsmen have increasingly turned to approaches that demand the utmost from them in terms of stealth, woodsmanship, marksmanship, and similar qualities. That explains in large measure the exponential growth in the ranks of bow and black powder hunters, and there has been an appreciable upsurge in the numbers of handgun hunters as well. In this chapter, the increasingly popular sport of hunting with the handgun is presented as seen through the eyes of two real authorities: Jeff Cooper and Charles Askins, Sr.

●

Taken from Jack O'Connor's Complete Book of Shooting *(1965), this treatment by Jeff Cooper looks at the use of the handgun by the hunter in* **Jeff Cooper** *all types of hunting — from small game to big. Some sensible questions about certain types of* *big game are raised, and the author suggests that the answer to the question of whether such animals are suitable for handgun hunting is a "qualified yes." Today that yes is no longer qualified, thanks to the development of better cartridges, the production of optical aids, and general technological advances.*

HUNTING WITH THE HANDGUN

Pistol hunting has been called a stunt, which it is, but hardly more so than any hunting which is not conducted strictly for meat. It has been called inhumane, but it is no more so than any other hunting if it is done with proper care. I have been told that, since the average hunter can't hit his rifle, he should not be encouraged to go around wounding things with a handgun. But the average hunter wounds plenty of game with his rifle. With a pistol he is more likely to miss, to the benefit of the game. There is no practical way to keep the incompetent bungler out of the woods, and he can foul things up as well with one weapon as with another.

A proper pistol is accurate and powerful enough for many types of hunting

Actually, a proper pistol is both accurate enough and powerful enough for a great many types of hunting. It will not do for tiny targets, long ranges, or pachyderms. Neither should it be used on lions, tigers, or the great bears. But there is plenty of hunting which does not fall into the foregoing categories, and a lot of it can provide excellent sport for the handgunner who is willing to work for it.

The three requisites for sportsmanlike pistol hunting are short range, proper equipment, and superlative marksmanship. A good range for a pistol is about 35 yards. Fifty yards is a long field shot; 80 is marginal; and 100 to 125 is strictly big league. Naturally this depends upon the size of the game — but the essence of handgun hunting is cover. The handgun is a "brush gun," and unless the cover is fairly thick it is not going to be the tool for the job. Certain game may be spotted from afar and then approached in cover — I'm thinking of the javelina — and this makes for good pistol situations, but the shot itself must always be a close one.

The requisites are short range, proper equipment, and superlative marksmanship

This range limitation is not, however, as serious as it might look. We do a lot of talking about those elegant 300-, 400-, and 500-yard shots but, if we're honest, we know they are exceptional. Most game is engaged at under 50 yards. At that distance an expert field shot with a good pistol can hit within 3 inches of his point of aim even under pretty adverse conditions. This will anchor a lot of game. On a recent prowl into the backwoods of Guerrero, one of Mexico's wilder regions, I had a rifle, a shotgun, and a pistol available. In seven weeks' time I fired the rifle three times, the shotgun seven times, and the pistol seventy-two times. This was thick country, and the largest game was small deer, a perfect setup for my old Super .38

and hollow-point ammunition. A .22 Jet would have been even better for the rabbits, birds, iguanas and pigs which constituted the main targets, but I needed something to serve a defensive mission as well, and I appreciated my *cuatro cargadores*.

Proper equipment means an adequate weapon, a carefully obtained zero, fine trigger action, and the right bullets

Proper equipment for the pistol hunter includes a weapon of adequate power and accuracy, a carefully obtained zero, a fine trigger action, and the right bullets. These matters are discussed in the sections on hunting arms, but I note them here again for emphasis. You should not blunder afield with a gaspipe under the impression that refinement is needed only on the target range. In the woods you stand to lose more than a high score.

Fine marksmanship is the ultimate key to handgun hunting, for while a mediocre rifle shot can do very well on a hunting trip, a mediocre pistol shot won't even get started. This corroborates the comparative efficiency of the two arms, for the master pistolero and the duffer with the rifle shoot just about in the same class — if you exclude such things as buck fever and mistaken targets, which will not bother the master. Theodore Roosevelt, who by his own admission was a very poor hand with a rifle, was a very successful hunter. I can't say how his hitting ability with a rifle would have compared to that of Ray Chapman with a pistol, who now has a string of seven clean, one-shot kills on big game to his credit.

As to standards, if a man can fire 135 x 150 on

the field course he is ready to go hunting. This is not too hard with a .22 but it's a chore with a full-house .44. Which is why pistolmen should stick to small game until they have attained quite a high gloss with their magnums.

SMALL GAME

Obviously small game is the most common objective of the handgun hunter. There is more of it, more time to shoot it, it's closer to home, and it's practical with a .22. Tree squirrels and rabbits, both cottontail and jack, are the most common targets, and they all provide most excellent sport as well as fine meat for the table. And they're not easy. One can easily be "skunked" in a whole day's hunting in good territory, especially if he tries only for head shots, as he should.

The marmot family makes excellent pistol targets. I consider marmots small game rather than "varmints" because I like to eat them, and edibility seems to be the difference. Marmots seem to call for a little more steam than a .22 Long Rifle provides, and will often make it down a hole when hit squarely with a service-type medium-caliber pistol bullet. Most of my experience with them comes from the goldens of the high Rockies, and I find that a .38 Super needs an expanding bullet to anchor them.

Any animal that is ordinarily treed with hounds is probably best taken with a pistol, as any man

Any animal treed with hounds is probably best taken with a pistol

who intends to follow a dog pack will do well to avoid the encumbrance of a long gun. The range is rarely over 30 feet, and at that distance a competent pistolero can hit a dime.

Treeable game in the U.S. includes the opossum, the raccoon, the bobcat, the cougar, and the lesser bears (*Euarctos*), and naturally the weapon used should be of adequate power for the game. Above all it must be loaded with proper ammunition. Brain shots are the most humane on a treed beast, but they are not always possible, and even the normally inoffensive black bear can work up a fair amount of justifiable indignation after being hazed to and fro across the countryside.

There are two major game animals which are often hunted with dogs but not into trees. These are the boar and the jaguar, and they are great prizes for the hand gunner. I confess to a certain reluctance to popping a treed quarry — the dim-witted possum, the charming and mischievous 'coon, the lithe and elegant cougar, or the quaint and comical bruin — but a burly hog or a massive, cattle-killing *tigre* is something else. Both tend to "come on" when the hunter shows up, and then comes the big moment for the pistol shot. The shot must be delivered coldly but very quickly. The range is short — too short — but the bullet must be placed with surgical precision, for you can't blast a furious, 300-pound beast to a standstill with pistol fire; you have to hit the central nervous system. Any man who has stopped a charging jaguar with his pistol rates a special feather in his war bonnet. This feat is to the pistol hunter as beating the drop is to the combat shot.

Varminting with a handgun is popular enough so that special weapons have been built for it; specifically the Remington XP-100 and the Ruger Hawkeye. The classical "varmints," in this country, seem to be woodchucks and crows, and hunting either with a pistol is a fairly specialized activity. As I said, I regard woodchucks as game, but I don't know about crows, as I have never eaten one. Both chucks and crows can get very cagey in regions where they are hunted extensively, and as a rule become essentially rifle targets, but in places where they are really pests they are fair game for a handgunner. A flat-shooting pistol is indicated, for distances can stretch out with either beast.

Rats are often found in large numbers in public dumps, and here is a really fine target for your .22. These repellant creatures are best jacklighted at night, and can provide a lot of tricky shooting in the course of an evening. Of course one checks the local ordinances first, but quite often a rat-shooter has the blessing rather than the disapproval of the city fathers.

Game birds are excellent pistol targets, but, except for the wild turkey, they are banned to the pistol shooter in the U.S. I have hunted ducks with a pistol in both Mexico and the Yukon, and believe me it isn't easy. One works to leeward along the shore, hoping to recover the birds as they wash up, and a slightly bobbing target flat on the water, with ripples intervening, calls for a fancy degree of elevation control. A hair high is an over, and a hair low is a short ricochet. You can try them on the wing, too, but don't expect much unless conditions are just right.

The king of the upland birds, for the handgunner, is the pheasant. You'll have to look pretty hard for a locality where it's legal, but taking ringnecks over dogs from the holster is a sporting enough activity for anyone. The rule is to keep your hand off your gun until the bird rises, and then to draw and track him as he goes out. A brace taken this way with a heavy pistol is somewhat more of an achievement than the same taken with an ounce and a half of number fours. A load of 1000 f/s or less is indicated, to avoid meat spoilage.

Taking turkeys with a pistol often offers good sport

Turkeys are the exception to the general prohibition on taking birds with a pistol, and often offer good sport. A fine account of a .38 Special on turkey may be found as the lead piece in the marvelous little book *Colt on the Trail*, published some thirty years ago by the Colt people as an encouragement to the field use of the sidearm.

MEDIUM-SIZED GAME

Of the medium-sized pistol quarries my favorite is the javelina of the Southwest and Latin America. Fast, excitable, diurnal, gregarious, and near-sighted, he is just right for the pistolero. When jumped, the flock is likely to explode in all directions, offering a series of difficult shots to several hunters at once. The .357 seems made to order for javelina.

However, when one thinks of American hunting one thinks of deer, and deer — whitetail, mule, or blacktail — are very satisfactory game for the handgunner. The best states are Alaska, Arizona, New Mexico, and Idaho; though Wyoming, Montana, and Florida are also good if you can get a positive ruling on pistol hunting out of their game departments.

Deer — whitetail, mule, or blacktail — are very satisfactory game for the handgunner

One of the really fine deer parks for the pistolero is the Kaibab plateau of Arizona, a state that specifies the .357 and the .44 (and now, presumably, the .41) as legal deer cartridges. The Kaibab is a high, rolling timberland and one of the world's most beautiful forests. It is inhabited by a carefully managed herd of big, handsome, well-fed mule deer that is hunted just hard enough to make it wary. The conifers and aspens provide enough cover for close shots without developing into a tangle, and each little draw has a jeep trail in its bed to permit easy hauling for your kill. You can camp out or hunt from a lodge, and packing and freezing facilities are only half an hour to the north on a paved highway. Altogether a fine spot, marred only by a one-to-a-customer limit that forces the handgunner to take the first thing offered rather than to wait for a trophy.

For when you hunt deer with a pistol you can't be very selective about your animal unless you are prepared to risk total failure. Considering that a handgun is three times as hard to hit with as a rifle, and has only one-third its range, one must regard any full-grown deer as a prize, and take a trophy rack as a gift of the gods.

The deer hunter works the same way with pistol or rifle, except that he simply avoids terrain that opens out too much. Setting 100 yards as his limit (remember, only an expert should take the field) he prowls the timbered ridges, glasses the edges of clearings, and waits at saddles if the woods get too full of other hunters. Particularly effective is an upwind course just below the crest of a main ridge, crossing the tributary ridges at right angles and searching the small bay at the head of each draw, where deer like to lie up in the middle of the day.

For handgunning deer, 100 yards should be the limit

Such matters are better covered in a book for deer hunters. The handgunner who hunts deer must simply remember to stick to close shots, to master his weapon, and to use the right ammunition; and he will do very well.

The deer cartridges are the .44 and the .41, though any big bore, properly loaded, will do the job up close. The trajectory of the magnums is their big advantage, for the hunter has enough problems without having to lob his shot at 75 yards.

BIG GAME

The question must eventually arise as to whether the pistol may properly be used on game larger than deer. I confess to a lack of first-hand experience in this area, but I think the best answer is a qualified yes. After all, it isn't so much the size of the target as the range at which it is shot. The .44, using the Norma bullet, will shoot right through both shoulders of a moose and out the other side. Not at 300 yards, but at pistol ranges. If the hunter insists on close shots, and passes up the foolish ones, he ought to be able to take fairly large animals with humane, one-shot kills. On big animals the .44 does not appear to deliver the instantaneous knockdown of a .30/06 on a deer, but for that matter few riflemen have ever seen a moose knocked off its feet by a rifle bullet either. As long as the quarry staggers and falls within 50 yards, the kill may be considered clean, and a .44 Magnum bullet, through the heart, will achieve this on animals quite a bit bigger than a deer. Thus I believe that elk and moose, together with the African antelope, may properly be taken with a handgun under special circumstances. By no means do I recommend this as a general pastime, but I hope I have made clear by now that pistol hunting is never a sport for the ordinary sportsman.

Since the pistol hunter is rather unusual to

Elk, moose, and the African antelope may properly be taken with a handgun under special circumstances

begin with, he has the advantage of being able to forget convention. Since he's not after a Boone and Crockett head anyway, he can branch out. There are a number of beasts which are not game animals in the strict sense, but which, in these days of diminished conventional hunting, may offer fine sport to men in search of the unusual.

Handgunning the crocodilians

Particularly I have in mind the crocodilians — alligators, crocodiles, caimans and gavials. These are big, rough, not uncommon in the right regions, and can be dangerous. They are scorned by the riflemen as they lie in mesozoic sloth on the sandbar, but how about tackling a 20-footer with your .44?

Experts claim there is only one good place for your bullet, and that is in the center of the short neck directly from the side. This will anchor, while anything else will let the beast make it to the water. It ought to be feasible to spot downriver, then land and make an inshore approach to a point just at the edge of cover. Then, if you can hit a half dollar at whatever distance you can close to, a 240-grain steel-jacketed soft-point should net you enough leather to fill a shoe store.

And keep in mind that these latter-day dinosaurs come in several degrees of impressiveness. The king is the saltwater crocodile (*Crocodilus porosus*) of Oceania. Up to 10 yards long, agile and aggressive, and notably fond of human flesh, a prime *porusus*, taken with a pistol, would be a trophy of which any hunter should be proud.

TOP PISTOL TROPHIES

Just as the rifleman gleans the world for its best and finest trophies, the pistol hunter can endeavor to establish a set of grand prizes which could stand as testimony to the special qualities of the handgun as a sporting weapon. I don't feel that it would be right simply to duplicate the rifleman's list, for while it is technically possible to secure an argali, or a tiger, or a white bear, or even an elephant, with a handgun, it is not a sportsmanlike venture. I realize that sportsmanship is a matter of opinion, but in *my* opinion one can go too far in attempting to do a job with "an instrument singularly unsuited to the task," as Mark Twain said of a golf club. It may be that any pistol is unsuited to the pursuit of big game, but I don't believe this to be true. I think there is a compromise area, where rare, burly, beautiful, or dangerous animals are sought at short range under conditions that make them especially suitable as pistol targets. In preparing my own list of top pistol trophies I realized that I immediately pose a legal problem, for in many jurisdictions hunting with a handgun is not permitted. I do not suggest breaking the law, I simply suggest that laws, especially game laws, can be changed. You can't win at Indianapolis without exceeding the speed limit. Likewise you'll find it impossible to collect the grand prizes of the pistol without securing certain legal dispensations. This can probably be done.

Some rare, burly, beautiful, or dangerous animals can be hunted with the pistol at short range

Jeff
Cooper's
choices of
the top five
big game
animals for
the hand-
gunner

The following, then, is my choice of the royal five for the pistolero, listed by continents. Naturally all specimens should be prime examples of the species, as near to the record as possible.

Eurasia — For this area I'll pick the European wild boar (*Sus scrofa*), found from the Eastern Alps to the Tien Shan. He is a short-range target, rugged and quarrelsome, and he is quite capable of killing you. Taken with a pistol as you come up on the dogs, his 300 pounds must be stopped by the most careful use of the heavy handgun. Since most of his habitat is presently behind the Iron Curtain there are fairly difficult problems to be solved in getting at him. (Imagine trying to get a visa for your .45 auto!) But he has been imported into the U.S., so let's accept an immigrant, especially if he is outstandingly big and bellicose.

Africa — Here again the current political situation is so unstable that it's hard to say what the rules are or how they are enforced. In ex-English areas the pistol is probably still viewed with horror, but in the Portuguese colonies, east and west, people are more reasonable if they are approached politely. Skipping the giants and the traditional, I'll choose the gorilla. You'll need a museum permit to take him, but such can be had. If you threaten his group he will charge, and a charging gorilla is a fearful spectacle, to stand your ground with a handgun and flatten him at 15 feet is man's work.

North America — Again I will bypass the traditional, because the big bears are not humanely taken with a pistol. For a creature that is large, wary, noble in aspect, and a lover of the deepest forests where the range is short, I'll pick the Roosevelt elk (*Cervus canadensis occidentalis*). Bigger in body, darker in color, and with shorter but heavier antlers than the better known Rocky Mountain elk (*Cervus canadensis canadensis*), he is a beast of the dense, dank, rain forests of the Pacific Coast. He must be hunted with great skill, for you have to move in on him like a ghost to escape detection by his marvelously sensitive ears. And if you succeed in this, his massive body calls for very precise use of your .44 if you are to secure a clean kill. As of this writing, it is practically impossible to get permission to hunt the Roosevelt elk with a pistol, but this may change as handgun hunting becomes more respectable.

South America — There is no argument here, as the jaguar takes the prize. Not just any jaguar, but a really prime cat of 250 pounds or more. Such are hard to come by, and though Mexico's famed Enrique Job tells me that size is not a function of range, I feel the chances for a really massive *tigre* are best in the Mato Grosso and southward. Siemel, the spearman, has a photograph of one he took, the skin of which is so big that a tall man can just reach the ear when the hind legs touch the ground. This was Brazilian, but I understand that Paraguay, Bolivia, and Argentina claim some huge cats, too. Few English-speaking hunters penetrate the upper reaches of the Paraguay-Paraná river system, so there is not much written material available to us on the big cattle-killing jaguars, apart from rumor. This is one of the few remaining unspoiled hunting countries. Happily, there is no special problem about handgun hunting in Latin America, where the authorities seem more worried about rifles than pistols. If you can get a weapon permit at all, it is good for any sort of weapon.

Australia-Oceania — The warm waters of the Malay Archipelago and the north coast of Australia are the home of *porosus*, the aforementioned saltwater crocodile, and he is the last big prize. What with the Australians' anti-pistol bias, and the Indonesians and Malaysians perpetually on the brink of war, there are plenty of technical difficulties here. Also, *porosus* does not appear to be common, to the relief of the indigenous population. Here is a project for a man with a sea-going yacht, plenty of time, and a .44 Magnum.

Charles Askins, Sr. discusses hunting with the handgun

Charles Askins, Sr., did considerable hunting with handguns during the first half of the twentieth century, although Elmer Keith is rightly recognized as the gun writer who did the most to popularize this type of hunting. Here Askins offers his thoughts on the subject in an interesting and informative fashion. Some of the equipment-related limitations he addresses no longer exist, but his thoughts on approaches and choices of firearms retain their validity. This piece comes from The Pistol Shooter's Book *(1953).*

HUNTING WITH THE HANDGUN

There is a great deal of misconception in the minds of handgunners regarding the true killing power of the handgun. People who should have better judgment spin many dangerous yarns about shooting big game with the onehand gun. There isn't a pistol or revolver in existence that is fit to use on game the size of deer. A number of years ago one of our handgun manufacturers developed a new cartridge and a new revolver for the load and in order to give the development proper ballyhoo he proceeded to stalk and kill a very small moose, an equally small and unimpressive black bear and an elk. When his exploits were given the proper splash in all the outdoor magazines it served no better purpose than to encourage a good many handgunners to go afield and cripple big game.

I am an enthusiastic devotee of the hunting handgun. I enjoy nothing so much as to stalk and kill game with the pistol, however, I limit my hunting to the small things. The handgun will kill rabbits, squirrels, birds, foxes, javalina, wildcats and similar game, but it distinctly is not for such beasts as coyotes, wolves, deer, antelope and those species even larger.

An enthusiastic devotee of hunting with the handgun

I recently saw published in one of our midwestern hunting-and-fishing magazines a series of letters from three Californians who were attempting to kill deer with the .44 Special revolver. The firearms editor in publishing the series of letters

was very lauditory of the purpose of the sportsmen (?). However, what was most revealing about
the accounts of the two or three deer shot was
that the game was running and hits had been luckily made in head or neck. How anyone could be so
utterly devoid of sportsmanship as to shoot at a
running buck with a handgun at distances of more
than 100 yards (as these birds did) is beyond my
understanding.

Experiences as a forest ranger in New Mexico
In 1929-30 I was a forest ranger in the north-
west corner of New Mexico. On one side of me
was the Jicarilla Apache Indian Reservation and
on the other side was a goodly stretch of land in
Public Domain. The Indians had a great many
horses and these they permitted to run wild. Since
only a part of my ranger district was fenced, these
broomtails fed as much off my grass as off the
Reservation. On the side which bordered the
Public Domain I had little grazing problem save
from nesters who wanted to slip a few head of
stock onto the forest when my back was turned.
The horse problem was the more serious. I estimated the Indians were running not less than
1400 head of worthless, runty, unbroken broncs
on the forest land.

With the tacit approval of the forest supervisor,
who was more than 100 miles away, at Taos, I declared war. Everywhere I rode, and for five
months of the year I averaged 30 miles a day; I
carried a sixshooter and a rifle and every time I
came upon a band of broomtails I left dead horses

in plentiful numbers. These animals were almost like deer. You could not ride up on them if the wind was in their favor. They would scent you and hightail it when you were a half mile away. I stalked them like a band of elk. I'd climb a hill and carefully survey the country ahead. If a band was in sight I'd get the wind in my favor approach on foot to within 50 yards, crawling the last couple of hundred yards, and then open up on them. At the first shot the band would take to its heels like antelope.

I killed several hundred horses and I used a variety of both handguns and rifles on them. I deliberately set out to prove all the larger calibers of pistols and revolvers. I used the .30 Luger, the 9 mm. Luger, the .38 Super Automatic, the .45 Auto, and even the .22 Woodsman. I also used the .38 revolver, the .38-40, .44-40, .44 Special and the .45 Colt. Unfortunately the .357 Magnum had not yet been developed. I believe it is the most powerful of all one-hand weapons and I would have enjoyed proving this contention.

As a result of my exhaustive experimenting on the Indian broomtails I hold a very low opinion of the pistol as a killer of any medium-size animal. These horses were not wild game, even though they were precious near to being so; they were born of domesticated mares. It can be safely assumed, for instance, that a runty three-year-old weighing 650 pounds could be killed more easily than a bull elk of the same poundage, or of a bear running about the same weight. Despite this, I could never kill these horses with any certainty. Many times the animal had to be finished with the rifle, which I also kept handy for that very purpose. I shot these animals everywhere, I shot them in the head, neck, shoulders, spine, through the heart, in the lungs and through the paunch. I shot them from directly in front and I shot them from behind. I had a pack of dogs that I ran lions with and so I butchered many of the jugheads for hound meat and traced the course of many of my shots.

Not only was penetration poor but the most disappointing thing was the lack of shock. This was apparent with all the calibers and with the high speed loads like the .30 Luger, 9 mm. Luger and .38 Super the lack of apparent blow was most noticeable. Of the several big calibered revolvers I liked the .38-40, .44-40 and .44 Special very much. I could see little difference in the performance of the three. It is now contended that the .44 Special can be souped up with heavy overloads so it is the best killer of them all. This is very probably true. With factory loads, which I was using, I couldn't see that it was any better than either the .38-40 or the .44-40. The .45 Colt distinctly will not kill like these other big loads.

As a result of my vast amount of experimentation on the Apaches' livestock I have a very poor opinion of the handgun as a killer of big game.

I eventually tired of living like a sheepherder

and hearing some exciting stories about the gun-fighting that was going on along the Mexican bor-der between the newly organized Border Patrol and the "contrabandistas" I resigned from the For-est Service and accepted an appointment in the Patrol. My pardner, George Parker, was already in the outfit and was into and out of one gun fracas after another whetting my appetite for a taste of the excitement.

Experiences as a member of the Border Patrol

After a year in El Paso I was assigned to a desert outpost about 25 miles west of El Paso. The part of the International Line to be covered by my pardner and I was ample for even the most space-loving; we had a stretch ranging from the outskirts of El Paso to Deming, New Mexico, 120 miles west. We ranged this area on horseback but after a few years we put the caballos out to pas-ture and commenced to cruise in an old sedan equipped with giant sand tires. For a hunter like myself it was rich existence, for every day I was tracking game — big game — the most dan-gerous and therefore the most exciting of all. We had frequent brushes with the smugglers, and since tracking gangs in an old car was a sure invi-tation to ambush we were kept on our toes most of the time.

Among other dodges that we employed to track down the border crossers, was a pack of hounds. These kyoodles worked fairly well if we put them on a track immediately after a rain, otherwise the sand was so barren of moisture it would not hold the scent for any length of time. If however, our quarry decided to strike for the Rio Grande Valley the dogs worked marvelously, for the valley was under irrigation and there the scent remained very well. Feeding the pack was a problem.

The desert was alive with jackrabbits and I killed the long-eared denizens with my sixshooter. We rode horseback about 30 miles daily, and after changing to the car drove 50-75 miles each tour. We always came in with enough jacks to feed the pups their daily big meal.

The desert jack is an animal weighing about 8-12 pounds and he is as tough as the country itself. While his body appears soft and certainly is easily penetrated with any kind of a pistol bullet, getting the game to lie down and die peacefully after you have done a thorough ventilation job is quite another thing.

During the 5 years I was stationed on the desert I killed several thousand jackrabbits. I shot them with every caliber of handgun in the book, mostly however I used the big calibers, .38 Special and larger. Unless a jack was shot through the heart or spine (I couldn't shoot well enough to hit head or neck except by sheer luck) he was dangerously apt to escape. A shot through the lungs or the paunch, or in one of the legs meant that he would run, if through the lungs not far, but if farther back he might get away entirely. One of the worst killers in this regard was the .45 ACP, a cartridge which I used in both the service automatic and in the S. & W. Model 1917 revolver. The 230 grain slug, heavily jacketed, would knock a rabbit down; he'd kick and twitch for perhaps 20 seconds and suddenly bound to his feet and be gone. I learned with this caliber that if I bowled the quarry over the thing to do was to drive in a following shot as quickly as I could.

Two of the best killers were the .44-40 and the .44 Special. When the .357 Magnum came along it killed jacks better than any of the others; the shock effect was noticeably greater. However, it left a great deal to be desired. While the gun has 1450 ft. seconds of muzzle velocity, the amount of upset to the slug when it encounters the soft flesh and flimsy bones of the western jack is insignificant. The .32-20, a low-powered rifle cartridge is infinitely better. After my many years of shooting rabbits observing as I have, the mediocre performance of even our most powerful handguns, it seems utter stupidity for anyone to consider shooting big game with sixshooter or auto pistol.

One year while returning from the National Matches I stopped off in Oklahoma and had a shoot-of-a-lifetime on bull frogs. I had with me two members of the Border Patrol pistol team and it was the first time either had ever shot frogs with the pistol. We used our regular match .22 automatics and match ammunition. We soon learned that although shooting distances were ridiculously short a high degree of precision was required in the placement of the shot. The bullet had to hit

A shoot-of-a-lifetime on bull frogs

the brain or sever the spinal cord directly behind the brain. Otherwise the greenback would give one last convulsive leap and be lost. It was exciting and interesting sport.

Probably of more fun to me was an annual pilgrimage I used to make back to Oklahoma every year to visit my father. In the woods about his place were tiny fox squirrels and these I used to stalk using a Colt Shooting Master and wadcutter loads. It was the custom — and an iron-bound one, believe me — that squirrels had to be shot in the head. If someone saw you bringing in a mess of squirrels shot anywhere except in the head you were "hurrahed," to use the vernacular of the section. I therefore endeavored to drill my game through the head. The wadcutter bullet when I did connect with a sly red ear was worse than lightning. I was at that time firing away about 35,000 rounds of pistol ammunition annually and so the business of hitting a mark about 2¼ inches square at distances of 60 feet was not as difficult as it might seem.

Squirrel hunting

For this shooting, the revolver I used was equipped with patridge type sights, but the front post was a red plastic made by King Gunsight Co. It loomed up in the woods beautifully; otherwise the gun was a standard target weapon.

During the years I was on the desert I lived in a tiny settlement where there were five American families and about one hundred Mexicans. About the water-pumping station (for the Southern Pa-

cific R.R.) were a number of cottonwood trees.
Here I used to shoot English sparrows. The sparrow, as everyone knows weighs about 3 ounces,
maybe less, and offers a target about the size of
the end of your thumb, an antimated, suspicious
target never given to lingering long in any one
place. I used to shoot sparrows daily and rich fun
it was.

Tommy Box, a regular member of the Border
Patrol pistol team, later killed in line of duty, came
out one day and with my old tomcat, Pancho Villa,
tagging at our heels we shot 17 sparrows. The cat
ate them one by one and upon gulping down the
last, I observed that the middle portions of the feline chassis were barely clearing the sand. Had
someone not nearly so familiar with his nocturnal
habits as myself seen him, they would most likely
have immediately jumped to the conclusion that
here was a pussy in the latter stages of feline preg-
nancy. Those 17 sparrows bulked up most star-
tlingly and while Pancho did not die of tomcat in-
digestion the meal made a lasting impression on
him. He never afterward could be persuaded to
eat a single sparrow.

For this shooting, Box used his Woodsman .22
auto and I used a H. & R. .22 single shot furnished me by Walter Roper, who had designed
the model for the Harrington and Richardson Co.
The .22 was the only practical gun to use on the
tiny marks.

Handguns for game shooting may be any cal-

**Handguns
for game
can be any
caliber from
.22 to .45**

iber from .22 to .45, the caliber depends on the wild things hunted. The .22 performs very well on such targets as small birds, crows, the lesser hawks, squirrels, cottontail rabbits, snakes, frogs, gophers, chipmunks and like small game. For targets like jack rabbits, the larger hawks, owls, fox, wildcats, javalina, mountain lions when bayed by the hounds, and game similar to this, I favor the very heaviest calibers. The gun may be revolver or automatic but should be of good weight, at least 36 ounces, and should have a barrel length running at least 5 inches. Custom stocks are a great help just as they are on target guns.

Part III

GENERAL CONSIDERATIONS

A myriad of considerations enter into the matter of marksmanship. Obviously, the functional qualities of a rifle or pistol form part of the accuracy equation, and this means that use of a firearm with first-rate capabilities is of great importance. However, once the marksman has chosen a firearm, and even as he practices, sights in, studies ballistics, and takes similar steps, he needs to keep more basic concerns in mind.

Among these, safety is foremost. Its preeminence in anything related to the use of firearms explains why safety is the subject that forms the basis and beginning point of any and all types of shooting. With that in mind, it might not be a bad idea to refresh your personal awareness in this regard through reading the "Ten Commandments of Gun Safety" and the NRA's insights on safety. There are a number of excellent sources of safety information available on line. Remington's web site offers an award-winning safety program and a test (www.remington.com/safety/safety.htm).

Safety is
foremost

The NRA's web site also provides considerable information (www.nrahq.org/education/guide.asp). Ultimately, the "three Cs" — caution, care, and common sense — should be a part of every marksman's approach to shooting.

Similarly, good guns deserve good care. The marksman should maintain his firearms in tip-top condition in order to get tip-top performance. Proper maintenance of firearms should be a given. With suitable care well-made pistols and rifles will last not one but multiple lifetimes. Cleaning should be a ritual, something that forms an integral part of a day's shooting or hunting.

Cleaning should be a ritual

Moreover, the proper tools of the trade — brushes, rods, bore cleaner, lubricant and the like — should form a part of every shooter's kit. It isn't necessary to do a complete job every time, but a few strokes with a brush through the bore, followed by patches, along with a wipe-down of exterior surfaces with a cloth impregnated with rust preventative, needs to always follow each use of the gun.

More extensive cleaning takes place at the end of the hunting season or when the firearm is to be stored for a lengthy period of time. Likewise, it is a good idea to check and clean any gun after it has been in storage and following sessions at the bench or target range where a lot of rounds were fired.

Today's solvents and lubricants work better and gunpowder burns cleaner as well as leaving less (and cleaner) residue. Moreover, fully functional and far less corrosive propellants have been developed for blackpowder guns, although this category of firearms still requires special care. Better tools are available for cleaning than ever before, although home-made rigs and handy substitutes (such as use of an old toothbrush for scrubbing or pieces of worn-out shirts for patch material) still have their place. The basic consideration, for any marksman, is simple. Clean, well-lubricated firearms perform better, more predictably, and are safer. Those are reasons aplenty to make cleaning an integral part of your shooting regimen.

Virtually anyone can shoot a firearm, but fitness, both physical and mental, figures prominently in how well one does it. Chapter XI deals with two key aspects of attitude and physical readiness and the ways they can lend themselves to accurate shooting. Similarly, accessories also have their part in marksmanship. Most of us love the paraphernalia of shooting, but beyond the ample measure of pleasure it provides gear nuts, it should be recognized that fine optics, properly fitted stocks, comfortable grips, and many other accessories have their place in improving performance. Chapter XII examines some of these subjects.

Collectively, while sometimes overlooked, considerations such as safety, proper cleaning, fitness, and accessories form the underpinning of all

Physical and mental fitness are important

proficient marksmanship. Keep them firmly in mind as you read the closing chapters of this work and take its information to the shooting range or hunting field.

XI
PHYSICAL AND MENTAL FITNESS FOR THE MARKSMAN

Conditioning, both physical and mental, figures prominently in marksmanship. Hand-eye coordination, razor-sharp reflexes, breath control, and even the ability to reduce one's pulse rate are all part of the physical equation. An ability to "think out" shots, confidence, analysis of conditions, and even an understanding of the potential (and limitations) of one's firearm all form part of the mental side of things. The marksman strives to be as prepared as possible, both physically and mentally, and the material that follows offers varied suggestions on how to achieve optimal readiness.

●

This incisive analysis of the reasons we miss comes from an accomplished hunter, marksman, and writer, Wayne Van Zwoll. It originally appeared, under the title "Missing in Action," in the August 2003 issue of Sports Afield.

Wayne Van Zwoll on why hunters miss

WHY HUNTERS MISS

If you've never fired a shot at big game, seek out someone in your community who hunts and ask him to show you a rifle. Shooting can be a lot of fun.

If, like me, you've missed often, you're apprehensive every time the crosswire dances tentatively into a shoulder crease. You know that when the trigger breaks, the die is cast, and you don't trust yourself to hit. Missing easy shots can shatter your confidence and predispose you to miss. Expect to miss and you probably will.

So the first step to better shooting at big game [is simply that] better shooting at big game. Here's how:

Five steps for better shooting at big game

1. *Acknowledge that you're in charge of each shot.* Hunters with alibis set themselves up to miss. If you know that wind and gravity and pine boughs bend a bullet's path, it's up to you to compensate or decline the shot. Remember: if you don't shoot, you can't miss. A couple of years ago, I passed a shot at the biggest bull elk I've seen on a public-land hunt. The animal was 250 yards off — easy range, had I been steady. But I was not, and he gave me no time to get steady. Filling the air with bullets when you merely *hope* to hit boosts your odds for a hit from zero to just above zero, while odds that you'll miss or cripple rise from zero to nearly 100 percent.

2. *Be ready to shoot, always.* And when the possibility of a shot pops up, act as if you will shoot. To decline a shot is easy; you can

do that anytime. Hitting usually requires that you make the most of every second.

3. *Anchor the rifle.* That is, shoot from the steadiest position available. Use a rock or limb as a rest, but pad it with your hand to reduce the rifle's vibration away from the surface during recoil. Tree-side support can throw your shot to the side. Learn to use a shooting sling. The loop transfers weight from your left hand to your left shoulder, which can better support the weight. A carrying strap doesn't work *because it pulls from the rear swivel, too,* tugging the rifle from your shoulder and twisting it. A sling helps in prone, sitting and kneeling positions because your left elbow is anchored. It's not as useful in offhand (standing) because sling tension moves your arm.

4. *Focus.* Thinking about what you'll wear at the Boone & Crockett awards banquet or how you'll have the taxidermist turn the head slightly left is distracting. Concentrate on the reticle as muscle memory from long practice brings the rifle on target. Breathe deeply a couple of times, to deliver oxygen to brain and eyes for clearer aim; then let your lungs relax as you pull the rifle firmly into your shoulder with your left hand and begin the trigger squeeze. Add trigger pressure when the reticle comes on target; hold pressure when it wanders. If your position

falls apart or the reticle is bouncing too hard or you run out of breath, start over. *Shooting* must command all your attention.

5. *Go gently on the trigger.* A hit is a slice of time. A tiny slice. The bullet has only one chance in its headlong flight to find the mark, and as you squeeze the final ounce from that trigger, you seal the outcome. All the rifle movement you see in the scope field before a shot matters not; what counts is the position of the reticle when the bullet leaves. If you hold a rifle still, then jerk the trigger, you're pulling the rifle off target during the eyeblink in time that locks in the bullet's flight path. The hit or miss occurs late; but after the trigger yields, there's no changing the result.

A lot of hunters set themselves up to miss even before there's a shot to take. They don't practice. Shooting is like any other activity. The more often you do it, the more natural it seems. Now, firing away at soup cans on a sandbank is only helpful if you mind what you're doing. A few careful shots benefit you more than a host of full magazines sprayed without regard to shooting fundamentals. Paper bull's-eyes help you most because the bullet holes tell you where your sight was when the rifle fired. Calling your shot, or predicting where the bullet will land before you see the hole, is an important skill. You'll want to know as an animal runs off where the bullet struck. Paper targets

Calling your shot is an important skill

confirm your calls — or show that you didn't pay attention.

If paper bores you, try metallic silhouette shooting. Knocking steel animal cutouts from pedestals, you'll polish your offhand technique. Small-bore silhouette shooting is a cheap alternative. Understudy rifles (high-quality bolt-action .22s like my Kimber) have the feel and accuracy of a big game rifle. They cost little to shoot; and they treat you gently, so you can refine skills without developing a flinch.

"Recoil makes you miss," observed one of my friends, an Olympic medalist in marksmanship who uses a .308 Winchester for hunting. It's true! Watch a fellow benching the latest high-octane ordnance. Pretty soon the groups open up. "Barrel's heating," he says. And it may be. More likely, recoil has him on the ropes.

Intrinsic rifle accuracy and power matter less than most hunters suppose. What counts in the field is shot placement. Ordinary bullets fired through the forward ribs at ordinary velocities kill game. A rifle well handled is likely to kill what you shoot at. And rifles that don't brutalize you are easier to shoot well.

What counts in the field is shot placement

Because you'll shoot mostly inside 300 yards (probably much closer on average), scopes of modest size and power make sense. Magnification shrinks field of view and reduces brightness. The big objective lenses that transmit more light also add weight and bulk to your rifle. They make it top-heavy and may put the sight line high enough to pull your cheek off the stock. One more thing: my sights are all mounted well forward, so I see the full field with my face all the way forward on the comb. Many hunters attach scopes too far to the rear for fast shooting, or for shooting uphill or from sitting or prone positions.

Tips for uphill and downhill shooting

A note on uphill and downhill shooting: If the animal is close, or the angle gentle, just hold as you would for a shot on the horizontal. Far away, steep angles can cause the bullet to go high. That's because gravity's effect on a bullet depends only on the horizontal component of its flight. Vertical doesn't count, so the effective range may be significantly shorter than the bullet's travel distance. Shade low.

Even when you're prepared, the pressure of time affects your shooting. Once you have fundamentals in hand, it's a good idea to practice under the clock. Remember that accuracy is more important than speed, and if you don't have time for a good shot, you really don't have time for a shot. [In] Hunting, you often have more time than you think, however, and many hunters miss because they rush.

A few more tips, if you don't like to miss: When hunting in cold weather, wear wool mitts that free your fingers through a slit. They're warmer than gloves; besides, it's hard to shoot accurately with gloved fingers. Make sure before season that you can shoot well when dressed in hunting gear. A heavy jacket or a backpack strap can increase your effective length of pull. Practice getting into a sling or using your bipod or shooting sticks, so you can steady your rifle quickly and without taking your eyes off the target. Adjust your trigger for minimum creep and a letoff of 3 pounds. If yours won't give you a clean, consistent letoff, replace it with an aftermarket trigger.

Odd though it seems, many hunters miss because they don't know where their rifle is shooting. Before you practice, you need a zero — at 200 yards, in my view. Next, fire at 100 and 300 yards to check bullet drop. In the field, hold center to 250 yards. A lot of bullets miss high because hunters overestimate distance or forget that zeroing has lifted the bullet's path (relative to the sight line) already. Once you've refined scope settings, leave the dials alone. Don't tweak that sight in the field unless positively necessary! Almost always, the best hold is very close to where you want the bullet to strike. Shading can get you in trouble.

Shooters commonly blame recoil, or kick, for misses. Although there is no denying that recurrent recoil or simple dread of it can cause flinching, the subject requires careful analysis by the studious marksman. Here Jack O'Connor, in a piece taken from The Hunter's Shooting Guide *(1978; second edition), looks at flinching in his typical no-nonsense fashion.*

Marginal notes:

Adjust your trigger for minimum creep and a letoff of 3 pounds

Jack O'Connor discusses flinching

THIS FLINCHING BUSINESS

Flinching on the part of the shooter is supposed to be a low and discreditable business, something which nice people simply do not do, just as they don't write bum checks, take dope, or have fits. Asking a man if he has any trouble with flinching is a bit like asking him if his child has two heads or if he has poisoned the well at the orphans' home lately.

Yet many shooters always flinch. All shooters sometimes flinch — rifle shots, pistol shots, trap-shooters, skeet shooters, big-game hunters. Flinching is one of the major reasons for bum shooting. Show me a man who can honestly say be has never flinched and I'll show you a man who has never shot a gun.

Show me a man who says he never flinched and I'll show you a man who has never shot a gun

Sad thing about it is that many a citizen is convinced that he holds like a rock and that he never flinches. This is one of the major reasons why some people shoot forever and never get any better, why some cannot successfully call their shots.

What a good flinch can do to an otherwise properly held shot is wonderful to behold. Results are most marked with a handgun with its light weight and short barrel, but flinching with a rifle can throw a shot wide and I am convinced that a nice well-executed flinch can even cause a miss with a wide-patterning shot gun.

I write this piece as an authority, by the way, as I have flinched with every sort of an instrument that burns powder and some that don't. I am free to admit it.

Sad thing about flinching, as I have said, is that most of its practitioners have no notion that they flinch. If they do not realize it, they cannot cure it.

First, what causes a flinch? The usual explanation is that flinching is caused by the fear of recoil — of getting hurt by the bump and scared by the muzzle blast and report. Our boy knows that when the gun goes off he is going to he bumped and socked and that his ears are going to ring. So, he cringes (flinches) just as he finishes his trigger pull and knows he is bringing about these bad and unpleasant things.

What causes a flinch?

This explanation is partly or even largely true, but flinching is also caused by nervous tension. I have seen men who almost never flinched in rifle practice but who always flinched in a match and whose scores went down accordingly. I have seen others who never flinched when shooting at a tin can yet who would flinch when trying to pop at a rabbit.

First step in curing this very common habit of flinching is for the shooter to realize and admit that he flinches. Until he does that his case is as hopeless as that of a man suffering from some undiagnosed physical ailment.

How do you find out?

Simple! Have a pal load and cock a gun and hand it to you to shoot, sometimes leaving the chamber empty and sometimes not. If you flinch you'll find yourself contracting the muscles of the shoulder, jerking the trigger of the empty gun. When the gun is loaded, the recoil covers the flinch; but when empty, it doesn't.

Not long ago a young man who had been away to college and who had not shot a high-powered rifle for some months was out with me. He sat down, took a pop at a stone with a diameter of about 1 foot, and about 200 yards away. He missed it, took another shot, and missed it the second time.

"You're flinching," I told him.

"I am not either," he said, insulted.

I took the rifle, pretended to load it, but instead handed it back with an empty chamber, and told him to take another pop at the rock. As the firing pin clicked down he jumped a foot. Grinning sheepishly, he admitted he had been flinching. I took the rifle again, but this time I eased a cartridge into the chamber.

"All right," I said. "You know the chamber is empty this time so squeeze her off with those crosshairs right in the middle of the rock." He did and white powder flew right from the center. Convinced that he had been flinching, he shot well from then on.

This was quick detection and quick cure, but the boy had fought his battles with flinching before.

Two ways of curing flinch

Once a man realizes that he flinches, he has two ways of curing it. The first — and the one which is recommended by the army — is for the marksman to squeeze the trigger so gradually that he does not know when the gun is going off. When the sights look right the pressure on the trigger is increased a bit, when the sights swing off, the pressure is held. When the gun goes off, the report and muzzle blast will come as a surprise and our hero won't have time to flinch. This method is sometimes called "surprise fire" and a very good method it is. The beginner should always be instructed to hold and squeeze them that way, and he should always begin either from a rest of some sort or from prone because then his rifle is comparatively steady and he does not have the temptation to make a grab at his trigger to catch a bull's-eye as it goes by.

"Surprise fire" is a good method

Some old and experienced and also very fine shots claim they always use this surprise-fire method of shooting anything and from any position. Others claim they always know when the gun is going off.

My own first love is the rifle. I am a rather fair rifle shot and not too bad with a shotgun. I know about when both are going off. But there is only one way I can shoot a handgun and keep from flinching and that is to hold as well as I can and squeeze off by the surprise-fire method. If I try to catch the bulls as they go by, I flinch — doggone it, I flinch!

Shooting offhand with a rifle, which is sort of a sister of handgun shooting, I have very little tendency to flinch, as shown by the fact that when I was doing a good deal of offhand shooting I almost never got one out of the 4-ring. *But* I have noticed that if I have difficulty in getting a shot off and take so long that my muscles get tired I sometimes flinch and throw a wild one. The idea seems to be that my muscles say they are tired so let's yank it off and get it over with. The remedy for that is to put the doggoned cannon down and rest the arms.

We have seen that one way to cure the flinch is to attempt to kid yourself and squeeze off so gradually you will not know when the gun is going off. The other way to cure it is by conscious exercise of the will, *by concentration on target and sight alignment instead of what's going to happen at the butt end.*

When a man *knows* he flinches and resolves to cure himself the battle is half won. Probably the best answer in the way of a cure is a combination of the two recommended methods. First he can train himself to apply the pressure on the trigger very gradually with no tendency to yank, concentrating on trigger squeeze, sight alignment, and target, and *not* on what's going to happen when the gun goes off. Second, he can train himself *not* to flinch by conscious desire not to, and by making it a point to follow through on his shot, to try to keep his sights aligned *after the trigger falls.* This business of letting go all holds when the trigger falls is highly conducive to flinching.

Don't over-gun yourself

Our boy also makes this business of curing or not developing a flinch much easier if he doesn't over-gun himself. Some people have much greater recoil tolerance than others. The average trained shot can shoot a .270 or .30/06 without much flinching trouble, but few can shoot a rifle of heavier recoil without jumping now and then. Most people, though, are afraid to admit that they are recoil-sensitive, apparently feeling that if they did they would be admitting they were sissies.

There is nothing disgraceful about flinching, then. It is done in the best families and by the best shots, but no one can cure a flinch unless he *knows he flinches*. When he realizes that, he can go about a cure by adopting a gradual trigger squeeze, by putting the kick and muzzle blast out of his mind and by concentrating on the sight picture and the follow-through. He can help matters by not over-gunning himself.

The man who makes up his mind that he isn't going to flinch and who then applies his pressure on the trigger so gradually that it slips off an ounce at a time and who does his damnedest to keep his sight aligned after the firing pin falls isn't going to have time to do much flinching!

There is nothing disgraceful about flinching

XII
OTHER CONSIDERATIONS

A wide variety of factors must be considered when striving for the ultimate in marksmanship performance. In addition to physical and mental fitness, all sorts of aids improve accuracy. Depending upon the situation, these include the manner in which the gun is stocked, the sling, open sights, optics (spotting scopes, rifle scopes, and binoculars), and other accessories. The two selections that follow address a pair of the key aids that can be used to produce better shooting performance.

●

Wayne Van Zwoll, an accomplished marksman and competitive shooter as well as an experienced hunter, takes a detailed look at the gun's stock in this piece that appeared in the winter 2003 issue of Mule Deer. *He rightly suggests that a grip that suits the shooter's hand can make a real difference in performance.*

Wayne
Van Zwoll
on grips,
stocks,
and fore-
stocks

GET A GRIP

Hunting isn't at all like target shooting. You don't just lift the rifle; you carry it. You don't merely support the rifle; you hold it. You don't maneuver around the rifle; you direct it.

Oddly enough, rifle makers have largely neglected the one component that makes rifles easier
to carry, hold and aim. It's the stock. Making a
stock lighter on the carry, quicker in the hand,
and steadier at the shot is easily done. Once a
stock pattern is fashioned, it takes no more work
or expense to produce an unattractive, impractical
stock than it does one of flowing, functional line.

The ideal grip and forend result from custom
fitting, but it's certainly possible to make a commercial stock that fits many shooters. Mannlicher-
Schoenauer did it, on carbines that almost pointed
themselves. So did Winchester, with its stock for
the M94.

Practical grips and forestocks aren't complicated in form; they needn't be checkered. They're
simply well-thought-out extensions of your hands,
with as little bulk as can be arranged, and curves
that enable your hands to quickly find their positions, then relax as the rifle settles toward the target. If you must adjust your hands on the stock, or
if you're even conscious of that contact, the stock
needs work.

My hands, roughly the size of memorable pork
chops, have to work at getting around grips and
forends like those on some rifles with beefy wood
stocks. If you must wrap your fingers to hold the
rifle, there's too much to grip. Point an English upland gun or, if like me you've easier access to a
broomstick, any long, slender handle. Quick, huh?
You'll want more weight in a center-fire rifle, but

not much more bulk. Notice, too, that the fingers of your right hand needn't take charge. The meaty part of your palm, in firm contact with the grip (or stick), can bring enough pressure to bear. Your cupped shoulder does the rest. So a deep, steep, thick grip is just an impediment on the carry, an obstacle to fast aim.

A grip too steep also puts your trigger finger too far forward. Result: you can't pull straight back with your first joint. Instead, your big knuckle is ahead of the trigger, and as you squeeze, you pull to the right. A long, sweeping grip is not only good for big hands; it allows little hands to find the most comfortable place to rest. Double shotguns with double triggers typically have straight grips so the shooter can slide his hand back with ease during the first-barrel recoil. Recoil on potent double rifles makes a pistol grip more practical, but the necessary control can still be had with a long, open grip that gives your hand some latitude in placement and allows it to slide back and forth or around the grip for fast handling.

Among my favorite rifles is an old Springfield 03A3 equipped with a homemade synthetic stock. Whoever fashioned it had his wits about him. The grip is very long, with a delayed radius — it comes almost straight back from the guard — and very slight thickening to the rear. It's thinner in cross-section than it is deep, though not by much. Radiused away from the sides of the guard, it gives easy access to the trigger. A broad, deep flute on the right catches the heel of my hand, and the comb nose retreats far enough to allow a quick thumb-wrap. The forend is pear-shaped in cross-section and is relatively shallow so the rifle rests low in my hand. The forestock tapers gradually in depth and width to the front, so my left hand gets help as it lightly tugs the rifle into my shoulder. Together, grip and forestock offer just enough bulk to give my hands control of the rifle. But the profile from all angles is slender and sweeping. Straight lines are straight; curves are segments of circles.

In a hunting stock, you don't want a flat-bottomed forend or a grip so steep that you find it comfortable shooting Metallic Silhouette matches. **Avoid "hand-filling" stock designs.** Avoid "hand-filling" stock designs. If you have trouble holding a rifle still, get a Latigo sling. Snug above your left triceps, it hauls the rifle back to you, while deadening pulse bounce. Properly adjusted, it will let you relax into a shooting position, demoting your left hand to a minor supportive role and reducing the pull required of your right. It works in all positions save standing.

Checkering, stippling or roughened finishes all help weld your hands to the stock. But you don't want them stuck there. The stock should be free to rotate slightly in your hands and should pivot easily as you swing the rifle on running game or take a steep uphill or downhill shot. On wooden stocks, I like modest checkering patterns cut 22 to

24 lines per inch. Diamonds should have the edge of a butter knife — not sharp to the touch or jagged, but never flat. Stippling is as functional, if not as attractive. "Blob" finishes on synthetic stocks don't help much if the exterior is smooth — especially in rain or snow. But avoid the sandpaper finish I felt on a rifle recently. My hands couldn't slide, rotate or otherwise fine-tune their position.

Keeping a rifle almost fluid in your hands is one key to hitting game on the move. Competitive shooters who swing at predictable targets on tracks excel with stocks shaped to lock their hands into a consistent grip. But on the hunt, you may shoot from a variety of positions, at game moving fast and slow, uphill and down. You may have to hold a shot until the target crosses an opening or interrupt or even change direction with your swing. A slender stock is more versatile and will still deliver high scores on mechanical targets.

Keep the rifle fluid in your hands

Many commercial hunting rifles could use new stocks — not because the originals give out but because they're built too stout to fail. A stock is a handle. Like the handle on a hoe or hammer, it must nestle easily in your palm. You'll want almost aerodynamic lines and more room than you think your hand needs fore and aft. Pick a delicate-looking stock over one that reminds you of target guns. A comb that seems too far back probably isn't. Ditto for the grip. On hunting rifles, a forend that appears comfortable to grab is probably too thick. So is any that accommodates a varmint-weight barrel or rests without rocking on a table.

You'll know a good stock when the rifle seems to find and track targets by itself, but you're smart to get a grip before the target is one you really want to hit.

C. S.
Landis on
stock
design,
style, re-
stocking,
and re-
finishing

Over decades of shooting and writing, C. S. Landis studied all aspects of rifles and rifle shooting. In this selection, taken from his book Rifle-Craft *(1923), he offers an insightful and somewhat different approach to stocks from that of Wayne Van Zwoll.*

THE STOCK AS AN AID TO ACCURACY

One reason for the existence of a stock on any sporting or target rifle is to enable the shooter to hold the weapon steadily while aiming. Another is to enable him to absorb the recoil without seriously affecting the aim. To do this properly the stock should fit the shooter and it should be supplied with a butt plate of such size and shape that the recoil will he distributed over the largest possible area and not merely on the bony protuberances that adorn the shoulders and chests of some men.

For many years our shotgun shooters and particularly the trapshooters, have recognized the value of perfect-fitting stocks and the pleasure and satisfaction that is to be derived from owning at least one really high-class weapon. On the other hand, most men strongly object to paying over one-third to one-half as much for a rifle that ought to be not only of equal, but of even better quality and fit than the shotgun as it is a weapon of greater precision.

As most rifles must be sold cheaper than shotguns, it follows that the standard grades of commercial weapons are not often supplied with stocks that are made to special dimensions at the *regular prices*. Many of them can be so obtained if desired, at an extra cost that pays for the work required. This fact, however, was not generally known or taken advantage of until the remodeling of military rifles became popular and many shooters began to give real attention to this question.

The standard sporting and military rifle stocks will fit a good many people reasonably well, but sometimes to some they feel much like the average income, which is entirely too small and has too much drop connected with it, to be desirable.

In these cases the effectiveness with which the weapon can be used, particularly for snap-shooting, may be greatly increased by fitting it with a stock that is made to different dimensions. Not everyone knows what these dimensions are. The best way to obtain them is to try out each of the rifles and shotguns that can be secured, to measure the drop at comb and heel; the length, width and pitch of the butt-plate; the length of pull, width, depth and circumference of the grip, and to note its position; and the distance through stock, or stock and cheek-piece, where it touches the face. Then choose and combine those dimensions which fit you the best.

Other things that should be determined are the distance in front of the trigger where the left hand grips the fore-end, the shape and size of the fore-end at that point, and also the distance through the receiver if a bolt-action, and the distance from the trigger to the front end of the fore-end.

Any woods hunter knows how difficult it is to align rifle sights at moving game, especially late in the evening or early in the morning, when the light is dim. Unfortunately a very large percentage of the best chances and the biggest heads are then presented. The advantage of a perfectly-fitting stock that will automatically help to align the sights on the mark is obvious.

Fit of the stock, and the balance and "feel" of the rifle

The position, shape, and size of the comb will very largely determine the fit of the stock, and the balance and "feel" of the rifle. The comb should provide a secure and comfortable place to rest the shooter's cheek, so that the weapon may be held more steadily, especially in off-hand, snap-shooting. If the comb fits the face properly the eye will then glance through the sights as soon as the rifle is thrown to the shoulder and it will not be necessary to hunt around for the sights while trying to aim at game.

By examining and trying the different styles,

both the full, rounded trap and the sharp, thin combs; and by measuring either from trigger or butt plate, to the point of the comb to see how far they extend up on the tang; it is possible to select a style that will be satisfactory under most conditions. It can also be determined whether it would be advisable to have the stock made with a cast-off and if so, its amount and direction. Now is the time to decide whether a pistol grip is desirable. Its shape, size and position and the amount and style of checkering it will receive, can then be most effectively determined.

The butt plate is another detail that should be very carefully considered. It makes no difference how many nick-nacks may be placed in a trap in its center. The important matters to consider are its shape, size, durability and cost. If it is too rough, its engraving or cross lining will be deeply embossed on someone's red and tender shoulder. Even a ten-pound .22 target rifle will leave its mark — a red bruise — caused by the pull on the sling.

The butt plate is a detail that should be carefully considered

An important and expensive hunting trip may be a success or a failure depending upon the interval of time needed to make a snap-shot at a rapidly-disappearing deer or goat. On such occasions there is no time to waste in adjusting a slippery, sticky, or uncomfortable or poorly-fitting butt plate. The time *to save time* in this instance is when making the design and adding the details.

It is important to wear the same quantity and

type of clothing as will be worn when hunting or target shooting when determining the dimensions of stocks and butt plates. Both the thickness of the clothing and the shooting position make a big difference in the fit of a stock. One that fits off-hand is usually too long and too crooked to fit properly when used prone.

The height and weight of a man have little to do with the fit of the stock of his rifle. The length of his neck, the width and fullness of his face, the length of his arm and fingers, especially of the trigger finger, and the breadth of his shoulder have a great deal to do with it. The way the head is held and the position of the arms and shoulders, while shooting, are all factors to be considered.

For a big-game rifle, no matter whether it is a bolt or a lever-action, or an automatic, the following dimensions will suit the majority:

Recommended stock dimensions for the majority of shooters

For men with *short* arms and fingers, wide chests and shoulders, short necks and full faces, a drop of 1½ to 1¾ inches at the comb and 2¼ to 2½ inches at the heel is ample. These measurements are taken from the point-blank sighting of the rifle. A greater drop will place the comb away from the cheek and will put the top or heel of the butt plate too far down on the shoulder. The rifle will then feel unsteady and awkward and be hard to aim.

A length of pull, center of trigger to center of butt plate, of 13¼ to 14 inches will be very comfortable. It will also enable the rifle to be held *steadily* and will cut down the severity of the recoil, particularly that part of it which is delivered on the jaw or lips, or the fingers.

A large, flat or slightly curved shotgun butt plate, 5 to 5¼ inches long by 1½ to 2 inches wide, depending upon the overall size of the rifle, should be chosen. If the length from trigger to toe is not much greater than the length from the trigger to the center of the butt plate it will eliminate a tendency to slip down off the shoulder.

If the distance from the center of the trigger to the front end of the pistol grip cap is 3¼ to 3¾ inches and the circumference of the grip is 5 to 5¼ inches, the grip should be very comfortable.

This still leaves the tall and graceful, thin brethren to be taken care of. Thin faces, long necks, arms and fingers, bony collar bones and an inclination to stoop or lean forward when shooting, must all frequently be allowed for.

A drop of 1⅝ inches to 2 inches at comb and 2½ inches to 3½ inches at heel with a stock length of 14 to 14¾ inches will please the majority. The pistol grip should be a bit *longer* and set farther back — 3¾ to 4 inches, trigger to cap; and thicker, 5 to 5½ inches in circumference, in most cases. Thin-faced people will also prefer thicker and more rounded combs and cheek-pieces.

The fore-end should be proportional in length and diameters to the size of the barrel when building for appearance, but when choosing for practicability it should be designed with respect to the length of the left arm and the size of the hand. If the forearm is flat on the bottom it will eliminate a tendency to roll in the hand and nearly all canting of the rifle will be avoided.

This type feels awkward when used off-hand, but is fine for prone target shooting. A gentle swelling of the sides and sharp, but fine checkering will usually eliminate a tendency toward slipping. Most forearms are too small in diameter, are too sharp and thin, and are too short for the best holding.

The first reason for re-stocking is to make the rifle fit better, but at the same time it supplies the opportunity to add greatly to its beauty. Nearly anyone admires and treasures beauty when applied to a possession of this nature. For centuries before the time of the flintlock, ornamentation, often of the most beautiful and elaborate types, was common on the weapons of celebrated hunters and warriors.

RIFLE OR SHOTGUN STYLES

In choosing the stock either the rifle or shotgun style can be selected, or a beautiful model combining the grace of outline and softly rounded curves of the rifle stock with the heavy comb and wide butt-plate of the shotgun. The modeling of the comb, grip, and under-stock from grip-cap to toe of butt, will very largely determine the beauty of outline of the finished job. The grain and finish of the wood will give these their proper setting and contrast.

RESTOCKING

The big rifle factories can usually supply fancy or specially-designed stocks for each of their own models of rifles. The private gunsmiths can provide almost anything that their experience has enabled them to design.

The addition of a special stock may sound like useless extra expense to many, but it is absolutely the greatest aid to off-hand, snap-shooting that can be applied to a rifle. It is permanent, if made properly, and is inexpensive compared to the cost of going- on an extended big-game hunting trip.

HOME-MADE STOCKS

Many shooters of a mechanical turn prefer to make their rifle stocks. While the results are not always as beautiful as the work of the professionals, still they are usually quite satisfactory in fit and balance and enable the shooter to do better game or target-shooting. The principal requirement is a block of good-grade and perfectly-seasoned black walnut and the knack of working in wood.

A very comprehensive article describing the making of rifle stocks was written by Major Townsend Whelen and printed in the April 1st and 15th, 1922, issues of *Arms and The Man*.

REFINISHING RIFLE STOCKS

Eventually all of the stocks that are used considerably for either game or target-shooting acquire a weather-beaten and battle-scarred appearance. Barbed-wire fencing is as hard on gun stocks as it is on trousers and results in the nicking and scratching of many a beautiful piece of walnut. Rock slides and briar thickets all add their quota of damage until in time the rifle stock acquires a pattern that is far from beautiful.

Procedures for refinishing

In refinishing a stock the first thing to do is to buff down the surface of the wood to remove the dents and scratches. If it is a varnished or shellacked stock, the remaining glaze must be removed before the sandpaper, or steel wool can reach the wood. This is accomplished by dissolving it with varnish remover. After the hard glossy surface has been removed, take coarse emery paper and buff out all of the scratches that can be effaced. Do not spare the deep cuts unless so much wood must be removed as to change the contour of the stock at that point. All scratches that remain will show up as distinctly as before, when the surface is again oiled.

Red putty, fiber or wood filler may often be used to fill exceptionally deep scars and do not, when the stock is refinished, show up in sharp contrast to the grain of the wood. Such cuts are seldom encountered, as the removal of a thirty-second or a sixteenth of an inch of surface wood will eliminate most of the scratches.

After each cut and scratch is buffed out so thoroughly that it cannot be traced when the wood is held up to a strong light, it is time to think about applying the final finish.

It is useless to attempt to buff out deep cuts by using *fine* grades of emery or sandpaper, as it takes too much time and work. Begin with the moderately coarse grades and gradually decrease the roughness of the abrasive material.

Cuts on the checkering may well be left alone or else filled up with red putty, or inserts of wood, and re-checkered, as emery or sandpaper applied to the checkering will ruin it.

The emery should be carefully kept off the metal parts of the rifle or else they will be badly scratched and marred. It is usually advisable to remove the stock from the weapon, as shellac, if it is used, will stick to the fingers and be transferred from them to the steel where it is very hard to get off.

After the scratches have all been removed, and the contour and outline of the stock is all evened up, take the finest grade of steel wool or sandpaper and finish the scouring. Fine scratches may be seen by looking at the wood from all angles and in a strong light.

The wood should then be wet with warm water and allowed to dry over a flame. This will raise the grain of the wood. These particles should be buffed off and the process repeated until no more spores are noticeable.

After the grain has been rubbed down and all

of the scratches have been removed, the stock is ready for the finish. The stock should never be set away behind a hot stove or close to a very hot radiator, because if the wood is not thoroughly dried it will crack or warp badly, especially at any place like the tang, that might be under heavy strain.

APPLYING THE DULL FINISH

The dull London oil finish is obtained by rubbing a solution composed of two parts of raw linseed oil and one part of turpentine, into the wood. The oil is applied on a piece of felt or by the hand.

The turpentine causes the oil to dry in faster and its use makes it possible to apply a large number of coats in comparatively a short time. The two things necessary are plenty of elbow grease and patience, as the wood will soak up an almost endless amount of oil. The addition of paraffin oil, later on, seems to make the color darker and richer.

THE GLOSSY SHELLAC FINISH

If a glossy finish is desired it is obtained by applying a coat of shellac.

Take a pad of cheese cloth or other soft material and rub linseed oil into the stock. Dip the pad in linseed oil, then into the shellac and then rub it on the wood. Repeat the process until the wood absorbs the mixture. The friction applied has much to do with the finish secured. Keep on applying the oil and shellac until the stock is saturated and will take up no more. Allow it to dry for two or three days and rub down with *fine* steel wool.

If there are bright spots on the wood, where the grain is not filled, repeat the operation. Let the stock stand until dry and then rub with fine steel wool until the bright spots have disappeared.

To obtain the glossy shellac finish, the final application of oil and shellac is applied until the desired effect is accomplished. It is *not* rubbed down with steel wool after the last application.

If the mixture on the pad gets gummy and stringy and a messy-looking job results, too much shellac has been used. If the pores of the wood do not fill up properly — use more shellac.

THE DULL SHELLAC FINISH

Proceed as for the bright shellac finish and finish off with pumice-stone or oil. This makes a very beautiful job.

CHOOSING THE FINISH

The finish to select depends upon one's personal preference and the quality of the wood. The dull, oily finish is the best for a really fine piece of walnut of close grain.

The glossy shellac finish is the showiest.

The dull shellac finish is probably the best one to use on a stock that is subjected to considerable wet weather. It is very beautiful and brings out the grain of the wood splendidly.

In refinishing stocks it is advisable to remove the butt-plate, if much wood is to be removed, to keep it from being scratched. It may be necessary to grind it off to make it fit properly to the refinished stock. It is also necessary to exercise considerable care to see that the wood does not warp while it is removed from the action. It should be replaced when you are not working on it. Care should also be taken to see that too much wood is not removed at those points where the stock fits up to the tang or receiver.

A very light-colored piece of wood may be stained dark by using wood filler. This often adds greatly to its appearance.

The actual refinishing of a stock is much simpler than the description would lead you to believe.

CONTRIBUTOR BIOGRAPHIES

CHARLES ASKINS, SR. — Major Charles Askins, Sr. (1861–1947), was probably America's leading firearms expert during the first quarter of the twentieth century. Before World War I, he contributed regularly to national hunting magazines such as *Outing, Recreation, Outdoor Life,* and *Field & Stream,* and during the same period he also wrote three books: *The American Shotgun* (1910), *Wing and Trap Shooting* (1911), and *Rifles and Rifle Shooting* (1912). His efforts expanded appreciably in the 1920s, and for many years he served as gun columnist for both *Outdoor Life* and *American Rifleman.* During this part of his life, he also wrote *Wing-Shooting* (1923), *Shotgun-Ology* (1926), *Shooting Facts* (1928), *Modern Shotguns and Loads* (1929), and *Game Bird Shooting* (1931). He was the father of another noted gun writer, Charles Askins, Jr. (see below), and his son's autobiography, *Unrepentant Sinner* (1985), includes some interesting comments on the elder Askins.

CHARLES ASKINS, JR. — The younger Charles Askins (1907–1999) was the famous son of an even more famous father. He followed in his father's footsteps as a gun writer, authoring a number of books and serving as field editor of *Guns Magazine* for many years. He was a colorful, controversial, and often cantankerous individual who in the course of his lifetime was a solider, lawman, firearms expert, noted big game hunter, and marksmanship instructor. He won the National Pistol Championship as a young man and taught marksmanship while a member of the U.S. Border Patrol. He also saw service in World War II and trained South Vietnamese troops in Vietnam.

His books include *Hitting the Bull's-Eye* (1939), *The Art of Handgun Shooting* (1941), *Wing and Trap Shooting* (1948), *The Pistol Shooter's Book* (1953), *The Shotgunner's Book* (1958), *Texans, Guns & History* (1970), *Gunfighters* (1981), and *Unrepentant Sinner* (1985; his autobiography).

JEFF COOPER — Jeff Cooper is a marine turned writer who was an expert pistol shot. After retiring at the rank of lieutenant colonel, Cooper wrote a number of books and contributed to national magazines. His books include *Fighting Handguns* (1958), *Guns of the Old West* (1959), and *The Complete Book of Modern Handgunning* (1961). He coached a number of intraservice pistol teams and personally won numerous first places in combat pistol shooting matches. He contributed the sections on pistol shooting to Jack O'Connor's *Complete Book of Shooting* (1965).

EDWARD C. CROSSMAN — In the words of one authority, Captain Edward C. Crossman (1889–1939) was among the "outstanding figures in the firearms field during the first half of the twentieth century." He made his first contribution on firearms to a magazine in 1904, when only 15 years of age, and from that point on was a regular contributor to the National Rifle Association's (NRA's) *Arms and the Man* and its successor, *American Rifleman*. Crossman could be abrasive and was always opinionated, and at times he seemed to take inordinate delight in irritating readers and editors alike. Yet there is no denying that he knew his stuff, and in the latter stages of World War I, he was the individual who, in effect, taught those who taught rifle instructors. He was also a first-rate competitive shooter and competed for his country in a number of international shooting matches in the postwar era.

Crossman's activities at the end of and following World War I led to the publication of all his books. These included *Small-Bore Rifle Shooting* (1927), *The Book of the Springfield* (1932), and *Military and Sporting Rifle Shooting* (1932).

JULIAN HATCHER — Julian Hatcher (1888–1963) grew up in Virginia's Shenandoah Valley. He graduated with honors from the U.S. Naval Academy at Annapolis, Maryland, but after a brief period in the naval service transferred to the U.S. Army. His career in that branch of the military stretched from 1910 to 1946, and throughout that time and beyond, he was recognized as one of America's leading authorities on firearms. He was an expert on everything from cannons and mortars to small arms, and he was also an inventor of some genius.

Hatcher first garnered major recognition in 1914, when he developed a highly functional breech mechanism; and in the latter stages of World War I, he oversaw military efforts connected with small arms and machine gun engineering and design. He would later be attached first to the Springfield Armory and then the Frankford Arsenal, before a stint as Army chief of ordnance, Small Arms Division, from 1929 to 1933.

It was during this period that he began to make his true mark as a writer and as an expert marksman with both pistol and rifle. Some of his earliest writing was done for the NRA's *Arms and the Man,* and he also later contributed to that magazine's successor publication, *American Rifleman.* He served as technical editor of the latter magazine for a number of years.

Over the course of his career, Hatcher wrote an impressive number of books, including *Pistols and Revolvers and Their Use* (1927), *Textbook of Pistols and Revolvers* (1935), *Handloader's Manual: A Treatise* (1937), *Hatcher's Notebook* (1947), *The Book of the Garand* (1948), *Handloading: An NRA Manual* (1950), and the posthumously published *NRA Firearms and Ammunition* (1964). Hatcher died on December 4, 1963, and, fittingly for a man who had done stellar duty for his country in so many ways, was buried in Arlington National Cemetery.

A. L. A. HIMMELWRIGHT — Abraham Lincoln Artman Himmelwright, an architect by profession, was one of the leading authorities on pistols and pistol shooting during the first part of the twentieth century. A marksman of the first order, he captained the Americas Shooting Team at one point and also served as president of the United States Revolver Association. His literary efforts include *In the Heart of the Bitter-Root Mountains* (1895), a description of a famed Montana elk hunt by the Carlin party; the section on pistols and revolvers in Caspar Whitney (editor), *Guns, Ammunition, and Tackle* (1904); and *Pistol and Revolver Shooting* (1915). He also wrote *The San Francisco Earthquake and Fire,* which looked in depth at building materials and the lessons the disaster had to offer.

C. S. LANDIS — Judge Charles S. Landis (1886-1961) was a prolific gun writer who specialized in rimfire rifles. From the appearance of his first book, *The Use of Rifles for Game and Target* (1922), through the 1951 publication of *Woodchucks and Woodchuck Rifles,* he wrote regularly on all aspects of .22-caliber rifle hunting and marksmanship, the wildcat cartridges that were becoming increasingly popular, handloading, and related topics. His articles appeared in magazines such as *Outers, Outdoor Life, Gun Digest,* and *Rod & Gun in Canada.* His full-length works include *The Shooter's Guide* (1925), *.22 Caliber Rifle Shooting* (1932), *Twenty-Two Caliber Varmint Rifles* (1947), and *Hunting with the Twenty-Two* (1950).

JACK O'CONNOR — Jack O'Connor (1902-1978) was born in Nogales, Arizona. After a short stint with the U.S. Army's 158th Infantry at the end of World War I, O'Connor obtained undergraduate and graduate degrees and then taught college in Texas and Arizona, all the while moonlighting by writing for newspapers and working for the Associated Press. He wrote two novels in the early 1930s, but as his family grew, O'Connor turned to writing for outdoor magazines to supplement his meager income.

It was in writing on guns and hunting that he found his métier. His love of guns and their uses in sport, along with a real feel for words and a transparent honesty that he could no more hold in check than he could hold his fiery temper, was what made O'Connor such a great writer. Most of his columns, feature articles, and books were written over the course of the three-plus decades, beginning in 1939, that he was associated with *Outdoor Life.* As the magazine's shooting editor, he was insightful, opinionated, and extremely influential. Almost single-handedly, he popularized flat-shooting, smaller-caliber rifles (most notably his beloved .270). Through his columns, he led adoring readers on hunts for all the species of North American big game, on safaris in Africa, and on shikars in Asia.

O'Connor was a complex, complicated individual. A friend, Jim Rikhoff, suggested that he was "a mixture of the sensitive and the sensible, of the ribald and reflective, of insight and inspiration, of instinct and intellect." As an author he was unquestionably a masterful stylist, and the same held true in the natty way he dressed, his feel for sportsmanship, and so many other aspects of his life.

His books are his most significant and enduring literary legacy. Here is a list of O'Connor's books, in chronological order by date of original publication: *Conquest* (1930; a novel), *Boom Town* (1931; a novel), *Game in the Desert* (1939; published with a new preface in 1945 under the title *Hunting in the Southwest*), *Hunting in the Rockies* (1947), *Sporting Guns* (1947), *The Rifle Book* (1949), *Hunting with a Binocular* (1949), *Sportsman's Arms and Ammunition Manual* (1952), *The Big-Game Rifle* (1952), *Jack O'-Connor's Gun Book* (1953), *The Outdoor Life Shooting Book* (1957), *Complete Book of Rifles and Shotguns* (1961; an excerpt was later published as *7-Lesson Rifle Shooting Course*), *The Big Game Animals of North America* (1961), *Jack O'Connor's Big Game Hunts* (1963), *Complete Book of Shooting* (1965), *The Shotgun Book* (1965), *The Art of Hunting Big Game in North America* (1967), *Horse and Buggy West: A Boyhood on the Last Frontier* (1969), *The Hunting Rifle* (1970), *Rifle and Shotgun Shooting Basics* (1986), *Sheep and Sheep Hunting* (1974), *Game in the Desert Revisited* (limited edition, 1977; trade edition, 1984), *The Best of Jack O'Connor* (1977), *The Hunter's Shooting Guide* (1978), *Hunting Big Game* (1979), *The Last Book: Confessions of a Gun Editor* (1984), and *Hunting on Three Continents with Jack O'Connor* (1987). The latter two works were published posthumously.

In addition to being the sole author of the aforementioned

works, O'Connor was a major contributor to a number of other books, most published or sponsored by *Outdoor Life*. Particularly noteworthy in this regard are his contributions to *Outdoor Life's Gallery of North American Game* (1946), *The Hunter's Encyclopedia* (1948), *The New Hunter's Encyclopedia* (1966), and *Sportsman's Encyclopedia* (1974). Selections from his writings have appeared in dozens of anthologies.

WILLIAM REICHENBACH — William Reichenbach was an exceptionally elusive figure. He does not appear in any of the standard biographical directories. Clearly he was an acquaintance of that publishing genius of the firearms world, Thomas G. Samworth, for both of Reichenbach's books, *Sixguns and Bullseyes* (1936) and *Automatic Pistol Marksmanship* (1937), were published by Samworth's Small-Arms Technical Publishing Company. He wrote in a chatty, engaging style, "blissfully ignoring all literary precepts" (according to Samworth), but his two books on pistols seem to be the extent of his work as an author.

JOHN TAYLOR — Widely known by his nickname, "Pondoro," John Howard Taylor (1904-1969) was born in Dublin, Ireland. Anyone interested in full details of his career should read his autobiography, *Pondoro: Last of the Ivory Hunters* (1955), or Peter Capstick's *A Man Called Lion: The Life and Times of John Howard "Pondoro" Taylor* (1994). Typical of Capstick, the latter work is somewhat sensational and probably pays undue attention to Taylor's homosexuality.

From the early 1920s until the outbreak of World War II, Taylor spent most of his time in Africa. There he enjoyed a remarkably footloose existence as an ivory hunter (mostly illegally), lion killer, mission farmworker, and officer in the British South Africa Police (he was dishonorably discharged). He also found a bit of time for sheep ranching in New Zealand and Australia and even poached birds of paradise in New Guinea. In short, he was something of a scoundrel, albeit a singularly engaging one. Two of his books, *African Rifles & Cartridges* (1948) and *Pondoro,* are true classics. He wrote two other hunting-related books, *Big Game and Big Game Rifles* (1946) and *Maneaters and Marauders* (1959), as well as a little-known novel, *Shame* (1956).

BRYCE TOWSLEY — Bryce Towsley is an award-winning writer and photographer who specializes in hunting and the firearms used for that sport. Over the past two decades, he has published hundreds of articles and thousands of photographs in most of the major outdoor and gun magazines. He is a field editor for the NRA's *American Rifleman* and *American Hunter* magazines and "reloading columnist" for *Shooting Illustrated,* and he holds masthead positions at *Petersen's Hunting* and *North American Hunter.* He is a member of the North American Hunting Club's Shooting Advisory Council. His books include *Big Bucks the Benoit Way* (1998), *Making Shots: A Rifle Hunter's Guide* (2000), and *Benoit Bucks: The Second Generation* (2003). An admitted gun buff and avid hunter with almost 40 years of experience, Towsley has hunted widely in the United States as well as in Mexico, South America, Africa, Russia, Austria, and Hungary.

WAYNE VAN ZWOLL — Wayne Van Zwoll is a full-time writer who specializes in hunting and gun-related topics. He is the author of more than a thousand articles and nine books.

Five of these — *Modern Sporting Rifle Cartridges* (1999), *The Hunter's Guide to Ballistics* (2000), *The Hunter's Guide to Accurate Shooting* (2002), *The Gun Digest Book of Sporting Optics* (2002), and *Bolt Action Rifles* (2003; coauthored with Frank de Haas) — deal with the technical side of guns. The others are *Mastering Mule Deer* (1988); *Elk Rifles, Cartridges, and Hunting Tactics* (1992); *America's Great Gunmakers* (1992); and *Elk & Elk Hunting* (2000). Van Zwoll assembles the specifications section of *Shooter's Bible* and is in charge of publications of the Mule Deer Foundation. A competitive shooter since his undergraduate days at Michigan State University, he qualified for the final Olympic small-bore tryouts in 1972 and has won two state prone titles. He was the Outdoor Writers Association of America Shooting Sports Writer of the Year in 1996. Van Zwoll earned a doctorate from Utah State University; his research focused on the effects of postwar hunting motives on wildlife policy.

TOWNSEND WHELEN — Once appropriately described as "a naturalist with a rifle," Townsend Whelen (1877-1961) was one of the twentieth century's most prolific outdoor writers. Born in rural Pennsylvania, he became a skilled shooter and hunter while an adolescent. He was greatly influenced by George Washington Sears ("Nessmuk"), one of the great naturalists of the late nineteenth century. Whelen's first outdoor article appeared in 1901, and he proved to be incredibly prolific in his contributions to magazines and as a book author. Over the course of his career, he wrote upwards of two thousand magazine articles, but it is his books that endear him to posterity. They include *Suggestions to Military Riflemen* (1906), *The American Rifle* (1918), *Cartridges and Loads for American Rifles* (1922), *The Care and Cleaning of Modern*

450 THE MARKSMANSHIP PRIMER

Firearms (1922), *Big Game Hunting for the Novice and the Expert* (1923), *Amateur Gunsmithing* (1924), *American Big Game Shooting* (1925), *Wilderness Hunting and Wildcraft* (1927), *Small Bore Rifle Handbook* (1928), *Telescopic Rifle Sights* (1936), *The Hunting Rifle* (1940), *Small Arms Design and Ballistics* (1945–1946; two volumes), and *On Your Own in the Wilderness* (1958; with Bradford Angier). Bradford Angier compiled a fine anthology of Whelen's work, *The Best of Colonel Townsend Whelen* (1963). He also compiled *Mister Rifleman* (1965), a blend of autobiography and Whelen's favorite articles.

Jack O'Connor, who could be acidic in his evaluation of fellow gun writers, thought highly of Whelen and stated that he was "certainly one of the best and most versatile outdoor writers that ever practiced the trade in the United States, and to narrow the field, he was probably the best writer on rifles and rifle shooting." When Whelen died, on December 23, 1961, O'Connor lavished further praise on him (although he could not resist a bit of prodding directed at others): "I consider him one of the most sensible, honest, and reliable gun writers ever to practice the rather doubtful trade in this country."

SELECT BIBLIOGRAPHY

Most serious marksmen realize that they can learn from serious study as well as from coaching and practice. The annotated bibliography that follows, though by no means complete, offers guidance to some of the best book-length studies of marksmanship from yesterday and today. In addition to these books, a number of shooting magazines contain regular features of note to anyone interested in marksmanship. Among these are *American Rifleman, Guns & Ammo, Guns, Gun World, The Rifle Magazine, GunHunter Magazine,* and, in England, *Shooting Times*. Three annuals of considerable note are *Shooter's Bible* (which includes a number of articles as well as up-to-date data on contemporary guns), *Gun Trader's Guide* (which offers much on the value of vintage firearms) and *Gun Digest* (which provides extensive information on all aspects of guns).

For anyone anxious to delve into the literature on marksmanship, there are a number of useful reference works that offer a solid start. Foremost among these, even though it appeared decades ago, is Ray Riling's *Guns and Shooting: A Bibliography* (Philadelphia: Ray Riling Arms Books Co., 1982; memorial edition). This comprehensive source covers only books published through 1950. Somewhat different in approach, but much more recent, is M. L. "Duke" Biscotti's *A Bibliography of American Sporting Books, 1926–1985* (Far Hills, NJ: Meadow Run Press, 1997). Compiled by a longtime sporting bibliophile, this work is particularly useful for those interested in marksmanship as it applies to hunting. More wide-ranging in scope, but noteworthy for its compre-

452 THE MARKSMANSHIP PRIMER

hensiveness, is Richard A. Hand's *A Bookman's Guide to Hunting, Shooting, Angling and Related Subjects* (Metuchen, NJ: Scarecrow Press, 1991).

Two books that will be of interest to anyone desirous of learning more about great shooters and authorities on guns are Sam Fadala's *Great Shooters of the World* (South Hackensack, NJ: Stoeger Publishing, 1990) and James Foral (editor), *Gun Writers of Yesteryear* (Prescott, AZ: Wolfe Publishing, 1993). Fadala's book consists of thirty-one biographical profiles of noted shooters and marksmen, whereas Foral dug deeply into the pages of magazines from yesteryear to find articles on all aspects of shooting by both famous and forgotten sporting scribes.

There are literally dozens of dictionaries, encyclopedias, and similar reference works on shooting. Among the more useful are Harold L. Peterson (editor), *Encyclopedia of Firearms* (New York: E. P. Dutton, 1964); *Firearms Encyclopedia* by George C. Nonte, Jr. (New York: Outdoor Life, 1973); *The Encyclopaedia of Sporting Shooting* by Robin Marshall-Ball (London: B. T. Batsford, 1992); and *Steindler's New Firearms Dictionary* by R. A. Steindler (Harrisburg, PA: Stackpole, 1985).

Army Marksmanship Unit Pistol Training Guide. Amsterdam, the Netherlands: Fredonia Books, 2001. Reprinted from 1980 edition. iv, 145 pp. Illus.

Askins, Charles [Jr.]. *The Art of Handgun Shooting*. New York: A. S. Barnes, 1941. 219 pp. Illus.

————. *The Pistol Shooter's Book: A Modern Encyclopedia*. Harrisburg, PA: Stackpole, 1953. [viii], 347 pp. Illus., index.

Askins, Charles [Sr.]. *Rifles and Rifle Shooting*. New York: Outing Publishing, 1912. 244 pp. Illus. No. 15 in the Outing Handbooks series. Several helpful chapters, most notably those on shooting positions and running shots and the chapter entitled "Two-Hundred Yard Sharpshooting."

Beginner's Shooting Guide; With Some Tips for Experts. Elgin, PA: Allegheny Press, n.d. 128 pp. Illus. Basic, but well done. Particularly strong on safety-related issues.

Bryant, Will. *Great American Guns and Frontier Fighters*. New York: Grosset & Dunlap, 1961. 160 pp. Illus. A popular look at the role of firearms in American history.

Chapel, Charles Edward. *The Art of Shooting*. New York: A. S. Barnes, 1960. 424 pp. Illus., index. A detailed guide to all aspects of pistol, revolver, and rifle shooting.

Cooper, Jeff. *The Complete Book of Modern Handgunning*. New York: Bramhall House, 1961. viii, 262 pp. Illus., index. Useful material from a frequent contributor to *Guns and Ammo* magazine.

Crossman, Edward C. *The Book of the Springfield*. Onslow County, NC: Small-Arms Technical Publishing Co., 1932. x, 451 pp. Illus. The chapters entitled "Accuracy and Safety Adjustments" and "Corrosion and Rifle Cleaning" are of note.

———. *Military and Sporting Rifle Shooting*. Onslow County, NC: Small-Arms Technical Publishing Co., 1932. xx, 499 pp. Illus. An enduring classic.

Enos, Brian. *Practical Shooting: Beyond Fundamentals*. Clifton, CO: Zediker, 1990. [iv], 204 pp. Illus. A useful guide.

Foral, James, ed. *Gun Writers of Yesteryear.* Prescott, AZ: Wolfe Publishing, 1993. vi, 449 pp. An anthology giving examples of gun writing from almost three dozen gun scribes.

Gould, Arthur C. *Modern American Pistols and Revolvers.* Plantersville, SC: Small-Arms Technical Publishing Co., 1946. 222 pp. Illus. A reprint of the 1894 edition written under the pseudonym Ralph Greenwood.

———. *Modern American Rifles.* Boston: B. Whidden, 1892. 338 pp. Illus. Written under the pseudonym Ralph Greenwood.

Gresham, Grits. *Grits on Guns.* Prescott, AZ: Cane River Publishing, 1987. xvi, 332 pp. Illus., index. Interesting collection of dozens of pieces by a true expert. Much on hunting, but also informative material relating to equipment that makes us better shooters.

Hatcher, Julian S. *Hatcher's Notebook.* Harrisburg, PA: Military Service Publishing Co., 1947. 488 pp. Illus. Later editions, revised and considerable expanded, were published by Stackpole.

———. *Textbook of Pistols and Revolvers.* Plantersville, SC: Small-Arms Technical Publishing Co., 1935. viii, 533 pp. Illus., index. Chapters 13 and 14, "Learning to Shoot" and "Practical Shooting," are particularly helpful.

Himmelwright, A. L. A. *Pistol and Revolver Shooting.* New York: Outing Publishing Co., 1916. No. 34 in the Outing Handbooks series. 223 pp. Illus., index. Outdated in most senses, but historically important.

Jennings, Mike. *Instinct Shooting.* New York: Dodd, Mead, 1959. 157 pp. Illus.

Johnson, Melvin M., Jr. *Practical Marksmanship: The Tech-*

nique of Field Firing. New York: Morrow, 1945. 183 pp. Illus. Still useful.

Kephart, Horace. *Sporting Firearms.* New York: Macmillan, 1912. 153 pp. Illus. An interesting little treatment in the Outing Handbooks series.

Keith, Elmer. *Big Game Rifles and Cartridges.* Onslow County, NC: Small-Arms Technical Publishing Co., 1936. 161 pp. Illus. A highly collectible classic.

————. *Sixguns Cartridges and Loads.* Onslow County, NC: Small-Arms Technical Publishing Co., 1936. viii, 151 pp. Illus.

Landis, C. S. *.22 Caliber Rifle Shooting.* Onslow County, NC: Small-Arms Technical Publishing Co., 1932. x, 414 pp. Illus. Several of the chapters in part 2 of the book are excellent.

————. *Rifle-Craft.* Cincinnati, OH: Sportsman's Digest Publishing Co., 1923. 124 pp. Illus. An early but still useful little work with some excellent practical advice on gun cleaning and a fine chapter entitled "The Stock as an Aid to Accuracy."

Lee, Kenneth Fuller. *Big Game Hunting and Marksmanship: A Manual on the Rifles, Marksmanship and Methods Best Adapted to the Hunting of the Big Game of the Eastern United States.* Plantersville, SC: Small-Arms Technical Publishing Co., 1941. 211 pp. Illus. Primarily of note for deer hunting. As is the case with virtually all publications under Thomas G. Samworth's imprint, the coverage is accurate and detailed.

Lind, Ernie. *The Complete Book of Trick and Fancy Shooting.* New York: Winchester Press, 1972. 159 pp. Illus. Although devoted to developing showmanship skills, the book is useful because of its hints on practice and improved performance.

Mann, Franklin W. *The Bullet's Flight from Powder to Target*. Huntingdon, WV: Standard Printing and Publishing Co., 1942. xxv, 384 pp. Illus. Issued in both deluxe and trade editions.

Newick, Glenn. *The Ultimate in Rifle Accuracy: Getting the Most Out of Your Equipment and Yourself.* Accokeek, MD: Stoeger Publishing, 1989. [vi], 210 pp. Illus., index.

O'Connor, Jack. *7-Lesson Rifle Shooting Course*. New York: Outdoor Life Books, 1982. 4th printing. [iv], 37 pp. Illus. Reprinted from O'Connor's classic Complete Book of Rifles and Shotguns.

————. *The Big-Game Rifle*. New York: Knopf, 1952. xii, 372, xi pp. Illus., index. Reprinted by Safari Press in 1994. An O'Connor standard. Although a solid list of O'Connor titles follows, those interested in complete bibliographical information will want to consult Henry van der Broecke's "Bibliographical Essay" in Robert M. Anderson's *Jack O'Connor: The Legendary Life of America's Greatest Gunwriter* (Huntington Beach, CA: Safari Press, 2003). The biography itself is uneven at best (the parts contributed by "Buck" Buckner are its saving grace), but this essay is first-rate.

————. *Complete Book of Rifles and Shotguns*. New York: Outdoor Life, 1961. 477 pp. Illus., index. Mostly on practical hunting and the characteristics of guns and ammunition, but the chapters on trajectory, using a rest, wind allowance, and his seven-lesson rifle shooting course all relate to marksmanship.

————. *Complete Book of Shooting*. With Roy Dunlap, Alex

Kerr, and Jeff Cooper. New York: Outdoor Life, 1965. [vi], 385 pp. Illus., index. This is an important work of enduring value. Cooper's contributions on the pistol are certainly as important as O'Connor's contributions on rifles.

——. *The Hunter's Shooting Guide*. With a preface by Jim Carmichael. New York: Outdoor Life, 1978. vi, 170 pp. Illus., index. Originally published in 1957 under the title *Outdoor Life Shooting Book,* this is a collection of pieces on rifles, handguns, and shotguns. Of particular note are the chapters entitled "This Flinching Business" and "Beginning with a Handgun."

——. *Jack O'Connor's Gun Book*. Chicago: Popular Science Publishing Co., 1953. 208 pp. Illus. Reprinted by Wolfe Publishing in 1992. A potpourri of the great scribes' thoughts on guns and hunting.

——. *Rifle and Shotgun Shooting Basics*. New York: Outdoor Life, 1986. 2nd printing. [iv], 42 pp. Illus. A useful little guidebook condensed from his *Complete Book of Shooting*.

——. *The Rifle Book*. 2nd ed., rev. New York: Knopf, 1964. xiv, 332, iv pp. Illus., index. A true classic by one of America's most revered gun writers. This is the fullest, most informative edition.

——. *Sportsman's Arms and Ammunition Manual*. Garden City, NY: Garden City Books, 1952. 256 pp. Illus., index. An overlooked O'Connor title with a three-chapter section entitled "How to Shoot Your Rifle", a six-chapter section entitled "Scopes, Sights and Sighting," and two chapters on handguns. Also published under the title *Arms and Ammunition Annual*.

vens, James R. *Sight Alignment, Trigger Control and "The*

Big Lie." Milwaukee, WI: JAFEICA Publishing 1996. v, 135 pp. Illus.

Petzal, David E., ed. *The Experts' Book of the Shooting Sports.* New York: Simon & Schuster, 1972. 320 pp Illus., index. Contributions from a number of leading authorities, with Gary Anderson's "Rifle Target Shooting" and Steve Ferber's "Handgun Target Shooting" being of particular note.

Reichenbach, William. *Automatic Pistol Marksmanship.* Plantersville, SC: Small-Arms Technical Publishing Co., 1937. viii, 140 pp. Illus. Interesting little book written in a decidedly lively style.

————. *Sixguns and Bullseyes.* Plantersville, SC: Small-Arms Technical Publishing Co., 1936. [xii], 145 pp. Illus. Quirky, written in an oddball style, and fascinating. Particularly useful on physical aspects of pistol marksmanship.

Rodengen, Jeffrey L. *NRA: An American Legend.* Fort Lauderdale, FL: Write Stuff Enterprises, 2002. 304 pp. Illus., index. A coffee table–type history of the National Rifle Association.

Smith, W. H. B. *The N. R. A. Book of Small Arms.* Vol. 1, *Pistols and Revolvers.* Harrisburg, PA: Military Service Publishing Co., 1946. [xxv], 638 pp. Illus., index. Comprehensive coverage devoted to various types of pistols and revolvers.

————. *The N. R. A. Book of Small Arms.* Vol. 2, *Rifles.* Harrisburg, PA: Military Service Publishing Co., 1948. [iv], 546 pp. Illus., index. Describes calibers and makes of rifles in detail.

Stebbins, Henry M. *How to Select and Use Your Big Game*

Rifle. Washington, DC: Combat Forces Press, 1952. xiv, 237 pages. Illus., index. The chapters on gun care, accessories, and practice are particularly useful.

————. *Teaching Kids to Shoot*. Harrisburg, PA: Stackpole, 1966. 96 pp. Illus. A useful little book designed to help parents and instructors who wish to develop sound, safe young shooters.

Taylor, John. *African Rifles & Cartridges*. Georgetown, SC: Small-Arms Technical Publishing Co., 1948. xiv, 431 pp. Illus., index. A classic in its field, portions of this book have general applications to marksmanship as it affects the hunter.

Trefethen, James B., comp. *Americans and Their Guns*. Harrisburg, PA: Stackpole, 1967. 320 pp. Illus.

Trench, Charles C. *A History of Marksmanship*. Chicago: Follett, 1972. 128 pages. Illus. A coffee table book that, though visually interesting, lacks depth.

United States Marine Corps. *Rifle Marksmanship*. Albany, GA: Marines Corps Logistics Base, 2001. Marine Corps Reference Publication MCRP 3-01A. Illus., glossary. The guidebook used by the Marines to train recruits in rifle handling and marksmanship.

Van Zwoll, Wayne. *The Hunter's Guide to Accurate Shooting: How to Hit What You Shoot at Every Time*. New York: Lyons Press, 2002. 332 pp. Illus., index.

————. *The Hunter's Guide to Ballistics: Practical Advice on How to Choose Guns and Loads, and Use Them Effectively*. New York: Lyons Press, 2000. 280 pp. Illus., index.

Wallack, L. R. *Modern Accuracy: The Story of Bench Rest Shooting*. New York: Greenberg, 1951. 151 pp. Illus.

Whelen, Townsend. *The American Rifle*. New York: Century Co., 1918. x, 637 pp. Illus., index. A true classic. Part 2, "Practical Rifle Shooting," is still quite useful.

————. *The Hunting Rifle*. Harrisburg, PA: Stackpole, 1940. 463 pp. Illus., index. An important work by one of the great authorities on the subject. Almost half the book, comprising the fourteen chapters of part 2, deals with marksmanship.

————. *Small Arms Design and Ballistics*. Vol. 1, *Design*. Georgetown, SC: Small-Arms Technical Publishing Co., 1945. vi, 352 pp. Illus., index.

————. *Small Arms Design and Ballistics*. Vol. 2, *Ballistics*. Georgetown, SC: Small-Arms Technical Publishing Co., 1946. ix, 314 pp. Illus., index. Helpful on a variety of topics, ranging from wind deflection to care and storage of arms and ammunition.

————, ed. *The Ultimate in Rifle Precision*. Harrisburg, PA: Stackpole, 1958. 328 pp. Illus., index. This detailed, useful work covers all aspects of rifle shooting — bench rest, target, and varmint shooting, along with use of the rifle for hunting.

————. *Why Not Load Your Own? Basic Handloading for Everyone*. Washington, DC: Infantry Journal Press, 1949. [viii], 215 pp. Illus.

a

Angles of Elevation

Cartridge	Bullet Point	Bullet grs.	M.V. f.s.	Minutes of Angle				
				100†	200	300	400	500 yards
.22 Hornet	Ptd.O.P.	46	2625	6.5	8.5	14.0	25.5	38.0
.220 Swift	Ptd.O.P.	48	4140	1.5	3.5	5.5	8.0	12.0
.25 Rem. Auto.*	R.N.	87	2700	2.5	5.5	8.5	13.0	18.0
.25 Rem. Auto.*	R.N.	117	2250	3.0	7.0	12.0	17.3	24.0
.250-3000 Savage	Ptd.	87	3050	2.0	4.5	6.5	9.0	13.5
.250-3000 Savage	Ptd.O.P.	100	2670	2.0	4.9	8.0	12.0	17.0
.257 Roberts*	R.N.	87	3200	1.7	4.0	6.5	10.0	14.5
.257 Roberts*	R.N.	100	2900	2.2	4.7	7.9	11.8	16.5
.257 Roberts*	R.N.	117	2650	2.6	5.5	9.2	13.5	18.7
.270 Winchester	Ptd.	100	3630	1.4	2.8	5.1	7.7	10.5
.270 Winchester	Ptd.	130	3160	2.0	4.0	5.5	8.0	12.0
.270 Winchester	R.N.	150	2670	3.0	6.2	9.7	14.8	20.5
7-mm Mauser	Ptd.	139	2800	2.0	4.3	7.3	10.0	14.0
7-mm Mauser B.T.	R.N.	175	2300	3.0	6.0	10.0	15.0	21.0
7-mm Mauser*	R.N.	175	2550	2.7	5.7	9.3	12.9	17.3
.30-06 U.S.*	F.P.O.P.	110	3500	1.5	3.0	5.0	7.5	10.0
.30-06 U.S.	Ptd.	150	2700	2.5	5.2	8.2	11.6	15.6
.30-06 U.S.	Ptd.	150	3000	2.5	4.0	6.5	9.5	12.5
.30-06 U.S. M.I.B.T.	Ptd.	172	2640	2.5	5.0	8.0	11.1	14.3
.30-06 U.S.	Ptd.	180	2700	2.5	5.0	8.0	11.5	15.0
.30-06 U.S. B.T.	R.N.	220	2330	4.0	7.2	10.5	15.5	20.0
.300 Magnum B.T.	Ptd.	180	3060	2.0	4.2	6.7	9.5	13.0
.300 Magnum O.P.E.B.T.	Ptd.O.P.	180	3060	2.0	4.5	6.8	10.0	13.5
.300 Magnum S.P.	R.N.	220	2730	2.5	5.3	8.7	12.7	17.3

† 100 yard angle includes jump.

* Factory calculations. Probable errors. Should be verified by a trained rifleman.

461

INDEX

ABOUT THE AUTHOR

Jim Casada the editor and compiler of this work, was a university history professor before taking early retirement to write full-time on hunting, fishing, and other outdoor-related topics. He serves as series editor of the Firearms Classics Library from Palladium Press and of the Outdoor Tennessee Series from the University of Tennessee Press. He is a senior editor of *Sporting Classics* magazine and a contributing editor for *The Hunting Magazine, Cabela's Outfitter Journal,* and *Sporting Clays.* He serves as editor at large for *Turkey and Turkey Hunting* and has contributed hunting and gun-related pieces to dozens of publications, including *Outdoor Life, American Hunter, North American Hunter, Sports Afield, Shooter's Bible, Deer & Deer Hunting,* and *Gun Hunter Magazine.* He has written, edited, or contributed to more than 30 books, including *The Best of Horatio Bigelow* (1994), *The Lost Classics of Robert Rourk* (1996), *Africa's Greatest Hunter* (1998), *Innovative Turkey Hunting* (2000), *Forgotten Tales and Vanished Trails* (2001); on Theodore Roosevelt as a hunter and naturalist, and a quartet of works bringing together the finest hunting writings of Archibald Rutledge. With his wife, Ann, he has coauthored a number of game cookbooks. Casada is a past president of both the Southeastern Outdoor Press Association and the Outdoor Writers Association of America.